DIARIES OF AN INTERNET LOVER

Dawn Porter

First published in Great Britain in 2006 by Virgin Books
Virgin Books Ltd
Thames Wharf Studios
Rainville Road
London
W6 9HA

A catalogue record for this book is available from the
British Library.

ISBN 9780753510094

The paper used in this book is a natural, recyclable product
made from wood grown in sustainable forests. The
manufacturing process conforms to the regulations of the
country of origin.

Typeset by Phoenix Photosetting, Chatham, Kent

Printed and bound in Great Britain by
CPI Bookmarque, Croydon, CR0 4TD

Dedicated to:

Jane, Charlotte, Louise, Tara and Lilu
My girls

We have so much fun!

I love you x

CONTENTS

CONTENTS

Acknowledgements

Special thanks to:
Adrian Sington – for loving my idea and making all this happen.
Stuart, Natalie, Kerri, Eleanor, Jamie, Stina and all at Virgin Books. Extra special thanks to Stuart who, even though I have only ever had one editor, is definitely the best editor I have ever had.
Luigi Bonomi (LBA Associates) – for being a brilliant agent.
Max Clifford – for the opportunities – very grateful.
Aroon Maharajh, Teresa Quinlan (U1st Media) – for believing in me 100 per cent.

Mummy – Miss you.
Daddy – Love you.
Aunty Jane, Uncle Tony and all the Rix's in Guernsey – especially my gorgeous cousins Kerry, Clem, Will, Louis and Elise – love you all so much x.
My thister – for being the truly most important person in my life (that's my sister by the way!)
Graham Smith – I adore you for giving me great advice and being a monumental drinking partner, and of course being a very good friend.
Don Bursill – for constant support and stupid chats – moron!
Graham Joyce – for all the advice, help and introductions.
Linda and Glen Kielty – for being so understanding.
Kooga – secret kisses x.
Mark Pontin, Ship and Crown, *best pub in town*, Guernsey – for being you.
Wynnie and Charlie – Charlie you are my biggest fan, so much so it actually scares me a little. You're the best friend/cousin I could ever wish for and I quite simply love your work!
Ed – still my bro.

Laura Elliot – for being my oldest friend.
Mel Stenhouse – because you're just so much fun!
Jamie Hill (my Bumble) – for all the help.
Ian – I adore you.
David F – you know why!
Angharad Alan – the sweetest thing.
Liz Thomas – little legend.
Lucy Johnston – for being all bendy and brilliant.
Dylan Todd – for being you. Eggy little nutter.
Michael Livingstone – for having balls of steel.
The ladies on the Independent Reception – for making me howl with laughter and being so great.
Guernsey in its entirety – I love home.
The Soldier – for making sure I know exactly what good sex is!
Everyone who features in this book.

LOGGING ON . . .

'Why does a good looking girl like you need to cruise a dodgy website for dates?' Are the words my daddy said when I told him what I was intending to do. And I understand why he felt confused. There is a stigma attached to Internet dating, which on many occasions can be justified – especially when you do it through the kind of site that I was intending to use.

Though the website I used is not specifically a dating site, it is notorious for its intimate adult connections. A section of the site, called 'Casual Encounters', is specifically designed for people who are looking for one off meetings with strangers; but we're not talking polite chats over coffee and muffins. It's about discreet, random and totally no-strings-attached sex.

Posts such as 'Wife is away for the weekend, come over and I will give you two hours of solid anal' are commonplace here. But before you snap the book shut thinking that this is a dark and sordid tale of my quest for the filthiest one night stand, just hang on. Call me old fashioned, but I would rather stay home and stub cigarettes out on my cheeks, thank you very much. There is another part to the personals section called 'Women looking for men', which catches the fancy of a much more mild-mannered cliental. It is here that I placed my posts, and, although I didn't actually advertise for sex, it's interesting to know that a subtle approach can achieve equally as successful results as a blatant plea . . .

Even though my healthy social life has always introduced me to multiple eligible lovers, here was a sure fire way for me to seriously satisfy my passion for all things fruity, and meet people who were totally disconnected from my life. I have now worked from home for three years, the chances of Managing Directors of international corporations who want to whisk me off my feet, or super beautiful French stallions with fixations for performing oral sex walking in the door are few and far between. But with a bit of captivating wording and a few clicks of my mouse, all these fantasies became reality, and I was introduced to a fascinating and diverse list of characters, who have all made the last six months of my life more colourful than I could ever have hoped for.

I suppose I should tell you a little bit about me before I continue with my tale. I'm a 26-year-old female, who lives in London's Marylebone with my Siamese cat Lilu. However, and to save any confusion later, when I started this journal in January 2005 I was 25 and lived in a warehouse conversion in Hackney with seven boys, and of course Lilu, who, as you will come to learn, is my most precious possession.

My background is in TV production and PR, but after losing my job just before Christmas, I knew I wanted to be a writer. Rather than go back into full time employment I decided to take the leap and devote my time to words. That's when the idea to keep a journal of my Internet adventures came to me. After being persuaded by a friend to give it a go last summer, I was amazed by the social opportunities meeting people in this way offered me. Sharing those experiences and opening people's minds to this implausible societal awakening seemed like the obvious next step. Thus *The Diaries of an Internet Lover* were born.

I was born in Scotland but raised in Guernsey and I have lived in London for three years. I love it here and every day discover something new that makes me feel so lucky to live in what I would consider to be the best city in the world. Well, apart from New York, which I think is equally as fabulous, but I'll get to that later on when one of my dates so kindly took me there . . .

I love socialising, eating (a lot), drinking (a lot), writing, talking, walking and dating. Oh, and I love having sex. Nope, I'm not ashamed to say that I love sex for all that it is. I think it's fun, it makes me smile and I could do it all day . . . everyday . . . twice . . . with bells on . . . and maybe a strap on . . . (ha ha, I joke – that's really not my thing!).

When I started to keep this journal in January I had the intention to get it published, but I never really believed that would happen. I presumed it would be one of those things that people would find under my bed when I died, which my kids would make millions from but I wouldn't see a bean. But at a dinner party on 7 March 2005, when the gentleman sitting next to me asked me what I did, rather than bleat on about my job loss and dire financial straits, I told him about the Internet dates I'd been on and the written accounts I was keeping of them. He thought the idea was fascinating and – what a result – that gentleman was Adrian Sington, the Executive Chairman of Virgin Books. He asked me to send over the little bits that I had done by that point and by noon the next day we were in negotiations for a publishing deal. I couldn't believe my luck; it must have been fate. The good thing about getting the deal then was that it gave me a block of time. It meant that I really did have six months, and six months only to get as much out of the experience as possible. And I have to say . . . I really did!

Meeting people on the Internet wasn't about being kinky. I'm not into meeting strange men in dark toilets and having them fondle my bits while I spank them with a paddle. It's dating, normal dating. Drinks, dinner then the prospect of something more – should both parties be game. It's just a slightly unconventional way of setting it up. People out there reading this through their fingers must relax. Yes, there are horror stories, and I'm not suggesting that there are not. But it can be very safe and legit if you are savvy and judicious about whom you meet. Which I was . . . most of the time.

When I Internet dated there was a genuine connection from the initial email contact. This connection could be anything from a common interest to a similar sense of humour, or even an unspoken sexual attraction that managed to seep its way through the words. This has happened on a few occasions and you'll see a fine example of it with The Wolf, my second date. It was clear we'd caught each other in a horny mood and the conversation couldn't have been anything other than suggestive. It was a real buzz when that happened and, man, did it make the working day go faster!

The banter usually went on for a couple of days, so conversation on the nights flowed well as we already knew so much about each other. So the only question when we met was: were we going to fancy each other? And I can tell you now, that although there were many unfortunate times when I didn't feel a sexual attraction, there were also many when I did, and they were excruciatingly saucy. It's like you share a secret, like what you're doing is a little bit naughty, like you are involved in a sort of underground dating gang that makes it all that little bit more erotic and gives you a sense of bravery that can result in a seriously engaging encounter.

Also, it's bloody exciting. Exchanging emails with a total stranger then arranging to meet them off the back of some tempting words was an adventure in itself. Every date I went on gave me an adrenalin buzz that isn't quite the same as when I've just gone to the pub, got off my tits, eyed someone up, snogged their face off for a few hours, gone back to theirs and then woken up in the morning doused in a crusty residue, remembering little more than the colour of their pillow. I'm done with that. For the time being anyway . . .

'It's a social experiment father,' I replied, while handing him a tissue to mop his brow. And it was. We put ourselves out there into the world and never quite know how other people perceive us. When I decided to try Internet dating I promised myself that I would remain true and constant in every scenario. What's fascinated me most out of all this is how I react differently to different people. With some people I may be the consummate lady, with others I'm a brazen hussy who can't wait to get my pants off; yet I'm always myself. Hey, I can't help the way that someone makes me feel and I *do* tend to act on impulse.

So, on this site that is most commonly associated with no-strings-attached sex, I placed simple postings along the lines of

Young, attractive, professional female wants to be whisked away. Take me on the date of a lifetime and let's see where it takes us . . .

I changed the posts a few times to attract an assortment of types. And occasionally, if they seemed appealing, I answered other people's.

It was a simple procedure. I decided what I wanted, advertised it and saw who bit my bait. The beauty of it was that I was in utter control of who I responded to. On the site I was anonymous, so no one knew anything about me. It was up to me how much information I divulged as there was no profile form to fill in, unlike many dating sites. And if at any time the banter made me feel threatened or uncomfortable, I could pull out instantly.

I won't lie, not every response was charming. But after sifting through the pictures of cocks – both hard and flaccid, yet all proudly naked – descriptions of sexual abilities or the many emotional outpourings from a load of divorcees, I managed to get some email banter going with some people who interested me enough to want to meet them. And sure, some were not quite who I thought they were going to be. One in particular sent me a picture of someone so far from their actual physical appearance that I actually lost the power of speech for a few hours. A very uncommon event I can tell you. But others – like The Gentleman who so unexpectedly stole my heart or Plato who has become one of my closest and most appreciated friends – are people who have undoubtedly affected my life in no other way but positively and who have made this whole experience so worthwhile.

You'll learn more about The Gentleman later, but for now let me just say that I never went into this looking for love. My singledom is precious to me and Lilu gives me just the amount of commitment that I'm willing to bear right now. I went into this looking for fun, adventure and some hot, steamy lovers who would be in my life as extras, rather than the sole focus of my emotions. I didn't want my life to change, but when something jumps up and bites you on the arse, you have to tend to the wound somehow!

I don't have a prerequisite with men and I certainly don't have a 'type'. I think it's ridiculous to say you would never fancy a blonde, or that anyone with a hairy chest is out. That defies the whole notion of chemistry. I have been out with tall, short, fat, skinny, hairy, bald, spotty, leathered and baby-faced men, and although I know which ones I favour, I would never say never on the others. Saying that though, I do prefer them to be the tallest, but that's only really so I can wear stilettos and not feel like a street light.

The only feature that I was keen to avoid was dating men in their 20s. This is just down to experience. I reckon they are not far enough out of 'lad culture' from their university years, so individually they are usually inept at being with women. Yes, yes, not all I know, excuse my sweeping generalisation. But remember I said I used to live with seven boys? Let's just say I'm talking from experience. As much as I love them as friends, lovers . . . NO! And anyway, my social life is full of twentysomethings – I did this to spread my wings and experiment with age, occupation, nationality and anything else that makes someone a bit different from my usual squeezes. Including sex . . .

I could never deny being a bit bi-curious. And I'm surprised at how many women actually responded to my post, even though I was appealing for men. It got me thinking. Here is an opportunity to experiment in a low key, confidential and incredibly sexy way. So on the section of the website called 'women looking for women' I placed a simple post that read:

26 yr old female, professional, intelligent, heterosexual yet curious. Looking for a chance to experiment. If there is anyone else who wants to see how it could be, the other way, then get back to me.

I was inundated. It would seem that there are hundreds of women out there with secret desires that they are looking to explore. Interestingly, just like when I appealed for men, I got numerous oddbods going straight for the 'look at my genitals' approach. A swarm of horny housewives chucked over naked bath shots, bum shots, tit shots and, wait for it . . . straight up the middle shots. But through the many pairs of open legs I once again saw the light and found myself a very desirable lady to enjoy an evening with . . .

On top of this there were other responses that caught my eye. One in particular from a young lady called Gillian, who asked me to join her and her boyfriend for a night of 'fun'. At first I simply read the email and moved to the next, but instinct took me back, and over the course of six months such a friendship developed that I actually did go and meet them, and it brought my adventure to a liberating and climactic close that I would never have foreseen when I set out to write this book.

It would have been impossible for me to include every person that I had banter with, or even all of the dates that I went on, but the following accounts of the ones that had the most impact on me are genuine and explicit. It's a humorous and sexy journey, a tale of lust, heartache, repulsion and risk taking which has taught me reams about who I am and who I share this crazy world with.

I hope you enjoy them. I did, but you'll see that for yourselves!

Post A

Young, attractive, professional female wants to be whisked away. Take me on the date of a lifetime and let's see where it takes us . . .

Post B

I don't know if I want sex yet. How would I know until I had met you? I want to be taken out for dinner, wined and dined the proper way in nice places. Treated like a lady then I will decide. I like dating and no one does it properly . . .

I have my own money, its not about that, I just want a Hollywood style scenario where I'm whisked off my feet by a guys charm . . . is that too much to ask?

I'm a creative person, interesting, funny and attractive. I want to meet someone interesting who is looking for a bit of an adventure.

I can't deny I have a fantasy of a suited city worker where the sky is the limit

I want to have some fun . . . any offers??

Post C

Hey

I'm 27, very attractive and professional.

January is just so dull, don't you think?

My social life is great but I fancy a random night of fun with a total stranger. If I'm honest I would quite like to be spoilt rotten and made to feel a bit special . . . we all need that once in a while and that's the one thing my life doesn't offer. Anyone want to whisk me off my feet and show me how a guy is supposed to treat a woman?

Post D

If you are:

MALE
27–35
Successful
Funny
Not a relationship retard
Just too busy or not sleazy enough to try to pull in bars
Charming
Graceful
Sexy but not pushy
Experienced
Preferably not divorced
Confident
Love pretty ladies
Love socializing
Flirty
etc. etc .

Then get in touch . . . .
Me? I'm in my twenties, kind, honest, intelligent and craving
someone to show me how exciting life can be.
Anyone out there??
Bring on the ideas for the perfect first date and I'll do my best
to be there!

Post E

The girl who seems to have everything is missing something . . .
any ideas?

FRIDAY 7 JANUARY

Monsieur Cunni
Bon Appétit!

Post A

07/01/2005   **13.23**
From: Monsieur Cunni
To: Dawn
Subject: Bonjour

Hi,
My name is **** and I am a 31 yrs old French.
I would love to take you to dinner as I know a few places and wines
is no secret for me.
What type of food do you enjoy most or would you prefer a
surprise . . .
Have you ever tried a French lover? If not then you must.
I am free all weekend hope to ear from you.
I have attached my picture x

07/01/2005   **13.39**
From: Dawn
To: Monsieur Cunni
Subject: Bonjour

You are a good looking man . . . very nice!
Look like you take care of yourself quite well . . . I like your
confidence, sexy!
What food do I like? French, for sure. If garlic had a willy I would
marry it . . . where you taking me?

07/01/2005   15.49
From: Monsieur Cunni
To: Dawn
Subject: Bonjour

I know one called Eire Brother very nice with Mediterranean food
and good wine and what is even better with room on Friday night!
Where do you want to meet?
Do you have a picture?

07/01/2005   16.58
From: Dawn
To: Monsieur Cunni
Subject: Bonjour

First question . . . what exactly did you mean by 'with room'?
Interesting!
Pic attached x

07/01/2005   17.08
From: Monsieur Cunni
To: Dawn
Subject: Bonjour

I meant that it is not always fully booked on Friday eve.
Tres mignone! (Very pretty)
Shall I book?

07/01/2005   17.14
From: Dawn
To: Monsieur Cunni
Subject: Bonjour

YES x
I can get to you for eight . . . that cool?

07/01/2005   17.48
From: Monsieur Cunni
To: Dawn
Subject: Bonjour

Eight is OK. Do you know the bar called The Electric
Showrooms near Hoxton square?

07/01/2005   17.50
From: Dawn
To: Monsieur Cunni
Subject: Bonjour

The Electric Showrooms? I know it very well . . . see you there at eight!
ps -how tall are you? It's important to know what height shoes to wear . . .

07/01/2005   17.57
From: Monsieur Cunni
To: Dawn
Subject: Bonjour

180cm you will have to convert!

The Date

One hundred and eighty centimetres? My maths concluded that this made him fifteen feet tall . . . don't ask – I still haven't managed to get my maths GCSE. The figure suggested that I might have calculated incorrectly, so I decided that 180cm was probably six foot and, as planned, chose to wear my three inch stilettos.

I liked his bold emails, his straight-up and confident style was appealing and his photo was very cute. He stared right into the camera, big, deep brown eyes that I instantly imagined looking down into mine. I was in a particularly horny mood that night and had some seriously naughty intentions; my imagination was on override before I had even met him.

'You do not need ayt,' he said as he stood to greet me. I was slightly unsure of what he meant, but his dance-like foot movements made it clear that he was referring to my high heels. We measured out at around the same height, which was something of a relief. I like it when I'm not the tallest.

He looked just like he did in his photo. Tanned and flawless skin, short dark hair, cheeky smile with a couple of dimples and a particularly massive conk – I said conk, Jesus, give me a chance! – which in a strange way, really complemented his face.

'Which drink would you want?' He asked as he turned towards the bar.

I said a Jack Daniel's and Diet Coke and he walked away. Worried about the language barrier I relayed the word 'Diet' to him approximately three times. He got it right. As you would if someone repeatedly shouted something at you. He was French, not stupid; I soon learnt that.

Conversation started very easily, he glugged on his pint and I sucked on my straw. It wasn't particularly flirtatious, work stuff, French stuff and social life stuff . . . the usual. He was quite huffy. Raised shoulders, arms crossed, legs crossed, protrusive bottom lip. Like he was constantly saying 'I don't give a sheet.' And he did that thing that French people do when they hold their hands out like weighing scales, while pushing their chins into their necks and raising their eyebrows. I liked it, it was sexy as all was performed with a constant smirk, which undisputedly said 'I want to take off your knickers and stick my Eiffel Tower up your Watford Gap.'

We finished our drinks and walked a couple of streets to the restaurant. He led the way, waving his hands at speeding traffic and not making too much conversation. I tried but he was concentrating on getting there, so I quickly learnt not to bother.

The restaurant was pretty quiet, he had been right again; there was lots of 'room' for a Friday. I joked that in his email I thought that he was telling me that the meal is much more fun on a Friday when you have a room booked in the hotel upstairs, but he assured me I had got it wrong. We looked at the menus but he took control of the wine order, and I let him decide on our starter – a Spanish ham that we shared and that he spoke about a little too much. I mean, don't get me wrong, it was delicious but there is only so much you can say about ham . . . no matter how expensive it is.

The waiter brought over a dish of what looked like two sausages, I happily dived in. He stared at them, but didn't touch.

'That's pig blood, and guts . . . it is clotted blood and guts,' he announced as I took my second mouthful. A menstrual sow came flowing into my mind and I almost projectile vomited it across the room.

'I'm sorry, I need to urinate, that is not once, but sree times I av gone . . . it is because of my pint.' He sauntered off to the toilets.

He didn't need to tell me that he had gone three times, I wouldn't have noticed. He had only been to the loo once since I'd been with him. But, I suppose all information is good information.

While he was away I had a chance to think. I wasn't feeling quite as naughty as I had been earlier on. I think that was to do with the pace of the evening so far. We hadn't been laughing lots, nor doing a particular amount of flirting, so my horniness had been tamed a little. However, when he returned from the loo the whole tempo of the evening changed when he burst out with the following comment.

'I just hate the way the British FAT!'

I choked on my rioja.

'Derr, um . . . baa . . . excuse me?'

'The way that they FAT! I was standing at the urinal, one British man on my right, one on my left. The one on my left did the biggest FAT I have ever 'eard, and neither of them reacted, like it was totally normal. I'm telling you it was the biggest FAT I have ever 'eard.'

Unsure of how to respond to such outrage at my country's gaseous habits, I did what any normal and slightly ashamed English woman would do in that situation and howled with laughter. It took him a few moments but he eventually joined in, and we chewed on the remains of our posh ham while giggling profusely and making the occasional raspberry noise.

He was a gentleman, in as much as he poured my wine, stood up when I stood up, looked at me when I spoke to him and laughed at my jokes (probably the most important thing). As we settled into the evening I fell more and more for him, his sweetness, usually a quality that irritates me in men, was so endearing and genuine. He wasn't one of those guys who do sweet things because that's what he thinks he should do; he did them because they came naturally to him and it was very welcome. He wasn't cringeworthy, even though he was very attentive. Lots of 'You are so beautiful's and 'I cannot stop but look into your eyes.' God knows how but it was working on me. It wasn't hard to refuse dessert so we could get somewhere else and be slightly less civilised.

After dinner we walked over to Catch on the Kingsland Road. It was packed and over the bar I could see someone that I knew. I did everything I could not to catch her eye as I couldn't bear it if she came over. Not because I was ashamed of him or how we had met, but because I could not for the life of me remember his bloody name. I had been racking my brains all night, but wasn't stressing too much as I didn't really need it. I knew that if I saw him again after that night I could just read my emails and get it, but it would have been awful if I had to introduce him to someone.

She saw me and I strained a smile. She gestured that she was going to come over. I panicked and did the first thing that came into my mind to detour her. When he asked me what I wanted to drink I launched myself at his face and kissed him. At first it was erratic; he was blatantly taken aback as I noshed away at his lips like a hungry dog. But soon I had forgotten all about my friend and was so involved with what I would comfortably describe as one of the most sensuous kisses of my life that my mind could only focus on one thing. Him.

We kissed for ages; it must have been about five full minutes, which is a pretty long time as far as snogging in public goes. I couldn't stop. When he did eventually put both hands up to my face and stroke my cheeks with his thumbs I was totally delirious. It took me about thirty seconds to come back into the room and open my eyes, when I did so he was looking right into them.

'What drink will you have?' He asked with his outrageously sexually provocative grin.

I shook my head slowly.

He knew exactly what I meant, took me by the hand and led me out the door.

We didn't speak as he steered me to his nearby flat. Behind his front door we collapsed onto some stairs where more kissing took place, yet this time much harder and more passionate. I could have eaten him alive right there and then, but he had other ideas.

'Come,' he instructed as he gestured me to walk up.

'That won't be a problem,' I murmured.

Up two flights and I was aching for him. As he put his key in the hole I stood behind him, kissing his neck and groping his crotch. It would appear that the feeling was most definitely mutual.

His flat was open plan with a small kitchen in one corner with an open door next to it that led into a bathroom. On the other side of the room there was a double futon. The sheets were red and it had lots of pillows. It looked very comfortable and so I was ecstatic when he led me straight to it. The lights coming through the windows from the street outside were ample so that we could see each other clearly, yet it was soft and inoffensive enough to be incredibly sexy.

We lay down and kissed again, I automatically manoeuvred myself so that I could get on top of him but he restrained me and saw me onto my back. He knelt between my legs and undid my jeans, occasionally lifting my top and kissing my belly.

He slid off my jeans but left my knickers on. I went to take them off but he stopped me and shook his head.

He moved down the bed so that he was lying flat. Both arms were under each of my legs so his hands were looped through and resting on my hips, leaving his face between my legs.

He looked up. My head, which was perched comfortably on his mound of pillows, was positioned perfectly so I could watch him. Even though our intertwinement suggested exactly what was about to happen, the fact that he had chosen to leave my underwear on left me with a sense of unknowing which was driving me crazy.

He remained motionless for a while. I kept subtly tilting myself towards him, desperate for contact but each time I thrust he pulled his head away. I shut my eyes, realising that what was going to happen next was entirely his call.

Then what seemed like hours later he kissed me. The cotton of my sodden knickers felt cold as it was pushed back against my skin. He planted various pressured kisses on them; as they got harder I could feel the warmth from his mouth.

Now my thrusts were uncontrollable and he granted me the liberty of gentle movement. He removed his right arm from under my legs pulled his face away as he moved my knickers to one side. My hands were on my face, motionless with anticipation.

He ran a finger over me. Slowly circling the bit that matters before slipping it inside. I sank deeper into the bed.

He licked the full length of me before locking his lips in place and putting his arm back under my leg, holding me so that I couldn't move again. It was just moments until I came. He stayed suckled onto me as I pushed into his face. I found it almost impossible to move my body.

Bliss.

'You see why you must 'av a French lover?'

I giggled.

'Yes, yes I see where your coming from now.'

I was trying to build up the power to return the favour, but when I gently pulled him up and kissed him he said.

'Tonight was for you. That was enough pleasure for me.'

Surely not!

I tried again.

'No, really, that was as sexy for me as it was for you. I'm 'appy!'

He lay back, linked his fingers and rested his palms on his belly. I sat forward and reached for my jeans. I hadn't planned to actually stay the night but I didn't think it was going to be quite so easy to leave.

I took my knickers off. They were soaking and I didn't want to catch a cold, it was freezing outside. I pulled on my jeans, stuffed my pants in my bag, gave him a kiss on the cheek and left one very happy bunny.

Bravo!

SUNDAY 9 JANUARY

The Wolf
He ate like a very clever wolf . . .

Post C

07/01/2005   **09.01**
From: The Wolf
To: Dawn
Subject: Your 80987979898 reply?

Hi, I'm at a loose end, saw your ad liked it . . . . my pic is attached.
Shall we get the ball rolling?

07/01/2005   **11.59**
From: Dawn
To: The Wolf
Subject: Your 80987979898 reply?

Ball is off at a steady pace
Tell me more about you x

07/01/2005   **12.05**
From: The Wolf
To: Dawn
Subject: Your 80987979898 reply?

Work in town, Live in Richmond. Work for a web design company
and have a free weekend. So what about u . . . tell me all . . . ?

07/01/2005   **12.12**
From: Dawn
To: The Wolf
Subject: Your 80987979898 reply?

25 years old, but that changes in a couple of weeks – aspire to be
astronomically successful – want to go out all the time, have loads

of fun, meet new people, get involved in things that will make my
life interesting . . . you know . . . the usual!
maybe we could squeeze a lunch in somewhere this weekend?
So . . . why you on here? What you looking for? Be honest, might
as well . . . have you done it before?? Any luck? Tell me your
stories . . .

07/01/2005   12.28
From: The Wolf
To: Dawn
Subject: Your 80987979898 reply?

Nice picture lady!
Why here? Well I kind of go there now and again and look at it and
go "Oh right . . . its all blokes/weirdoes" Then I realise I'm weird for
looking but I like to think that I'm a good weirdo as opposed to a
gun/knife collector weirdo.
What am I looking for? Dunno. Food, wine, snogs, arm wrestles . . .
whatever.

I do have a strange/naughty side to me that pops
up now and again . . . .
Met one person a while ago, which was cool. She was nice and we
had some fun. We still speak now and again.
What about u?

BTW, u look v cute in that foto

07/01/2005   12.34
From: Dawn
To: The Wolf
Subject: Your 80987979898 reply?

Why here? Because it sounds like fun . . . whenever do you get to
meet total randoms in a totally disconnected way from every day
stuff . . .
Friends of friends . . . blah blah blah . . . I like meeting new people,
with new stories etc . . . I was raised in Guernsey – it's nice when
people are totally disconnected – the Internet offers that . . . who
the hell are you?? I dunno, who cares lets meet up, get drunk have
an arm wrestle (great idea by the way but please can you let me
win . . . I'm a terrible looser!)

It's weird. I'm on here writing to a stranger but I still think you must be weird for replying to my post . . . it makes no sense . . . sorry!
You shall have to prove me wrong over lunch!
How you prepped for tomorrow?

07/01/2005   12.52
From: The Wolf
To: Dawn
Subject: Your 80987979898 reply?

I'm prepped well.
My arms are small like a child's so it's cool. U should win
So. Where do u live?

07/01/2005   13.26
From: Dawn
To: The Wolf
Subject: Your 80987979898 reply?

I live in Hackney at the moment
What time? Where??

07/01/2005   13.31
From: The Wolf
To: Dawn
Subject: Your 80987979898 reply?

OK. Well what about Sunday? 13:00 – Richmond.
Oooo this is all very exciting . . . are we allowed to kiss?

07/01/2005   13.34
From: Dawn
To: The Wolf
Subject: Your 80987979898 reply?

Fine!
Yes we can kiss . . . why the hell not! (Air kisses . . . right?)

07/01/2005   13.39
From: The Wolf
To: Dawn
Subject: Your 80987979898 reply?

Get a train to Richmond I can meet u there, and then we can air
kiss and walk to mine . . . and go from there . . . i.e.: to the park,
then pub, and then to bed, then to Jamaica and then Gretna green,
then the moon . . . sorry bored.
My mobile trumpet number is ***********
So . . . tell me a secret, a naughty one. I will if you will . . .

07/01/2005   14.42
From: Dawn
To: The Wolf
Subject: Your 80987979898 reply?

A naughty secret . . . so soon? OK
Not very long ago I had sex with one of my best friends in a toilet in
Soho . . . SHE hasn't spoken to me since!

07/01/2005   14.44
From: The Wolf
To: Dawn
Subject: Your 80987979898 reply?

OK well I once had a 3 some with 2 girls at a xmas party . . . .I think
about it at least 8908908 times a day . . . nearly . . .
booze and other influences didn't help . . .
You're naughty!

07/01/2005   14.51
From: Dawn
To: The Wolf
Subject: Your 80987979898 reply?

Yes I am . . . see you Sunday x

The Date

I didn't wake up until 11 a.m. that morning and I was feeling a little crazy from a night of wild dreams. A tiny part of me thought that I should cancel and see The Wolf when my head felt straight, but from our email banter I had a pretty good feeling that he was going to be equally as mental. So in my dazed state I made my way over to Richmond, one hour behind schedule.

When I got to the station I called him to let him know I had arrived, the phone call was short and to the point – I'm here, how long you gonna be? Can we go eat? I'm starving; see you in a minute then. He had a slightly posh, deep and sexy voice, which somehow oozed cheekiness.

I was still feeling insane, like I'd slept too much and my brain was still passed out but my eyes and body were awake – dense is the best way to describe it. I felt very, very dense, and the extreme hunger in my belly was adding to my lightheadedness. I waited for my date feeling completely off my face and ready to devour absolutely anything that was put in front of me.

My heart sunk when I was tapped on the shoulder by a very small guy who could very well have been the person in the photo. He looked dreadful, dressed in a black T-shirt, teamed with a black leather waistcoat and the tightest pair of black stonewash jeans I have ever seen. We held eye contact for a few seconds, during which I contemplated pretending to be foreign or simply bolting around the corner. But I was saved from having to perform my getaway when the poor little weirdo asked me kindly for directions to the nearest cash machine. Relieved, I extended an arm in what I think was the right direction and watched him scuttle away, wondering how the hell he was managing to negotiate movement in those trousers.

'I couldn't even get my arm into those jeans,' said a voice to my side. 'I take it you're Dawn?'

He was taller than me, brilliant! He had longish scruffy dark brown hair, a round face and a body to match – but it was cute, not fat. He had the cheeky grin I had expected and I fancied him pretty much straightaway. On first impressions I was very happy.

I told him of my lightheadedness and he explained that he'd just left his flat, dodging three bodies on the way in the aftermath of a particularly large night the evening before. So we drifted to a pub by the river, bouncing hilarious one-liners off each other and relishing in the ease of each other's total randomness. Both of us were comforted by the fact that we spoke as much shit as each other.

We ordered our food as soon as we got there, there was no need to look at the menu, it was 'Two roast chickens please, and can we have it yesterday?'

A large glass of red wine and a much desired Marlboro Light, took me from crazy to pissed in a nanosecond. He too was pretty quickly affected by his pint of lager, so as was so far the norm with us, the chat got more and more ridiculous.

Time passed and passed, people were being fed all around us but there was no sign of our food. Conversation had turned to imagining what it would be like if we cried wax, an argument about whether shrews lived in the underground and what would happen if Bigfoot was gay and wanted to wear stilettos. But no matter how serial our inane blabber got, our focus was essentially on the waitress who had appeared to have lost our order. On asking, we discovered that indeed she had, so when her back was turned we discussed our appreciation for the word cunt and decided that she most certainly was one.

'When my food comes, I'm going to wolf it down in seconds,' I said, dribbling.

'Yes, I'm going to devour mine just like a very clever wolf,' he replied.

'A clever wolf? That's ridiculous.'

'Yes, but I will do so nevertheless.'

Our nonsensical tripe was reaching extreme levels, and the date looked like it was going to be more like an inmate's day out from a mental asylum than a successful romantic encounter.

But lo and behold when the food arrived, via the previously labelled cunt who was now one of our favourite people in the world, our heads wafted slowly back down to earth and some actual intelligent conversation began.

He was a genuine, kind natured, cute, cuddly and bladder-shatteringly funny bloke, whose company I was thoroughly enjoying. Whether we were talking about our troubled pasts or hairy bikini lines – which was a topic that somehow kept on popping up, amongst other things . . .

He asked me questions like, 'What's your favourite word?' I said something gay like 'discombobulated', and he told me that he had recently become very fond of the word 'plinth'.

I was taken aback at the coincidence, as the word plinth also holds substantial significance for me. (I once found myself masturbating on one outside the Anglican Cathedral in Liverpool while heavily under the influence of LSD. The congregation got more than a sermon that Sunday, I can tell you . . .) His mentioning of the word had a particular reaction in my knickers as the memories of that highly sexual moment came flooding back. It changed the direction of the evening for me. Suddenly it wasn't about laughing and funny one-liners, I actually wanted to sleep with him.

Three bottles of red and a whole lotta chicken later, he announced that he needed to get home to 'feed his dog'. Now, I'm a pretty good judge of character, but all those stories that you hear from victims of attack like, 'He seemed so nice' and, 'I thought he really liked me' were ringing in my head. But I went anyway and en route we picked up two bottles of red wine, so we could carry on drinking before going back to the pub again later.

It was at his house that a hyperactive King Charles spaniel sucked my face until my cheek looked like a bowl of spaghetti. The Wolf reacted mildly hysterically, and my head was soon numb from the effects of the bag of frozen peas that he'd squashed against it. He suggested that I may have tapeworm, then offered to dangle a piece of raw meat around my anal area to try and entice it out. I called the process a bum fondue and we laughed hysterically . . . nice!

The Wolf sat on the couch rolling a spliff, while I let my eyes wander around his living room, not being able to avoid a five by eight photograph of him with a very attractive woman.

'Your sister?' I asked.

'No, my girlfriend.'

His girlfriend? A lump the size of a potato formed in my throat – in fact, it could have been a potato, after all, I had eaten my lunch very quickly . . . A momentary pang of guilt overcame me, but then I realised that it wasn't my problem, cracked open another bottle of wine and toasted his ability to retain his independence.

After an hour or so I wanted to go out again. He'd suggested numerous times that we should watch a DVD but I refused.

'Why the hell would I meet a guy then sit in silence for two hours and not get to know him?'

I knew exactly why he wanted to watch a DVD, saucy bastard! But I felt pretty certain that we didn't need dim lighting and a movie to take the night to the next level. I wanted to go out, so we got ourselves together and went to his local to get some more booze.

In the pub my sexual desires were getting stronger. You may well be noticing a pattern here. Get Dawn drunk and she gets the horn? Yes, that's very often the case, but I'm actually surprisingly selective about who I get it on with, it just so happens that both dates were with guys who I fancied. I mean, after all, that's the idea with dating isn't it? You go out, then if you like each other it may progress to something sexual, whether it just be a kiss or something more, so I don't feel guilty; I'm just doing what you do when you date . . . ha, ha, listen to me trying to convince myself that I'm behaving myself . . .

After a few attempts at serious conversation involving the Koran, parenthood, adoption, the Tsunami and George Bush's issues with the English language, I eventually managed to pull the chat back to the level that I preferred, in this case our mutual appreciation for masturbation. I knew from the moment I met him that he was someone with a high sex drive, and imagined that with his girlfriend being away a lot, he most likely spent a great deal of his time playing with himself. I was right and the conversation was colourful – to say the least . . .

It was information that I was happy to share with The Wolf, as well as a blatant attempt to turn the vibe more sexy. So when I leant forward to kiss him and he pulled back and said 'This is my local.' I can't deny that I was disappointed. But I sat back and continued with my drink, excited about the prospect of getting outside and having a nice big snog somewhere less conspicuous.

Being only moments away from St Margaret's Station, we hurried onto the platform and found a little alcove to shelter us from the rain. We were kissing passionately for a matter of minutes before I applied pressure to the top of his head, steered him down, leant my back against the wall, copped my right leg over his left shoulder and let him bring a fabulous day to a fabulous climax.

Only moments into my journey I received a text message.

Text Message From: The Wolf

I really want more of you.
Get a taxi to mine, NOW!

Text Message From: Dawn

You're outrageous!
Thanks for the perfect end to the perfect day, but . . .
I need to get back. My sister has locked herself out.
Gutted!
Soon though x

Text Message From: The Wolf

I can't stop
wanking.
Thanks! x

The Couple: One

Part C

11/01/2005   **14.35**
From: Gillian
To: Dawn
Subject: Hello

Hi

I saw you online and liked the sound of you. I'm not sure if you would be up for this? My boyfriend and I would love you to join us for a night of pleasure. We are quite new to this, having had one previous experience with a female friend of ours. We enjoyed that so much we would love it to happen again. I am 26, 5'4", slim but curvy, with red hair, Gavin is 33, 6'2", slim and toned. I have attached some photos so you can see if you like us. If you want more graphic ones we can send some. We would be able to accommodate you in a hotel in London for a night. We are trying to arrange a night next Tuesday 18th January in a 4* hotel near docklands. If not we can arrange for a different date.

We both have very high sex drives and love to experiment. We can bring toys with us, and I have a few outfits that normally get Gavin going quite well!!!
We also like to get tied up and blindfolded, as it adds to the excitement. We are very genuine, and really would love this to happen. Please send us photos so we can see if we like you.
I hope to hear from you soon.

Gillian
x

TUESDAY 11 JANUARY

Action Man
Anyone here called Action Man?

Post D

07/01/2005   10.15
From: Action Man
To: Dawn
Subject: City gent

Hi there,
I work in the City, but not in a bank. I run a publishing company.
I'm 35, love fine wine, company, conversation, manners, sport, film,
fun and would be delighted if you would accept an invitation to
lunch sometime soon at a beautiful restaurant.
Perhaps first things first we should meet somewhere lovely to
share lunch, conversation, some wine and find out if we relax with
each other at all.
I like lively conversation, humour, open mindedness and natural
people, which I believe are my qualities and generosity is good too.
I look forward to your reply and perhaps realizing your dream.
Best wishes
p.s picture attached, I'm the one playing football, obviously!

07/01/2005   11.56
From: Dawn
To: Action Man
Subject: City gent

Well hark at you Action Man! How could I refuse an offer from such
a gentile sportsman like yourself . . . ?
Lunch sounds fabulous let me see where I'm at next week . . . if
lunch is tricky would an after work type scenario be agreeable?

07/01/2005   12.43
From: Action Man
To: Dawn
Subject: City gent

Hi there Dawn,
You have my photo, how about yours?
Lunch would be preferable for a first meeting as it is an
easier opportunity to get to know a person first without any further
implications. After that then fine.
You are the lady so you decide when you are free, happy to extend
the invitation to whenever.

07/01/2005   13.35
From: Dawn
To: Action Man
Subject: City gent

I know what you're saying about lunch . . . good idea! How you set
for Monday?
Pic attached x

07/01/2005   14.55
From: Action Man
To: Dawn
Subject: City gent

I am around Monday
What time and how posh would you like? What type of food do you
like?
Lovely pic, I have someone here who I work with who is the spitting
image of you, (not the puppet of course) and I nearly fell off my
seat when I opened it. They say media is a small world, but that
would be scary.
Okay back to you . . . .
And I'm keeping an eye on my colleague to see whether she gets
an email and I find this is a beautiful wind up . . . lol. I hope not
though . . .

07/01/2005   15.05
From: Dawn
To: Action Man
Subject: City gent

No. I'm currently in my house in Hackney -just off Mare Street so really close to City and looks like I should be around Monday so . . . nice!
Ha ha, imagine if it was your colleague . . . how embarrassing for you
What food do I like? Sushi is my favourite x

07/01/2005   15.45
From: Action Man
To: Dawn
Subject: City gent

Nope she didn't touch her PC and here I have your reply. So that's that answered then . . .
I wouldn't have been embarrassed, possibly charmed but more likely I would have descended into a fit of laughter.
Okay, we have two venues to choose from, a rather bijou Sushi restaurant at The Great Eastern Hotel or a grander Asian fusion restaurant at The Great Eastern Dining Rooms.
Both are Liverpool Street way so close for you to get to. Let me know which and I'll book for 1pm under my name Jonathon Baits.
I will be wearing a Blue pinstripe suit with a pink shirt.

07/01/2005   15.42
From: Dawn
To: Action Man
Subject: City gent

Great Eastern Hotel 1pm is perfect. See you there Action Man
p.s I love boys in pink x

10/01/2005   11.45
From: Action Man
To: Dawn
Subject: City gent

http://www.streetmap.co.uk/newmap.srf?x=533190&y=182445&z=0
&sv=EC2A+3QR&st=2&pc=EC2A+3QR&mapp=newmap.srf&searc
hp=newsearch.srf

Thought I better send you the map – 54/56 Great Eastern Street. I
thought it was next to Liverpool Street but is further up the road
towards Old Street.
See you later

10/01/2005   11.49
From: Dawn
To: Action Man
Subject: City gent

Yeah, don't worry I know where it is . . . been there lots of times x x

10/01/2005   12.15
From: Action Man
To: Dawn
Subject: City gent

Cool. Leaving in 15 mins, so to be early for you.

The Date

Monday morning and I felt like I wanted to die. I had possibly one
of the worst – if not *the* worst – hangovers I've ever had. The night
before with The Wolf was an adventure, but something told me
that my date with Action Man was going to be worth dragging
myself out of bed for. The picture he'd sent me of him, mid-kick,
in some rather fetching football gear, had struck a chord. So, even
though the idea of eating raw fish made me want to vomit into my
cowboy boots, I tottered there regardless.

I arrived at five to one, looking surprisingly respectable considering my internal battle. I went into Miyabi, the Sushi restaurant
underneath the Great Eastern Hotel on Liverpool Street. It's small

but the food looked amazing and by this time my fear of raw fish had vanished and I was suddenly ravenously hungry.

'I'm here to meet a Jonathon Baits, table for two, 1 p.m.' I said quietly to the very busy manager. He took a little time to study his list of expected diners, before turning back to me and insisting that no one of that name had booked there.

'May I?' I asked, glaring over his shoulder at his clip board, determined to see his name on it. But no, he was right, it wasn't there.

I peeked my head around the corner, but there was no man in pink sitting alone, so I stepped back, pondered my next move and went to leave.

'Try The Fish Market, next door. There are four restaurants at the Great Eastern.'

Ah, I thought, phew, I'm in the wrong place. I said goodbye to the manager, and all of the delicious food and made my way round to The Fish Market.

'Hi there, I'm here to meet a Jonathon Baits, table for two, 1 p.m.' I said to one of the girls on reception. She scanned her list of names, then looked up and informed me that there was no booking for a Mr Baits.

I turned to leave.

'Wait, maybe he is in one of our other restaurants, there is Aurora and Terminus in the main hotel.'

Ah, I thought, he must be in one of those. What a palaver! I waved farewell and walked through the rain to the main hotel entrance.

As I walked into Terminus it was packed. This must be it, I thought to myself. Instantly I was smothered with overly keen waitresses all wanting to seat me as quickly as possible. I did the usual and said I was meeting some guy called Jonathon Baits; they looked through their lists and once again came back at me with the same answer: 'No Jonathon Baits here I'm afraid.'

I went next door to Aurora, which seemed wrong. It was very formal and as I walked in I just knew it wasn't the place. A friendly waiter bounced over and asked me if I had a booking. Bugger it; I thought I might as well ask.

'Yes, I have a booking with Jonathon Baits at 1 p.m., table for two?'

His list was checked and I was once again sent away.

'Wait,' he screeched just as I started to leave. 'Let me just check the whole system, I'll see if he's booked anywhere into the hotel today.'

Great, this would find him. I was so hungry and must have looked a little desperate.

'Do you have his mobile number?' He asked as he flicked through the pages on his computer.

'No, it's a meeting. This is very unprofessional of me, I've been out of the office all morning so he won't have been able to get hold of me, and I left my diary at home so I don't have his number.' I waffled on, wishing somehow that I could just tell the truth: 'No, actually I don't have his number; he's just some guy that I picked up on the Internet. He could be anyone . . . really, I have no idea . . . is he on the system?'

'Nope, sorry, he's not here. Pete, I'm just going to help this lady, back in five.' And he whisked me out of the bar, up the stairs, into the lift and back into the Sushi restaurant, where we had a brief chat with my friend the manager, once again confirming that there were no guys on their own, dressed in pink and waiting.

Following this we went back into The Fish Market where the same girl rushed over to announce that Mr Ian Baits had arrived and was sitting at his table.

'Could be him I suppose,' I said as I followed her, my bouncy little waiter still in tow.

'This is Mr Baits,' she said as she introduced me to a mammoth grey-haired beast who sat alone at a table by the window.

My heart sunk. Action Man's photo could have been from when he was younger, and maybe I'd been lied to. He looked bemused as I pulled back a chair. Luckily I was interrupted by the arrival of an equally grotesque gentleman, who was in fact Ian Baits' expected lunch guest.

Many apologies were made as my two companions and I

hurried back out to reception, all feeling a little embarrassed yet as determined as ever to find Jonathon Baits.

'I'm going to get the sack for this,' I announced, just to make sure that everyone knew I hadn't been stood up by a guy I'd never met. I was starting to feel very stupid.

'Don't panic, we'll do one more round,' said my bouncy little waiter.

So off we went, up the stairs, up in the lift, down the stairs and into all four of the fabulous restaurants that served what I imagine to be absolutely delicious food. But no, there was no sight or sound of my Action Man. No pink to be seen. He'd stood me up.

'I hope you don't get fired,' said my friend as I moved to the exit and into the rain. We shared a sorrowful wave and I left.

I walked passed Miyabi and glanced in the window on the off chance that he was there, panting with guilt from being late. But no, there were small groups and couples devouring sashimi, but no one alone and waiting for the woman of his dreams to walk in.

So to the bus stop it was. I stood there freezing, quivering, starved and demoralised; accompanied only by my disappointed expression and a tramp who insisted on telling me the complicated bus route to the Angel. I gave him a pound because I empathised with his loneliness, and then sat on the bus, about to throw up because I was so hungry.

I'd had high hopes for that date, but I was wrong. In the words of The Wolf, and at that moment in time, Action Man was definitely a massive cu . . .

10/01/2005   14.58
From: Action Man
To: Dawn
Subject: City gent

Do you know on days like this I wish I was a duck! Absolutely soaked through . . .
Well I go to the restaurant at 10 to 1pm. I sat, drunk some water, sat some more. The clock ticked to 1pm. No problem. Then 10 past 1 and I thought fashionably late you might be. When it got to 20

past 1 the waitress wondered 'Perhaps your guest has gone to the Great Eastern Hotel? I assured her that my guest knew where one would be. At 1.thirty it seemed a lost cause. I know we hadn't exchanged numbers, the weather was doing its best to rival Noah's flood, but at 25 to 2 I decided to pay up and leave. A long walk to the Great Eastern Hotel found it busy, but no Dawn. I did pass a girl in a checked coat who looked a little like your photo, but not your height, and not used to stopping total strangers in the street, even after exchanging eye contact, I moved on.

So back to my desk, dripping wet, wondering if feathers would have saved me and wondering whether you decided late in the day to take a rain check.

10/01/2005   15.05
From: Dawn
To: Action Man
Subject: City gent

I was there, so so excited to meet you but your waitress was right . . . I was at the Great Eastern Hotel – because last week when you asked me where I wanted to go . . . I said the Great Eastern Hotel would be great – so I just went with that, because I know the sushi restaurant there. Thing is, when you sent me the street map earlier on, I didn't even look or read cause I new that I knew where the Great Eastern Hotel was . . . I had the most bizarre encounter, walked in and out of all four restaurants there at least 6 times, made amazing friends with all the staff and even pulled up a chair next to an obese geriatric who was called Ian Baits . . .

I left hurt by you, cold and wet and so so hungry

I have no idea what to do now . . . I feel terrible, can we establish that maybe, in small ways we both made little mistakes and re arrange?

We are both wet . . . disappointed . . . a little shocked.

Actually if I'm honest I feel devastated and entirely responsible . . .

Why are they both called that? Stupid stupid stupid places!!!!

I wish I was a duck to, if for no other reason than to waddle off and be stupid enough not to be so stupid! – but then who would want to be a duck . . . you'd just get shot!

10/01/2005   15.15
From: Action Man
To: Dawn
Subject: City gent

I didn't leave hurt by you. What will be will be, I suppose I'm pretty relaxed in nature.
My sincerest apologies for you having to walk in the various restaurants a number of times.
I think we should choose a place that does not have a similar name. I'm busy this week, but we could rearrange for next Tuesday?
I was so looking forward to meeting you, and then it all washed away too quickly. What are you after from this? I guess a meeting would help . . .
I hope you are now drying out nicely, sorry for the misunderstanding.
Now how do I get dry?

10/01/2005   15.24
From: Dawn
To: Action Man
Subject: City gent

I'm dry now . . . I dried my face on my kitten, Lilu, who is always good when I feel a little down (excuse the pun, quack quack!)
I suggest that you angle yourself nicely under the hand dryer in the loos; it's a little uncomfortable but is fast and effective . . .
What do I want out of this? I'm not looking for anything to change my life, just fancy making it more colourful for a while . . . you??

10/01/2005   15.53
From: Action Man
To: Dawn
Subject: City gent

Yes I like the excitement of it too, but I don't make a habit of this. Okay how about tomorrow? The Argyle Pub in Argyle Street, Oxford Street. Then if we do meet up we can go to Mash for lunch. Let's say 1pm shall we?

10/01/2005   16.38
From: Dawn
To: Action Man
Subject: City gent

Perfect – I will be seeing you at Argyle Pub at 1pm tomorrow . . . I
promise x x x x
Book a table at Mash, under your name . . . not Ian Baits . . . he
sucks!
See you tomorrow Action Man, I really am looking forward to it x x x

The Date

I walked into the Argyle and through into the main bit with the
bar. He was sitting to my left, tucked neatly into a little alcove. I
wasn't sure that it was him; he looked a lot older than I had
expected. Short, grey hair which surprised me as he said he was
39. Do people really go grey in their thirties? Shit! He stood up,
obviously recognising me.

'Hello Dawn,' he said. There was no mistake to be made, he
was my Action Man.

Conversation was a little bit slow until my first JD/DC had been
consumed, then my motor mouth was off and there wasn't one
thing I didn't want to know about him. He was indeed the kind,
gentle and genuine guy that I imagined. I didn't have to dig very
much to work that one out.

'It's so good to finally meet you, I was so upset when we missed
each other the other day,' he said.

'Me too, and thanks for being so kind to me after I ruined your
day and got you soaked in the rain.'

'You didn't ruin my day at all. Your emails were fun. It made
meeting you now all the more exciting.'

Again, my hopes were very high for this date. A part of me worried on the way there that this might be the end of my Internet
adventure, and that I might come away blissfully in love. His
emails revealed him as a mature, down-to-earth, caring man. I
hoped that more humour would be apparent when we met, but I
was pretty certain I was going to marry him. I was mildly

hysterical after the hiccup with our first meeting, but his emails were so calm and understanding that my frenzy didn't last very long. I like it when people make me feel manic; it always pulls me back a bit and sorts me out.

His complexion was pale yet he had nervous colour in his cheeks. Untidy shapes of reddish purple appeared where the blood was rushing to the surface. His nose carried the occasional broken vein and his eyelashes were entirely free of curls. He wasn't a good looking man, but somehow he was a pleasure to look at.

We talked a little about dating sites and the risks you take, but he wasn't the kind of person who was scared. He spoke very openly about the fact that he saw no shame in meeting people on the Net and, judging by my success so far, I agreed wholeheartedly.

I was a little surprised by the extreme lack of flirting. He looked at me almost lovingly but he didn't actually 'flirt'. By flirting I mean that there were no cute smiles, no gesticulations, no provocative lines of questioning and no suggestive winks or random leg touches. He was pretty still, and his eyes were kind yet unrevealing. It was hard to work out if he was very comfortable or extremely nervous. When I put a match to his cigarette and saw how violently his hands were shaking, I had my answer.

There wasn't the thunderbolt that I had been expecting but conversation was easy and there was something very calming about his company. So when he invited me to MASH for lunch I gleefully accepted.

Upstairs in the restaurant we ordered starters and mains. I went for a crayfish salad, followed by a large green salad. He insisted that I be a devil and have something more adventurous, but as I had another date that evening, which I was sure was going to be wild, I chose not to. I explained my healthy choice by lying that I was attempting to be good after the Christmas indulgences. He understood, of course.

He ordered a bottle of wine of which we both enjoyed a glass. I say 'both' and 'a glass' purposefully as he reverted to water after one, leaving me to tackle the rest of the bottle myself. It being lunchtime, and only having eaten a belly full of leaves, the effects of the three and a bit glasses were quite dramatic. The lack of flirting became even more frustrating and although the conversation was interesting and fluid – mostly about magazines or football leagues – I wanted to know if I could get my Action Man to give me some action.

Drunk, but aware that he needed to be approached with care, I chose not to frighten him with my verbal enticements and instead opted for a more subtle approach. I forked up each of the remaining peas individually, seductively rolled each one onto my tongue and occasionally held one gently between my teeth. I was doing my best. But though I was puckering my shining, salad dressing drenched lips while practically fellating my fork, it wasn't working. He didn't move closer or even acknowledge my attempts, but did express his views on Jen and Brad's break up and the perils of Hollywood marriages. Interesting stuff, don't get me wrong, but I would have preferred a knee tickle and a bit of kinky chat.

Worried that I was intimidating him with my pea eating technique, I pushed my knife and fork together and joined him in a page by page account of that week's *heat* magazine. He knew his shit, yet I must say that I prefer to have those conversations with my girlfriends. There is something mildly gay about a guy that studies gossip mags.

I was with my Action Man for nearly two hours and I thoroughly enjoyed it, even if he wasn't the confident aphrodisiac I'd predicted. He led an active life as a keen football player and was a successful businessman. He dressed excellently and was honest and attentive but he was too old for me. Not in age but in manner. I got the impression that a night at the pictures would be more his style than a night at a strip club, which would be more mine.

We got the bill, paid up and went outside. On the corner of Oxford Street we kissed on each cheek and I knew that would be the last time I saw him. There was no spark, he was too low energy for me and I think I intimidated him a bit. The goodbye wasn't uncomfortable, we both knew it wasn't worth pursuing.

For me it was the flirting. I love it, and although I like subtlety from men, I do like to know that they are at least trying it on a little bit. I left sad – and drunk. I wasn't expecting to be able to walk away from that one so easily. But alas, I almost skipped.

The Couple: Two

11/01/2005   **00.47**
From: Dawn
To: Gillian
Subject: Hello

I can't say you haven't whetted my appetite a little, but just bear
with me until I can give you some dates, next week is no good for
me but I would love to get involved.
This wasn't what I was looking for but it sounds rather interesting!
I will be in touch
Pic attached, hope you like x

12/01/2005   **00.12**
From: Gillian
To: Dawn
Subject: Hello

Hi Dawn,

I like your picture very much! And look forward to arranging a night
together (at least!). I'm sure we will be able to work out a date that
would be convenient to all of us.
Look forward to hearing from you again
Gillian
xx

12/01/2005   **01.49**
From: Dawn
To: Gillian
Subject: Hello

A few more pics . . . no naked ones I'm afraid .
You look hot by the way, strokable . . . amongst other things, may be
paying most
attention to you . . . if not all . . . that OK?
We will get a date in the diary soon, it sounds very exciting – I like
sexy lighting and sexy tunes . . . can you arrange?

TUESDAY 11 JANUARY

The Little Leprechaun
Pocket Rockets, Love Eggs
and a Bug with No Anus

Post D

07/01/2005   **10.05**
From: The Little Leprechaun
To: Dawn
Subject: Hi

I would love to take you out, wine and dine you . . . that sort of
thing!

07/01/2005   **11.30**
From: Dawn
To: The Little Leprechaun
Subject: Hi

This sounds exactly what I want . . . but tell me a little more about
you . . .
Why so generous?
Married?
Bored?
Rich?
Where do you live?
Where would you take me?
What exactly are you looking for? Be honest, you have nothing to
loose here . . .
Really – the idea sounds fabulous x

07/01/2005   14.00
From: The Little Leprechaun
To: Dawn
Subject: Hi

hello . . . .
Well it might not be that generous – we're not talking trips to Paris
here . . . well come to think of it is only 3 hours from Waterloo . . . .
Not married – bored definitely bored.
January is such a dull month don't you think.
Rich – not rich not poor I do OK.
so many questions Dawn . . . I fancy going to see what that Gordon
Ramsey is all about . . . .so the Boxwood cafe maybe.
What am I looking for – fun and adventure I think. You?
Now what about a picture?

07/01/2005   14.34
From: Dawn
To: The Little Leprechaun
Subject: Hi

Here you go . . . your turn!

07/01/2005   16.39
From: The Little Leprechaun
To: Dawn
Subject: Hi

Ding dong!
Very nice ;-)
Oh balls – you are not going to believe this – and I wouldn't blame
you – but I can't get at my pictures as our server is down.
I could do one on my phone I guess . . . sorry about this.

07/01/2005   16.41
From: Dawn
To: The Little Leprechaun
Subject: Hi

How old are you?
Server down my arse! Come on . . . get it over!!

07/01/2005   16.45
From: The Little Leprechaun
To: Dawn
Subject: Hi

I turned 32 yesterday – the grave beckons – I swear to you.
I just took a picture of myself on my phone, like a right eejit!
It's a bit dark and wee – the picture as opposed to me.
But here you go.

07/01/2005   17.11
From: Dawn
To: The Little Leprechaun
Subject: Hi

You look fun – what are your stats?
I'm 5 10", comfy size 12, size 7 feet, all pretty well proportioned, no
major complaints, other than a slightly over zealous Christmas
tummy, but I'm getting that under control

07/01/2005   17.14
From: The Little Leprechaun
To: Dawn
Subject: Hi

Oh I'm a bundle of fun me.
You are very candid. Me, same height as you. That was close. Used
to go to a gym – do a bit of sport. All limbs intact and well
proportioned as you put it.
Size 7 feet eh – my favourite size.
I'm Irish but have been in London for a good few years now – about
eight on and off.
Oh . . . hows about dinner on Charlotte Street maybe – some very
nice places down there.

07/01/2005   17.23
From: Dawn
To: The Little Leprechaun
Subject: Hi

Dinner on Charlotte Street sounds lovely – I love that street . . .
When you free, any nights next week?

07/01/2005   17.27
From: The Little Leprechaun
To: Dawn
Subject: Hi

Charlotte Street is a lovely spot. Let's do Tuesday x
Looking forward to it.
So where do you live – and what brought you here?

07/01/2005   17.47
From: Dawn
To: The Little Leprechaun
Subject: Hi

I live east – what brought me here?? The lights and the dream that
one day my name will be written in them
I have to go . . . lets meet at 7pm at The Marquis, end of Charlotte
Street . . .
Have a great weekend x

07/01/2005   17.48
From: The Little Leprechaun
To: Dawn
Subject: Hi

You too Dawn – I liked that – the lights and the . . .
bye until then (exciting isn't it)

The Date

I had no idea what to expect from him. In his photo he looked
quite small, with little eyes and a big nose. There was something
comical about him, which is why I chose him for a date. I have
quite high standards when it comes to guys, but they are not about
looks. I like attitudes, good ones, and humour is vital. Yet it has
to be sophisticated and clever, I'm not up for dating fools. His
emails were sharp, he seemed on the ball, and from the speed at
which he hurled text messages at me while I was on my way to the
pub, I knew he'd have a lot of energy. All in all I expected to giggle my way through a few hours, at the very least.

As I walked up Rathbone Place I could see the Marquis in front of me, and there was no mistaking that the guy in a three-quarter length charcoal coat sitting outside was him. He assumed an uncomfortable masculine stance that he kept adjusting and was pretending to read a newspaper. I knew he was pretending because his head was facing down but his eyes looked up, darting in every direction trying to spot me.

I sat down at the table and he jumped to his feet, firing me with questions like, 'Would you like to go inside?' 'Can I get you closer to the heater?' 'My God, are you OK?' 'Can I make you any warmer?' All of which I didn't answer, not out of rudeness but because he didn't leave enough spaces in between to let me. This went on for the best part of four minutes until I reached out to him and in the calmest of voices said 'I'm fine, but you can get me a Jack Daniel's and Diet Coke.' To which he took a deep breath, put his hands on his hips, nodded and bolted into the pub, giving me a few seconds to come to terms with his performance.

As to be expected he was back in a flash, but with only one drink.

'Are you not drinking?' I asked, a little confused.

'Ahh, shite, I forgot that, yes, hang on, wait there, I'll go and get myself one.'

So there I was again, happy to have another two minutes to sit still with a look of total bewilderment on my face before my hyperactive Little Leprechaun came springing back to join me.

Conversation wasn't sparse. Oh no, not with him, his choice of ice breaker was fabulous: the fascinating subject of the Cnidarian, the bug with no anus. Yup, that's what I said. On our date, the first thing we discussed was how on earth the bug with no anus excretes toxins from its body – I presumed through sweat; he suggested that it simply didn't and therefore has a very short life span. I still haven't discovered how, but I'm sure that when The Little Leprechaun finds out he'll let me know straightaway.

I liked him very much, and though he was nervous I wasn't going to judge him for that. He was constantly in motion, I'd be talking and he'd be bobbing around like a jack in the box that had just had the lid opened for the first time in a million years. It was quite hard to keep a straight face because all his nervous energy was being launched over to me and was making me react with laughter as opposed to unease. I had to keep cracking really hilarious jokes so as to give myself an excuse to laugh. For example, I did my Irish accent, which is appalling but makes me chuckle every time. He didn't laugh – I'm not sure why . . .

We finished our drinks and I suggested that we got another. He was starting to settle and I was worried that if we tried to walk anywhere he might lose balance. Off he skipped again to retrieve another JD/DC and a pint of lager.

'So, where did you go to university?' I asked, as he spilt his pint all over himself.

Another trip inside to get a roll of blue paper gave me an opportunity to do a runner. But alas, I remained out of decency, and when he returned he went on to say that he'd studied in Liverpool. This was good as I did too, so a mutual interest made conversation flow well for a time – but it was just a short while . . .

I should have thought twice about telling him of my ex-football hooligan pals who promised to 'kill' anyone that ever hurt me. It was just a little too much for his nervous little heart to take, and very soon we were back to the erratic head movements and uncontrollable eye rotations that had previously greeted me. I eased the situation by showing off my Scouse accent, which by the way is exceptional, until eventually he had to stop me . . . I had never thought that was going to happen. Slightly discombobulated from the knock back, I suggested that we move on, unable to resist saying it in Liverpudlian.

Thinking he'd booked a place to eat, I asked him where we were going. His face made it abundantly clear that he hadn't made any kind of reservation. I didn't mean to be presumptuous, but considering his early emails had mentioned Gordon Ramsey's gaff, I'd just supposed that he'd got it all sorted. I felt somewhat cheated, especially when he announced he wasn't even hungry and didn't want to break up the evening by going for food. A very odd thing to say in my opinion, seeing as we met so early and had blatantly agreed on dinner. I was absolutely starving as I'd only eaten a plate of peas all day, so I was pretty pissed off.

'Well I need to eat so we're going to, let's find somewhere with finger food.'

We walked towards Soho, my mood slightly darkened and his even more elated because I hadn't run away yet.

Just as we reached Oxford Street, we both totally randomly said, 'Pitcher and Piano' at exactly the same time. I wasn't too freaked about it, but what did rather spin my brain was when, approximately five seconds, later we both shrieked 'Perfecto!' Once again, at exactly the same time. Not only had we both said two identical things within minutes of each other but I had said 'Perfecto!' A word that I'm sure had never passed my lips before and one that I was pretty unaware I was saying. It created a bizarre and strangely psychic feeling, but one that I didn't want to revel in as it was becoming clear that he was more attracted to me than I was to him. The last thing I wanted to do was spend the next few hours discussing how we were probably soul mates, and let him believe that we would end up having sex. So I did my best to avoid elongated periods of laughter and opportunities for him to sling his arms around me in joy, and I upped the pace to the pub.

At the Pitcher and Piano we found a quiet table and ordered a bottle of wine, which he paid for. I took off my coat to reveal my leopard print vest top. His eyes almost knocked my nipples off my chest when he saw how low cut it was.

'Wowzer, you sure wear that well,' he dribbled.

Wowzer? Do people really say that?

I ordered and paid for a sharer platter of roasted vegetables, which he presumed was a romantic gesture – it wasn't. In no uncertain terms I let him know that there was no way we were going to be sucking on the same piece of aubergine.

I am always amazed and slightly irritated by people that pick up on signals that simply aren't there. I was doing about as much flirting as I did with the tramp who chewed my ear off while I was waiting for the bus after Action Man stood me up. But somehow The Little Leprechaun was taking everything in totally the wrong way. As soon as the vegetables were gone, he was sitting beside me clutching my hand.

I didn't know how to respond. Maybe I'd got it wrong, maybe he felt like me. Maybe this was a person who was relatively easy to get along with and a friendship was possibly forming, how could he possibly be thinking that I fancied him? I was talking about other men and doing everything I could to make it clear that this was not and never would be a passionate relationship.

As he got drunker the dance moves came out again, and if ever there was a personified version of the move 'jazz hands' then he was it. He was clapping and waving all over the place, looking incredibly proud of himself and coming out with comments like, 'Finally' and, 'I knew this would work out.'

I was becoming more and more aware of glances falling on us, so made a last grave attempt to revert the energy from his finger-tips to his lips and get a normal conversation out of him. I asked him what his success rate so far had been from the website. It was obviously a topic that he was happy to discuss.

'Seven women, most mad, I had sex with three of them but none worked out,' he said, with total ease.

I was pretty impressed, he'd obviously done something right to get three shags but I couldn't imagine how. It did make me feel slightly less sorry for him. If I'd denied him sex thinking that he'd not had it in years, I would have felt meaner than if he'd got some action a few months before.

The conversation, once again, was frank and most definitely sincere. I had no doubt that he was telling me the truth. Physically he might have acted like he'd just hovered up five grams of fine Colombian cocaine, but his mind was sound and his honesty wasn't something I ever considered questioning. It was hard for me to be entirely focused though, as the drunker he got, the more he would finish a phrase, drop his chin down to his left shoulder and expose all of his teeth in anticipation of my reply. I couldn't work out whether it was supposed to be a huge grin or a stressful clench. Equally as frustrating was the gargantuan piece of parsley that had wrapped itself around one of his incisors. It was almost like he was presenting it to me. I just couldn't be the one to tell him about it, he seemed so proud.

Giving me a few moments to collect my thoughts he hopped off to the toilet, where he remained for a slightly longer length of time than seemed normal. Hoping that this was due to him undertaking the huge task of removing the tree from between his teeth, I sat and watched the waitress mop up the gallons of wine that he had managed to spill on our table.

'Thanks,' I said as she walked away.

Clearly unable to restrain herself she stopped, turned back and asked 'What are you doing with him?'

My mouth opened, but no response came out. I had no answer.

Soon he was skipping back over like a Shakespearean nymph bearing news. With said shrub still firmly in place.

'They sell love eggs in the toilet,' he declared.

'Wot?'

'They have a vending machine in the toilet that sells love eggs, lust fingers, pocket rockets and lots of other kinky sex toys.'

Oh Jesus, I thought, as I felt the presence of his penis become overpoweringly prevalent. I had no idea where to look – was I going to have to watch him do his impression of someone with love eggs inserted into their anus? Or was I supposed to try to avoid the subject altogether? All I could do was give into my intrigue and make a trip to the ladies to see this genius machine for myself.

Indeed it did exist. Rummaging in my bag for five pound coins I was disappointed to realise that I wasn't able to purchase a toy for my own use later on. However, when I returned to my seat he'd somehow managed to make a sneaky second trip to the gents and bought me one himself.

Not being able to hide my elation I grinned from ear to ear, obviously this caused him to believe that I had plans for the two of us to use it together. I needed to make my escape before his tongue followed suit of his hands and landed somewhere on my body.

The waitress came over to clear our glasses, but before I had the chance to grab my bag he'd already ordered two more drinks. By this time he was playing twister and using me as his mat. Somehow I had an arm around me, another one on my leg and a leg between mine. It was quite a tangle and trying to escape it would only have caused a scene. So I remained enveloped and proceeded to drink as quickly as I could, managing amazingly to stay stone cold sober, even though he was so pissed I worried for his safety.

I don't think I have ever been so grateful to hear the phrase 'last orders' in my life. The lights came on and I finally had the right to move. I grabbed my coat and made my way for the door faster than you could say 'Is that a pocket rocket in your pocket or are you just pleased to see me?'

He walked me to my bus stop where I insisted he didn't need to wait. With one swift move he kissed my lips harder than a punch and bounced back from the force of my shove so quickly that he ricocheted off one of those stupid ticket machines that never work. Out of politeness I placed a neat kiss on each of his cheeks and steered him toward Oxford Street tube. He went pretty painlessly, and I watched him dance all the way down the road like Dick Van Dyke on ecstasy.

He was gone, I was free. It was just me and my pocket rocket and the memories of a night that I was trying to forget. I now realise that not flirting can cause a man to believe that you want him. From now on, if I don't fancy someone . . . I'll get my tits out!

The Couple: Three

13/01/2005   **00.08**
From: Gillian
To: Dawn
Subject: Hello

Hi Again,
Love the photos, you are very sexy.
I will not mind you paying me lots of attention. That would be great.
I'm sure I will want to reciprocate! However I do want Gavin to be
there. You don't have to get involved with him, but it would be good
if we could all have fun together. He also thinks you are very sexy,
and can't wait to see
us together.
If you let me know when you are free I'm sure we can arrange a
suitable venue, with sexy lighting and music.
Would you like to see more photos of me and Gavin? We did take
some naughty ones last year.
What things are you into? Are you dominant, or submissive? Do
you like uniforms, sexy underwear, Basques etc? It would be good
to know, as I will know what to bring with me on the night we meet.
Look forward to seeing you soon
Gillian x

13/01/2005   **00.13**
From: Dawn
To: Gillian
Subject: Hello

Would love some more pics . . . .
I like all sorts of stuff, it depends on the mood I'm in I suppose -
outfits are not something I choose to do but being an ex actress I'm
willing to take on any role. And of course Gavin will be involved but
I have no problem pulling guys . . . I'm more intrigued by the
opportunity to fiddle wth a lady for once. However, and I'm sure you
understand . . . there comes a point where a
girl needs a nice big cock to play with so all is welcome. I'm excited
but next week or so is manic so please bear with me on dates.
Oh lord how exciting!
You're fit, by the way . . . get those pics over

Am I dominating? Can be yes. Toys are very welcome. And if the outfits fit I will wear them. All up for new experiences!
Licking and good use of hands are very appreciated . . .
glad to believe you guys are genuine . . . meet, drinks, laughs and sex . . . perfect evening x x

13/01/2005   00.45
From: Gillian
To: Dawn
Subject: Hello

Here are some more pics. Hope you still like?! They are a few months old, and the one of us dressed is over a year old, but I just think it is nice photo.
Good to know you are willing to join in with Gavin. It will be great. We are both very excited at the prospect!
I was meaning what outfits would you like me to wear for you actually, unfortunately I don't think they will fit you as you said you are 5'10", and me only 5'4", guess they would be very short, although that isn't a bad thing!!! I have a couple of nurse's uniforms, one in PVC, and we have handcuffs and blindfolds, toys etc so I'm sure we can have lots of fun indeed!

You can be sure there will be lots of licking and good use of hands by both of us.
We are very genuine, and are glad you seem to be too. It is fantastic, I can't wait!
If you have anymore pictures it would be great to see more revealing ones? I would love to see your figure.

Gill
x

FRIDAY 14 JANUARY

The Gentleman
Whisked Away!

Post A

07/01/2005   00.55
From: The Gentleman
To: Dawn
Subject: Whisk Away

Hi. I found your ad online. I'm in the process of opening an office in London and there all the time but never have anyone to explore the city with and actually enjoy the fine dining type of life style . . . .
I could even be talked into a play, followed by dinner at the Ivy (or Savoy), followed by Martini's. (Although if the play is a musical . . . I refuse to sing show tunes . . . that's my limit!). I will be there starting on Monday for 2 weeks.
I'm 36. Never tried this type of thing, but why not?
Here's a pic. Let me know if you are interested. Do you have a picture?

07/01/2005   01.20
From: Dawn
To: The Gentleman
Subject: Whisk Away

Yeah, why not indeed . . . .
It's just nice to meet new people I think and I'm willing to embrace this as a way of doing so.
Pic attached

07/01/2005   **03.30**
From: The Gentleman
To: Dawn
Subject: Whisk Away

Hi Dawn,
Have you met people this way?
What is your ideal 'whisked away' scenario?
I'm sure you have gotten loads of offers. Great pic by the way, very beautiful!

07/01/2005   **14.12**
From: Dawn
To: The Gentleman
Subject: Whisk Away

Yes, lots of responses. Most sordid but a few sound decent. I don't really know what I'm looking for with this. To be honest I'm not really sure I'm looking for anything; I just like the idea of meeting someone nice, in whatever capacity. You are definitely the only gentleman so far . . . or so it seems.
For the record . . . I would love to go to The Ivy x

07/01/2005   **14.17**
From: The Gentleman
To: Dawn
Subject: Whisk Away

Same here. Wow . . . I'm a gentleman . . . .must be doing something wrong!
I will try to get reservations at the Ivy. If not, Gordon Ramsey's at Claridges?
Did you grow up in London?   I'm from New York City but have lived in many places across the globe which makes me not your average American.
Where in London do you live now?

07/01/2005   19.06
From: Dawn
To: The Gentleman
Subject: Whisk Away

Well I grew up in Guernsey, a small island not far from France.
Been in London about 3 years now and absolutely love it yet hope
to one day spend lots of time in other places.
Ooo, you can tell me all about New York, I'm so desperate to get
there soon.

07/01/2005   19.32
From: The Gentleman
To: Dawn
Subject: Whisk Away

I love New York, it's a great place . . . .actually a lot like London.   I'll
have to tell you all about it.
Have you been to the Ivy?   I called them and looking to get a
reservation. I'll let you know when/if they get back to me, so I'm not
sure what night.
I'll make sure I wear a tailored suit so you can have your whisk
dream!!

12/01/2005   00.40
From: The Gentleman
To: Dawn
Subject: Whisk Away

OK, I couldn't get The Ivy for Friday so I made reservations at
Claridges. Looking forward to it.

12/01/2005   00.48
From: Dawn
To: The Gentleman
Subject: Whisk Away

Ooo, me too I can't wait to meet you. I have to say that I think you
are lovely – oh, and I should also probably say that I'm drunk!

12/01/2005   00.49
From: The Gentleman
To: Dawn
Subject: Whisk Away

ahaha . . . I think you are lovely too and I think I like drunk Dawn.
I've heard great things about that restaurant . . . but I'm equally
looking forward to meeting you.
Pic attached for you!

12/01/2005   00.51
From: Dawn
To: The Gentleman
Subject: Whisk Away

LOVE that one!!!!
You look American – it's the fabulous grin and sturdy build x x
How tall are you?
Big KISS!

12/01/2005   01.03
From: The Gentleman
To: Dawn
Subject: Whisk Away

I'd say I'm sturdy . . . .at 6'4", not many people will topple me.
How tall are you?

12/01/2005   01.06
From: Dawn
To: The Gentleman
Subject: Whisk Away

5ft 10 . . . I'm so excited . . . when I go out with you I can rejoice in
my heels . . . I love tall men!
Thanks for the opportunity to break in my new shoes x x x
I'm so sleepy, my kitten is calling me for cuddles

12/01/2005   01.09
From: The Gentleman
To: Dawn
Subject: Whisk Away

Absolutely!
Do you have good body?

12/01/2005   01.14
From: Dawn
To: The Gentleman
Subject: Whisk Away

Wait and see x

The Date

When I walked into Claridge's bar I knew straightaway which one he was, because he stared right at me and walked straight over.

'You're beautiful,' he said.

I blushed.

I hadn't been expecting a disaster by any means, but I certainly wasn't expecting to be amazed. My Gentleman was huge, so tall that I was still tiny in my stilettos and his build was broad and firm. I felt delicate and petite next to him, a feeling that I seriously enjoyed. The features on his face were rounded and small but perfectly proportioned. I wouldn't have described him as really good looking, but I was enraptured with what I saw.

He confidently kissed me on each cheek and led me by the hand into the restaurant. As we entered the dinning room, he presented me to the room and already I felt astonishingly special. We walked around the entire span of the restaurant to reach our table, while the waiters formed a line and greeted us in a way that made me feel like diamonds.

I was wearing a knee length skirt with a huge split all the way up my right leg, a silver fishnet top that hung off my shoulder with a black silk vest underneath. It was a glamorous get-up and when I took off my jacket he looked me up and down approvingly. This simple gesture caused my vertebrae to shudder and I transformed from a girl who had a grip of herself to a girl who could hardly hold her glass straight.

A glass of champagne got our conversation off to a great start. I don't recall one moment where our chat didn't flow, yet there was no haste involved at all. The waiters, incredibly attentive as they were, came over quickly to give us the menu, yet after ordering a particularly delicious bottle of American wine, The Gentleman told them that we would be taking our time this evening so to come back later. I loved the way he did that. He took control. This wasn't a date that I was in command of and it was the sexiest feeling. It was a dream date, like the ones you see on the movies, where the man treats the lady like a precious gem and ensures that her every desire is met. I felt so beautiful that I could have taken all my clothes off and lay naked in the middle of the restaurant, having everyone stroke me and kiss me. Well, actually I wanted to lie naked in the middle of the restaurant and let The Gentleman stroke me and kiss me, even though the waiters were particularly beautiful.

He taught me all about New York, how buzzy the city is, how when you're there you have the feeling that you can achieve anything – but he also praised London and said he loved it. He was 36, though I would have maybe thought he was a little older than that. Not because he looked it, but because of his maturity; he beamed success and was extremely graceful with it. There wasn't a shred of arrogance or pretentiousness. He was softly spoken, charismatic, polite, attentive and calm, but most of all frank. He had no inhibitions about flirting. When I got up to go to the ladies he said 'Ha, cool, I can check you out!' I could feel his eyes on me until the moment I left the room, which was quite a walk, and I relished every second of it. I couldn't help holding my shoulders back, dropping the top I was wearing down to reveal as much flesh as possible, pushing my chest slightly out and wiggling my bottom just a tad. When I got back to the table I think we had both enjoyed the experience. Especially him.

'Right, well I can't stand up for another ten minutes,' he said.

Golly!

It must have been close to an hour before we ordered. I hadn't even looked at the menu so I told him to order for me. My knickers swelled when he said 'I shall have the fish and the lady will have the duck.' I felt elite and my heart was making my breasts look like they were pulsing.

Unlike Action Man, The Gentleman found the balance between flirting, getting to know each other and interesting story telling a breeze. He didn't struggle with letting me know he fancied me, yet at no point did I find him sleazy or overbearing.

I'm a very tactile person but I try to be selective as to when I touch, and of course where. From my experience, and it's fair to say that that's a lot, men are not so good with their hands. Touching can often be overpowering, slimy and presumptuous. They either launch themselves at you in a nervous flap, run their hands over your limbs like they're about to eat you, or alternatively look at your body like it's made of fire and panic if they touch it at all.

But not The Gentleman. His hand touched my knee every time he asked me if I had everything I wanted. He touched my shoulder when I spoke about things that I didn't like, and he squeezed my hand whenever I said something funny. Which, by the way was very often . . .

We ate from the chef's choice menu. A selection of small portions in an eight course extravaganza, which was perfect as it lasted for ages and kept the evening moving, not that we needed food to help with that.

Conversation throughout the meal mostly revolved around our pasts. There was no need for him to tell me that he had had a wealthy upbringing. I wasn't really interested in that to be honest. I was more intrigued by the stories of his father, whom he hinted at as being Mafia, and the complex stories he told me about his relationship with his parents. Being the eldest sibling, there was pressure on him to perform, yet something made me think that he would have been successful anyway. He was intelligent and had a depth to him that was drawing me in. The only way I can describe it is that unlike other guys who speak with their heads, he spoke through his body. Right down to the tips of his toes. Everything he said came through him in an indisputably true way. He was warm, and considering I had only just met him off a dodgy website, I felt remarkably safe.

Eight delicious courses, two bottles of wine, lots of ice cream chocolates and half a cheeseboard later, we were both entirely at ease in each other's company. Just opposite from us sat an old couple who had hardly said a word to each other. They just sat and ate their food, almost as if the other person wasn't there. The Gentleman made a joke about how much fun they were having and I said that I hoped we never got like that. After a moment's silence he looked at me. I thought I'd said something a little too full on but he said, 'I could never run out of things to say to you.'

At that moment, Shazam! Drunk Dawn made her appearance. The lip gloss came out and as I applied it seductively he said, 'Don't do that, it's not fair.' Which it clearly wasn't judging by the twitch under the tablecloth on his lap.

'Come on, let's get out of here,' I suggested, so we left the restaurant, desperate to get somewhere more appropriate for snogging.

In a taxi on our way to Leicester Square we drove past the Cheers pub. Insisting that it was authentically American, The Gentleman made the driver pull over and we went in. It was dreadful – a load of townies gurning, sweating and giving each other what I presumed to be kisses, all to the soundtrack of some hideous house music. But my Gentleman loved it, and, at that moment in time, I would have been happy anywhere as long as it was with him.

At the bar he ordered our double Jack Daniel's and Diet Cokes and a couple of shots of God knows what. I was pleased to see that we both drank as quickly as each other and, before I knew it, another full glass was being shoved in my face. He took his jacket off and I saw his chest bursting out of his shirt for the first time. I dread to think what my face looked like as I ogled over his body.

I took my seat on a stool at the bar and he stood between my legs, appreciating the split in my skirt which allowed me to accommodate him properly. We talked for a bit, I can't remember what about, then he kissed me. I remember every second of that.

The bar was pretty hectic but our little patch at the bar was serene and I was revelling in the fact that I seemed to have found the perfect man – classy, genuine, funny, sexy and a gorgeous kisser.

What happened next, and how I ended up back in his hotel room at the Hampshire Hotel in Leicester Square, is a bit of a blur, but what happened when we got there is lodged securely into my memory. And as I'm sure The Gentleman would never kiss and tell, I shall be a lady and do the same.

SUNDAY 16 JANUARY

The Gentleman: Part Two
Honesty is definitely *not* the best policy!

15/01/2005   16.00
From: The Gentleman
To: His Lady

This morning was fantastic!!

15/01/2005   16.23
From: His Lady
To: The Gentleman

Yeah and we all know why you liked it!!!
Naughty!

15/01/2005   16.27
From: The Gentleman
To: His Lady

Yes, we both know. It was the affection and cuddling . . . and the . . .

15/01/2005   16.45
From: His Lady
To: The Gentleman

Now now! I'm off out. Speak later . . . don't forget about me

15/01/2005   16.50
From: The Gentleman
To: His Lady

Forget about you? Not a chance . . . not after this morning!
X

16/01/2005   10.05
From: The Gentleman
To: His Lady

I have a dinner reservation at The Ivy tonight . . . care to join me?

16/01/2005   11.30
From: His Lady
To: The Gentleman

Oh bloody hell, do I have to? I hate that place!

16/01/2005   11.45
From: The Gentleman
To: His Lady

I know, isn't it a bind!
Table booked for 6.30 – meet me in the All Bar One across the
street at 6 x
How often do you masturbate?

16/01/2005   12.32
From: His Lady
To: The Gentleman

Great!
Pardon?

16/01/2005   12.36
From: The Gentleman
To: His Lady

Oh drats . . . I thought I could just sneak that question in there . . .
see you at 6 x

The Date

He was late. Not a problem though, it gave me time to sit at the bar and the opportunity to buy him a drink for once.

Text Message From: Dawn

I'm here. You are not
What would you like to drink?

Text Message From: The Gentleman

You x

OK, I couldn't buy him a drink, so I just sat and waited.

At 18.06 he walked into the bar wearing jeans, shirt and a light brown jacket. It wasn't a trendy outfit but he looked hot in it. We kissed, on the lips, which I loved and kind of made me want to sack off dinner and just go back to his hotel, but no, The Ivy was calling me.

Sitting in All Bar One, I was pleased to discover that he was equally as fantastic as he had been a couple of days before. That's always the fear with second dates, was the first one just so good because you were excited and you were both making lots of effort? And when the novelty has worn off, are they actually as sexy as you thought they were? Very often not, which is why I usually fear it so much. Yet on this occasion I didn't fear it at all, and when it was in progress I didn't experience one shred of disappointment. He was lush and getting lusher.

As we walked into The Ivy he had his hand on the small of my back, a simple gesture that was driving me wild. His hands were huge and firm and his ease with me made this date so real. I had forgotten all about the idea of keeping a journal, this was just about me and him.

Something was going on in my head that I had never expected would happen, but I was happy that it was, and I was in no doubt that he was feeling the same way.

At our table we sat next to each other enabling our tactile

natures to be fully expressive. One of his hands was on my knee and we were leaning forward, elbows resting on the table, so that the many kisses that were taking place were easily accessible. He ordered a bottle of wine called 'Frog's Leap' which was American and absolutely delicious, and as we drank our first glass he once again said 'Let's take our time again tonight.'

I don't know what it was about it, but when he said it my chest quivered. I think it was just knowing that he was happy to be there and we were enjoying each other's company so much that we didn't want to hurry a second. Most people in London are so hectic. As I looked around the restaurant everyone looked manic, eating quickly, talking at super speed. The waiters were running around flopping plates about the place, and then there was us, calm and slow, in a little bubble totally disconnected from everyone else.

Once again I let him order for me. I'm the kind of person who'll eat just about anything, so I was happy to let him make the selection. We had caviar to start. Then scallops in garlic, then the most delicious steak in the world, and some sort of fish that I wasn't really bothered about. In fact, I wasn't really that bothered about any of it – I didn't even feel the urge to rotate my head on a celebrity hunt. I was with The Gentleman and I really cared about that. We could have been anywhere. Well, not anywhere, but it didn't have to be The Ivy, although it was very nice, anyway . . .

During dinner we must have kissed over a million times. He kept looking into my eyes then leaning forwards to plant little ones on my lips. Anyone watching would never have imagined that it was only our second date. We looked blissfully in love, and at that moment in time I think I was.

He mentioned that he'd be back in a few weeks for another business trip, which might involve a trip over to Jersey. Before I knew it I was texting my uncle to ask if he would come and pick us up in his plane and take us to Guernsey. I was so excited about him seeing where I was from and telling him all about my life, so I spent a short while describing my beautiful island and all the places I wanted to show him. He kissed me throughout my mono-logue and I worked hard to stay focused.

We were moved into the bar at around 10 p.m., where the dou-ble Jack and Cokes came quickly. We sat on separate chairs yet practically on top of each other. I couldn't get close enough to him and my hands were glued to his leg.

It was then that it all went horribly wrong.

'Well, I'm pleased to say that you're not a freak. And compared to some of my other experiences so far that's saying something. You're certainly the best person I've met so far,' I said, slightly droopy eyed and particularly drunk.

'But the other night you said you hadn't met anyone else. Which is it?'

I panicked, I thought that in my early emails I'd mentioned some of the other people I'd been out with, but it would seem not. Unfortunately for me, alcohol means memory loss and as I scrab-bled around in my brain I had no idea what I had and hadn't said. Then the guilt kicked in as I thought of all the dates that I'd been on in the last week. So, in a moment of total madness and extreme honesty, I told him everything: the other men I had met, the jour-nal that I'd been keeping and my hope that I could get the accounts of my experiences published.

He looked devastated. His posture slumped as he felt more and more that what we had wasn't exclusive. But it was. I had no sign of a publishing deal at that point so it really didn't matter – the journal was just a personal diary and could have stopped right there. But, I couldn't be made to feel guilty for meeting people before I had even met him, and I certainly was-n't going to be made to feel like a bad person for wanting to be a writer and having an idea. I did my best in my drunken state to convince him I genuinely wanted to be there, but every word seemed to dig me deeper and deeper into a cavernous hole, and he became more and more distant. He paid the bill and we went back to his hotel.

For a moment I thought he was OK about it. That moment largely involved my head being in his crotch with some extraordi-narily horny sex to follow. Yet afterwards, in what should have been a loving embrace he moved to the edge of the bed, put his head into his hands and said, 'I'm just Chapter Three to you.'

I left.

17/02/2005   10.30
From: Dawn
To: The Gentleman

I'm sorry. I can't have you hate me. I can't explain how I'm feeling – it's weird.

17/02/2005   /   11.15
From: The Gentleman
To: Dawn

Well at least you don't feel like freakish research.
I don't hate. I'm leaving today; I don't think we should speak anymore.
Good luck with, whatever it is you do . . .

TUESDAY 18 JANUARY

Plato
Making a spectacle of yourself!

Post D

07/01/2005   **21.57**
From: Plato
To: Dawn
Subject: How could I refuse!

Hi
A very intriguing posting. I'd just about given up on the amount of drivel on the site and then I happen upon you.
Well, I very much enjoy dining in London's finest restaurants (what's your favourites?), enjoy travelling, and believe in working hard but making the time for quality leisure. I'm a bit old fashioned, I guess, in that I send flowers, check that you got home safely (that is unless we ended up together of course!) and treat a woman with respect – I'm interested in learning what life experiences you've had and what your thoughts and feelings are on all topics under the sun.
I also like being spontaneous – whether whisking you off at the last minute for a weekend in a European city to (well, that would be telling . . . . . .).
I love comedies – The Office, Little Britain, Phoenix Nights etc and am a big movie fan.
Hope I've whetted your appetite, would be great to hear from you.
Take Care

08/01/2005   **02.43**
From: Dawn
To: Plato
Subject: How could I refuse!

You sound cool – I'm drunk, just got in from a night out . . . you still up???

08/01/2005   **12.55**
From: Plato
To: Dawn
Subject: How could I refuse!

Hi Dawn
Guess you might have a hangover when you read this?? Hope you had a good night, afraid I had an early one – needed to be bright eyed and bushy tailed for a day in the office today. If you do feel a bit fragile, I find a day on the Bloody Mary's helps.
I've been on the wagon all week, not sure how long my New Year's resolution will last though – am meeting an old friend in Cambridge tonight so I could end up falling off.
Hope you have a great day. I'd be really interested in finding out more about you.
PS – remember these wise words
A good thing for a hangover is drinking heavily the night before.
If I had all the money I've spent on drink, I'd spend it on drink.
Never eat on an empty stomach.

08/01/2005   **13.45**
From: Dawn
To: Plato
Subject: How could I refuse!

Hangover . . . yes, very much so but I'm getting over it slowly – love the Bloody Mary idea, that is my all time favourites way to survive a day like this.
So what do you do? What do you look ..like . . . come on . . . tell me more about you . . .
Got a pic? I know it seems odd to send pics but I kind of like it . . . don't you think?

08/01/2005   **16.00**
From: Plato
To: Dawn
Subject: How could I refuse!

OK – a few facts before I send any pics (don't want to scare you too quickly!).
I'm the MD of a marketing company, have worked my way up from sales exec, to be a boss. Do a fair amount of travelling through

business as well as socially. Originally from Yorkshire but have lived in London – and here's the bit that I give my age away – for over twenty years. So at the ripe old age of 40 I find myself at the start of a new year with a great circle of friends, good job but with the feeling that something missing.

Since my divorce, don't have any kids by the way, I have dated some great ladies but ultimately the relationship(s) have fizzled out. I'm not saying that I want to run head long into a serious relationship but I really liked the sound of you.

I'm 6ft 2" tall slim build reasonably fit. Still want to see a pic?

Tell me more about you . . . .

08/01/2005   16.19
From: Dawn
To: Plato
Subject: How could I refuse!

Absolutely yes . . . get it over you . . . loving the sound of you x

Me? I'm 25, just about to turn 26 (two weeks). Live in Hackney but also about to move house, to a beautiful flat in the west end – Marylebone area . . . can not wait!!

I feel that London, despite its variety, is actually quite a hard place to meet new people. Bored of the friend of friend scenario . . . I get excited when I meet people who are totally disconnected from my life and the Internet offers me that . . . would you not agree?

I don't know what I'm looking for here . . . . I don't really feel that to much is missing from my life apart from my need for new stuff . . . you sound like a really interesting person and I already think I would love to meet you . . . I'm sorry you feel something is missing. I can't say that I might be that thing but I have a feeling that we could have quite a pleasant evening . . . don't you think??

p.s – now send that pic!

09/01/2005   13.34
From: Plato
To: Dawn
Subject: How could I refuse!

Hi Dawn

Just got back from town (only four bottles of lager all night – not bad eh?). Just had an opportunity to read your emails, certainly empathize with what you say. I meet a lot of new people through my job, but London isn't the greatest place to meet people on a social basis.

Pic attached . . . yours??

10/01/2005   09.32
From: Dawn
To: Plato
Subject: How could I refuse!

Hey there
Well done you for only sinking four bottles . . . I wish I could learn that skill . . .
What am I on about? I probably did only have 4 bottles last night . . . of WINE . . . ouch!

10/01/2005   14.00
From: Plato
To: Dawn
Subject: How could I refuse!

What a beautiful smile – you look lovely. Been stuck in a long meeting all morning, feel cheered up now. Hope your head is feeling better as the day wears on.
Dinner Tuesday? What food do you like?
x

10/01/2005   23.01
From: Dawn
To: Plato
Subject: How could I refuse!

Great for Tuesday – how exciting
What food do I like? Um, pretty much anything really but it would be quite cool not to have Italian – My tummy hates me when I eat wheat, an unfortunate by-product of a bad student diet I'm afraid, but anything else is fine. I love French and I love sushi and I also love themed places with loads of character.
Up to you though, I'm just looking forward to meeting you x

11/01/2005 **22.06**
From: Plato
To: Dawn
Subject: How could I refuse!

Good morning
I feel like I'm having a protracted near death experience today.
I fell out of a bar at 2.30 this morning, got a cab home.
Unfortunately I fell asleep in said cab only to wake up as he drove into the street where I used to live 5 years ago. Took some slurred explaining that I got the address wrong and an extra £15 to put it right!
Anyhow, I've booked a table for 7.30 pm at a restaurant called Bam Bou, not sure if you know it, they do French-Vietnamese cooking which if memory serves was OK the last time I was there. The address is 1 Percy Street W1 (just off Tottenham Court Rd). We've got the table for 2 hours and can either move into the bar there or go elsewhere – that's unless I haven't bored you senseless!

14/01/2005 **18.19**
From: Dawn
To: Plato
Subject: How could I refuse!

Wow what a story! I always fall asleep on the bus and end up in the dodgy Hackney depot, being prodded by old men, then having to walk home as I have no money, usually being followed by someone large, mad and drunk and with a massive dog . . .
Yes I know Bam Bou and love it . . . see you there x x

The Date

Before the whole Gentleman palaver I'd been very much looking forward to meeting Plato. I thought he sounded brilliant in his emails. Clever, charming, witty and silly, four excellent attributes. But as The Gentleman had left the country without saying good-bye, my excitement had been somewhat shat on from a great height and I nearly cancelled a few times. What stopped me was the ridiculousness of the situation. There was me, the girl who set out to have nothing but fun, getting all stupid and emotional over someone who I had only met twice, lived on the other side of the world and had a passionate affinity with melodrama.

With things in perspective I made my way to my date with Plato, determined to enjoy it, yet angry with myself for not turning my phone off during dinner and willing it to buzz.

I walked into Bam-Bou and saw him sitting alone at a corner table. He was fiddling with a fork. As soon as he saw me he leaped up to greet me. He knocked the table but nothing fell off it. We were both relieved. He rolled his eyes and huffed, I got the impression he was quite used to being clumsy.

'Miss P, finally we meet,' he said – sorry, shouted.

His nerves were practically popping out of his pores. It was really quite sweet. Our kiss on each cheek was awkward and we kept talking at the same time, but I adored him instantly. He apologised constantly and I could almost hear his brain process saying 'Shut up you fool, just stop talking. Be cool, be cool.'

I put my hand on his hand and smiled. 'It's really good to meet you.' He relaxed a little.

'Right, we better get the drinks in before my heart jumps out my mouth. Champagne?'

'That would be lovely.'

I expected a glass but he ordered a bottle. We toasted and both took a couple of very large gulps.

'So, Dawn, have you met anyone else on the Internet?' He asked in a voice that filled our quiet restaurant. A woman who sat alone at a table two along from us laughed and Plato sunk his shaking head into his hand.

'Don't worry; I have no shame in it.'

'Dawn, I'm so sorry that was so stupid.'

'I actually thought it was quite funny.' There was a moment's pause then we both had a good giggle.

His nervous disposition matched his appearance. He was tall and skinny with a head of orange hair that also played host to some definite signs of grey. His nose was long and pointy and comfortably held the weight of his rather thick corrective eyewear; his smile was so wide and constant that it could very well have been drawn on. I realise that sounds predominantly unattractive but taken together it kind of worked. He was no looker but I loved looking at him. He dressed well. In his slick black suit, white shirt and smart tie, he looked elegant and smooth. Yet, it wasn't his aesthetic qualities that I focused on; it was all about his character. He was eloquent, polite, attentive and extremely friendly. Despite my state of mind re: The Gentleman, I couldn't have been spending my evening with anyone more amiable.

He wanted to know all about me but he wasn't intrusive. On occasions he'd ask odd questions which got him in a bit of a fluster. My story of how my family were involved with setting up the Guernsey pottery, for example, elicited the question, 'Do you like dishes?' He fumbled over it, said sorry and admitted that he meant 'throwing clay'. I thought it was quite cute and was enjoying his efforts. What I liked about him was the way that he acknowledged every time he said something a bit stupid. It was almost like watching someone with Tourette Syndrome. When I was at school, every single school report I ever had said, 'Dawn has a tendency to speak before she thinks and this often results in mindless statements.' I never quite knew what they were getting at. Now I know exactly what that means.

When we ordered our food, he was keen to make sure that I was happy with his choice as well as my own, in case I wanted to try some. He also used my name a lot when he spoke, which I liked. He would say things like 'You see, Dawn' and 'Well the thing is, Dawn'. There's something really personal about it that makes you trust that the person is genuinely interested in what you are saying.

Every single thing that happened over dinner, from the choice of wine to the stories he told were all run by me first. He couldn't have been any more conscientious, or indeed hilarious. I got him to tell me again about the time when he got the taxi driver to take him to his old house and he told me another brilliant one about how he'd been for a big night out on a business trip and was back in his hotel room after getting undressed. In his drunken state he'd wanted to know whether the door to his room opened from the outside without the key, so, in his pants, he jumped out into the corridor, shut his door and discovered that it didn't actually open without the key. But where was the key? In his jeans on the bathroom floor . . .

So there he was, pissed out of his face, unable to see because his glasses were also inside and wearing nothing but his underwear. (I didn't ask what kind of pants they were but for the sake of comedy I decided they were probably Y-fronts).

After contemplating his next move, he decided to go down to reception and find someone who could let him in. So off he strutted, angry and drunk – still in just his pants. After a brief detour to the kitchens, he eventually found reception. A young woman sat behind the counter and was confronted by a naked ginger beauty storming towards the desk.

'I appear to have locked myself out of my room. Do you have a spare key? I need to get to sleep.'

He wanted to sleep – the fact that he was in his undies and addressing a woman he'd never met was totally irrelevant.

Unfazed she replied, 'Certainly sir, what's your room number?'

'My room number?' It was a rather vital piece of information that had managed to escape his memory.

He checked three different floors before he recognised his corridor. Squashing his head against a number of doors to get a clear view of the numbers, he eventually got to his room. Still very drunk, and now exhausted from his Herculean endeavours, he took a moment to relax on an armchair with all the intentions of heading back downstairs to inform the lady of his room number. But that never happened. Four hours later he was woken by the sound of a Hoover, as various cleaners were pushing trolleys full of dirty crockery past him. To make matters worse his room door stood wide open.

Looking down he quickly managed to tuck himself back in, aware of the fact that most people in rooms 326–350 had probably had a good look at his morning glory. Then he went into his room, where his clothes were now neatly folded on the bed.

I thought it was hysterical. I could visualise it so clearly, like a scene in a silent movie. He was the ultimate dufus, yet totally adorable. I loved the way he told me the story. He shook his head throughout in shame but had no problem with laughing at himself. This was the managing director of a huge company, who must be excellent at his job to have achieved his status, but who was still that much of a Muppet that he felt the need to step out of his hotel room at 4 a.m., without his key just to see if the door locked . . .

The story had been a good ice breaker and he relaxed a little. That might also be due to the fact that we had drunk the champagne and were now on a lovely bottle of white. Nevertheless he still apologised for talking too much about himself and insisted that I tell him a story.

'If you keep telling stories like that, you can talk about yourself all night, you nutter!' But he was adamant it was my turn.

He'd mentioned earlier that he'd recently done some work in Marbella, so I told him about the time that my cousin Charlotte, my friend Fiona and I were on holiday there and how we got kidnapped by a Serbian prince.

We'd met him in a bar during the day and had had lots of fun, so when he asked us to join him for dinner at an Indian restaurant just up from Puerto Banus, we happily accepted. We met him at a roundabout as arranged and got in his car. Clever, huh? I know Marbella very well as I used to live there, so when he carried on driving in the opposite direction to the restaurant I started to realise that something was not quite right. My cousin and I were on the back seat, which was in the open air, but Fiona was in the front which was under cover, and so we couldn't hear their conversation. Our imaginations were running wild as we came to terms with the fact that it was getting dark, no one knew were we were, we had no mode of communication and that we were probably going to die. I think I really started to panic when I turned around and realised that about five Range Rovers full of bodyguards (that I recognised from the bar during the day) were following us.

When we got to his house three Dobermans came bounding towards us but sat instantly on his command. He then made us sit around a large dinner table with himself, a woman that couldn't speak and three massive and very scary looking men. He fed us curry that gave us all the shits and could have been laced with anything from Rohypnol to Cyanide, but which we all devoured within seconds. Let it just be said that my cousin and I have very similar appetites and if someone feeds us then we eat it, regardless of the consequences. After dinner he ushered us into a drawing room where I sang an a cappella version of 'Don't It Make My Brown Eyes Blue', and he recited some poem that he had written about eyes which made no sense and went on for ages. My cousin and I got the giggles, which was horrendously inappropriate as I'm sure that somewhere in this million dollar villa was a place where he could keep us and no one would ever find us. But it was so funny.

After about three hours, I announced that we had to leave and that he was wrong to have driven us all the way out there without our consent. He offered us the opportunity to travel around the world with him while he was on business, and said that all we had to do was keep him company and he would let us shop all day. We thought about it for a couple of seconds, declined, then one of his body guards took us back to our apartment. It was a rather bizarre experience.

Plato loved the story, but I was adamant that he told me another one. He did, and followed that with another, and another, and another after that. He had loads – all based around that fact that he finds himself in crazy places, with crazy people, doing crazy things. He really made me laugh and I had the biggest smile on my face throughout the entire meal.

By the end of our main course we'd drank a bottle of Champagne, a bottle of white wine and a bottle of sparkling water. I'd been to the loo twice and couldn't help but wonder how he was managing to breathe, let alone talk, as he hadn't been once.

'Excuse me for being rude,' I said, 'but do you have the bladder constitution of a camel or something?'

'Oh God you're right, I'm dying over here. I was just being polite. Excuse me.' And off he shifted, clearly about to burst.

When he got back I told him not to worry about being so polite – I understand that the body needs to micturate and I had no problem with it.

'It's good you don't smoke,' I said after dinner, 'I've been trying not to, I don't take cigarettes out with me so if the other person isn't smoking, I won't either. It's tough though.'

'I do smoke, and I'm gagging for a cigarette, was just being polite about that too.'

'Well stop it!'

Approximately two minutes later, the waitress brought over a saucer with a packet of Marlboro Lights on it and we each smoked two in succession.

After dinner we got a taxi to a gorgeous little members bar on Poland Street called Milk and Honey. It's very small and dark, with mellow jazz music and big leather seats, perfect atmosphere for us – not too smoochy and romantic, but calming and chilled. I got straight on the JD/DCs, he joined me and we started to chat about his divorce.

He wasn't downbeat about it and didn't go into a big woe-is-me-I-need-to-talk-about-this type scenario – in fact he was quite the opposite. He'd married someone a lot younger than himself and it hadn't worked out, but they were still friends. Now he was single and looking for the next stage in his life. All pretty straight-forward really.

In Milk and Honey I told him how incredible I thought he was and we had a really open moment about how good it feels when you meet someone that you adore. I wasn't sure I fancied him. Well, I think I knew I didn't, but I knew I had to see him again. He's one of those people whom I feel honoured to know. So genuine and kind and fantastic company. So when he asked me to join him for dinner again in a few weeks I jumped at the chance.

We left at about 1 a.m. and he saw me into a taxi for which he gave me the money. I insisted that I'd be fine on the bus but he wouldn't have any of it. Saying that he would kick himself if any-thing happened to me on the way home. We kissed on each cheek and promised to see each other again soon. I couldn't wait.

In the taxi I was so happy. That evening could have been an absolute disaster because of how I was feeling about The Gentleman, but in fact it was probably my favourite date so far.

Text Message From: Plato

You are wonderful
Thanks for a fantastic
Night. Don't forget to
Let me know you get
home safe, can't wait to
see you again x

Text Message From: Dawn

Home safe!
You have no idea
what a pleasure tonight
was. You are great.
Looking forward to next time

The Couple: Four

19/01/2005   **22.58**
From: Gillian
To: Dawn
Subject: Hi

Hi Dawn,

Haven't heard from you in a few days. I know you said you were busy so it is understandable. I just hope you aren't getting cold feet, or have been put off by our photos?
We are really looking forward to meeting you and having a night of pleasure together.
I hope to hear from you soon

Gill
x

WEDNESDAY 19 JANUARY

Del Boy
Without the class!

Post A

12/01/2005   **17.57**
From: Del Boy
To: Dawn

Hey Attractive professional Lady Aged 25
I think I may have just what the doctor ordered:
* Martini's at Dukes
* Cocktails at Sketch
* Dinner is up to you – but perhaps staying at Sketch or The Wolseley as an alternative
* All you need to provide is stimulating conversation and plenty of fluttering of your eyelids
* Complete chivalrous male behaviour is assured
* Package available immediately
* Hopefully you will be feeling a bit special already! (a youngish 35)

12/01/2005   **18.30**
From: Dawn
To: Del Boy

Wow that all sounds amazing
I would have been happy with a glass of Blue Nun and a bowl of chips but hey . . . Sketch is probably my most favourite place so I would love to . . . Got a pic for me?
Wednesday?
Dawn x

12/01/2005   19.45
From: Del Boy
To: Dawn

Wish I'd offered Blue Nun and Chips now . . . !
Wednesday the 19th as an option to meet?
(I also have a great social life but the thought of a night out with a total stranger sounds great!)
I guess we have to get past the hurdle of the photo-scan first though! (Mine's the result of a day out at Ascot and I'm the one on the right)
Well . . . . You still there?

13/01/2005   09.01
From: Dawn
To: Del Boy

OOOO, Ascot, how exciting! You shall have to tell me all about it
I think this might be fun!!
How random is this!!
Pic attached – it is the result of muchos muchos Jack Daniel's and Diet cocks . . . and don't worry, the wind didn't change, my face is actually quite normal x x

13/01/2005   09.07
From: Del Boy
To: Dawn

Dawn,
Nice photo . . .
It's uncanny but JD & DC is my drink to. Welcome to the square-bottle club! I notice how you spelt "cokes" by the way . . . Freudian slip??
Will tell you all about Ascot later, shame theirs no meeting this year though. The racecourse is being modernized. It's an annual pilgrimage for me.
Will get a booking for Wednesday – you look like you might be worth it x

13/01/2005   **10.30**
From: Dawn
To: Del Boy

Well you sound right classy so I hope Wednesday is a date!!

13/01/2005   **12.00**
From: Del Boy
To: Dawn

Well it's not often a right classy man gets a chance like this so where and when do you want to meet . . . .??
Shall I book a table at Sketch (seeing as it's your favourite) for say, 7:30 ish . . . ??
We could meet in the bar before-hand for some ice-breakers!

14/01/2005   **16.00**
From: Dawn
To: Del Boy

You just tell me where and when . . .
Can't think, been drinking Champagne at the boat show all day . . . dahhhling!!!!

16/01/2005   **20.17**
From: Del Boy
To: Dawn

The coincidences are racking up fast and furious. I was sooo nearly at the boat show on Friday as well as a guest of a good friend of mine who works for Moody. Would have been pretty freaky to have seen you there. (Pretty impressive too, recognizing you from that photo!) You'll have to tell me all about what I missed.
How about we meet outside Sketch at about 7. I've booked a table for 7:30 if that's OK.
Maybe we can start the evening with a couple of JD & Cocks! Champagne may have to follow though . . . .?

18/01/2005   12.45
From: Dawn
To: Del Boy

Absolutely!
You sound really good fun.
7.30 is fine, perfect in fact . . . oooo, what the devil shall I wear!
BIG kiss x x x x

18/01/2005   14.00
From: Del Boy
To: Dawn

To help you I'll be in dark suit, pink shirt so you'll be able to
recognise me!

18/01/2005   15.23
From: Dawn
To: Del Boy

Oooo . . . I LOVE BOYS IN PINK!!!!!

18/01/2005   17.01
From: Del Boy
To: Dawn

That's a good start.
Drum roll please . . .

The Date

Del's emails and photo gave me the impression of a 35 year-old
city gent who enjoyed fine things and was probably quite cultured
– I got that from the Ascot photo. But when I met him it was clear
he was a small town salesman who couldn't tell his Shakespeare
from a pig's ear, which, as it happens, is exactly what he made of
our date.

As I walked towards Sketch I was pleased to see that facially he
looked exactly like his photo. And, although there were a few
issues with height – i.e. there wasn't much of it – he wasn't bad
looking and seemed nice enough.

There wasn't any real acknowledgment of me though. I was

wearing the skirt with the obscene split up the side that I wore to Ramsey's with The Gentleman. It's a head turner, there's no doubt about it, but Del didn't seem to notice it at all. I felt like stridently crying, 'Um, hello, I'm half fucking naked here!' But I restrained myself.

Initially I was quite turned on by his reluctance to admire me, a girl likes a challenge and he was giving me one. I did my best to act demure and presumed that after a few sherbets he would succumb to gazing at my thigh.

A drink in the bar to begin with set off the conversation. When he told me he worked in sales I could see straightaway that he was successful at it. Not so much because of his gentle persuasions or convincing descriptions but because he talked shit and rarely allowed me to say a word.

'So where were you brought up?' he asked. Allowing me to eek out all of four words before he cut me off and started telling me how he knows when he's stressed because he gets cold sores. A delightful point to make fifteen minutes into your first date. It left me examining his mouth for blemishes and pretty much secured the fact that I was never going to kiss him.

I'd heard so much about eating at Sketch; the service, the food, the atmosphere . . . the prices. But, alas we weren't eating upstairs in the plush restaurant, but downstairs, which was still lovely, though he didn't really need to tell me that he'd got a deal off last-minute.com – it just kind of took the glamour away.

As he doesn't actually live in London he was soon bumping his gums about the perils of public transport. However, his complaint was not of its often disputable punctuality or overcrowding, but the tube's habit of making him sweat buckets. How very charming! He continued to say that once he sweated so much that when he arrived in the office his light grey shirt had turned dark grey and he'd to go home to change. We both agreed that he should most definitely stick to driving in future.

I was experiencing another one of those drinking-a-ton-but-not-getting-drunk nights. Trying not to yawn was torture. We had nothing in common, apart from that I do occasionally get a sweaty face on the tube . . .

'So, do you go to galleries at all?' He asked.

I don't really, but I've been and I would like to go more, so I took this as a chance to be taught a little about art. But no, he didn't seem to know what art was, it was a totally random question that he had no idea how to follow up.

I think he was intimidated when he discovered that I worked in the media. He was about as cultured as a block of extra mild value cheddar, but I was OK with that. There's nothing worse than a person that doesn't know about art, trying to sound like they do. Comments like, 'I saw the *Mona Lisa* when I was six and thought it was really nice' are best not said. But he proceeded to list every painting, play, street-performance and TV program that he'd ever seen in a grave attempt to prove that he had a clue. He didn't.

As if things couldn't get any better, our beautiful Japanese waitress became the brunt of his racist and homophobic jokes.

'Where about in Thailand are you from then?' He asked as she served me my raw fish. She looked puzzled, and more Japanese than you could possibly imagine.

'No, I'm from Japan. You think I look Thai? No one has ever said that before.'

As she walked off, he leaned into me conspiratorially, 'Actually, I didn't think she looked Thai,' he said, 'I thought she looked like a man!' He then roared with laughter and nudged me so hard that my elbow flew off the table and my fork crashed to the ground, taking my perfectly proportioned mouthful with it.

His laughter jolted to a close, but my squirming continued.

I know that London can be intimidating. The high-energy people, the fashion, the diversity of most things, but there are different ways of dealing with that intimidation. Being a Guernsey girl I understand how one can feel, but I'm unsympathetic towards people who react judgementally to things they don't understand. For example, the Maître d', a young attractive man probably in his early thirties, was wearing a suit with a white T-shirt and trainers. I thought he looked great, not too trendy but a perfect balance of smart and casual. Yet my subtle as a smack in the fanny dinner date insisted on laughing at him every time he walked past. When the poor bloke realised and turned to look, Del straightened his posture and made an 'It wasn't me' face.

I was so embarrassed. While he insulted our surroundings I did my best to look like it was a business dinner as opposed to a date. I made sure that my posture and mannerisms were formal and I nodded a lot, like I was taking in important information. I also blew out the candle to ensure that minimum romance was suggested. When he got up to go to the loo I downed the wine that was in my glass and poured myself another one, which I hoofed just as quick. All done with the sole intention of preventing him from getting any drunker and embarrassing me further.

After the meal we went back into the bar to have a few more JD/DCs. He mentioned the early email I had sent him when I wrote 'Cock' instead of 'Coke'. We laughed; he was pleased to have finally said something that I reacted to with more than a minor lip tilt. But really I was laughing at the fact that I'd been thinking what a cock he was all night and it was funny to hear him say it.

The bar was full of people who looked like much more fun. Opposite us were three men, all of whom were quite good looking and relatively trendy. He insisted on staring at them and mimicking their gestures. This final indignity caused me so much discomfort that I headed for the sanctuary of the toilets. When I got back, Del was talking to the guys – well actually he was talking *at* them – taking the piss out of one of them and calling him 'The moody one'. It was terrible, I either thought he was going to get hit or asked to leave. It was bad of me to do what I did, but I couldn't stop myself. I was so ashamed of the way that he was behaving that I didn't want people to think I was OK with it, so in a moment of sheer desperation I blurted 'We met on the Internet; this is a blind date.'

Slightly winded from my announcement he finally shut up and opened the way for me to eye up one of the guys who was now sitting with us. He got back to me straightaway with his flirtations, and before I knew it I was talking to him and totally ignoring my date. My new guy mouthed 'Get rid of him', and I willingly obliged. Putting my hand to my forehead I began to groan a little.

'God I feel so drunk, my head is spinning,' I said, building up to the big 'See ya!'

'You don't look drunk.'

'Well I am, and I think I need to get out of here. Yup, I do. Thanks for dinner, thanks for the drinks, thanks for chewing my ear off all night, thanks for embarrassing me to high heaven, I'm outta here!' I left.

Obviously I was a little more subtle than that, but I did make a hasty exit nonetheless. Making sure that I mouthed, 'I'll be back in a sec' to the guy I'd been flirting with.

Outside I hurried up the road, hid myself in a doorway and waited until I saw Del leave. As soon as he was out of sight I ran back into Sketch where my new guy was waiting for me, a drink already poured. I ended up having a very pleasant evening indeed ...

TUESDAY 15 FEBRUARY

Tash

Cigar Smoke, Body Hair and Dogs' Willies!

Post B

14/01/2005   23.01
From: Tash
To: Dawn
Subject: Re: A modest proposal . . .

Samuel Johnson once said 'When a man tires of London he has tired of life, for in London there is the best of all life has to offer.' That being said, as a frequent visitor to London, I know that sometimes, especially January (after the sales . . .) it can get pretty boring. I'm a 33yo, 6'2 195lb black hair/brown eyed Male (with a woman's weakness for shopping). I ski a bit, dive a bit more, and travel a lot. I read enough to stock a small library, and can carry a conversation about most subjects. You sound like a great dinner date to start . . . . . . and there's so much to enjoy in the city that I doubt I'd have too rough a time spoiling you rotten for an evening. As for whisking you off your feet, provided you don't weigh more than about 150lb . . . .no problem at all :) I'll be in London this week working on a film deal and would love to speak with you, see if we 'click'?
I'd be flattered by your response, and am available in the west end both Sun/Mon. nights, and would love to hear some about yourself?
Thanking you in advance,

15/01/2005   13:21
From: Dawn
To: Tash
Subject: Re: A modest proposal . . .

What a lovely email . . . thank you very much.
Sunday evening may be a strong possibility . . . what would you
have in mind?
I'm mid 20's, 5 foot 10, dark brown hair, bit posh, sophisticated,
lively,
bloody hilarious and particularly gorgeous!
I write and prance around like I own the place.
So . . . what shall we do?

16/01/2005   11:17
From: Tash
To: Dawn
Subject: Re: A modest proposal . . .

I was thinking of dinner (early?-5-6 or so), and perhaps you'd be so
good as to assist me @ the blackjack table (I do have SOME bad
habits:) . . . .drinks . . . -and see where the night takes us ?
I don't know London very well, but I know we can find something
interesting (it'd be my pleasure to facilitate any of your wishes I can
– I like to give people I'm with as good a time as I can afford), and I
can guarantee you this – you will not be bored !
Sorry don't have a pic online, professional discretion (business
related) doesn't allow it, but I'm said to be quite good looking, and
my description was totally accurate. We can talk, my number here
is ***********, and if you get my voicemail, please leave a
number/name & I'll call you as soon as I get off the other call.
Can't wait to hear from you,

16/01/2005   11.59
From: Tash
To: Dawn
Subject: Re: A modest proposal . . .

On second thoughts, my reply was probably inadequate . . . If
you're only half the person you sound like, I'd be more than happy
to just have dinner with you, go wherever you want, but most of all
just listen to you and try to figure you out – quality people are few

and far between, and I have a pronounced weakness for rare &
beautiful things – you sound like you might be both.
I know it's a little rude to ask, considering I don't have one to send
you, but until we talk next, could you possibly send me a pic?
Thanks either way, and talk 2 u soon.

16/01/2005   12.06
From: Dawn
To: Tash
Subject: Re: A modest proposal . . .

I liked the casino idea. I have just finished a two and a half year
contract working for an online gambling company. My favourite
place in the world is Vegas and you just try and get me off the
Black Jack table.
I will call you in a bit. X

16/01/2005   12.25
From: Tash
To: Dawn
Subject: Re: A modest proposal . . .

You get better by the second. A lady that gambles. Next you will be
telling me you love Jewish men and smoke cigars!
That's a shame about this week. I leave for Arizona on Tuesday. But
I'm back in a few weeks. When you call me, we can arrange a date
for then.
Speak in a 'bit' can't wait!

The Date

Christ this dude could talk. I was shocked when I heard his voice.
For someone who was only 33 he sounded a lot older, it was very
deep and brilliantly New York. Very Robert de Niro. The voice
was sexy but the character was odd, it didn't take me long to
realise that he was properly crackers, but in an interesting way.

'Do you like Americans, Darn?'
'Yes, I do.'
'Do you mind cigar smoke Darn?'
'Not if you don't mind me having a drag!'

'Do you like, Jewish men, Darn?'

'I do, yes.'

Really what I wanted to say was: 'Yes, I have no problem with Jewish men but I don't really know how to masturbate a circumcised willy. Is it best just to give it a good suck then get it in as soon as possible? Or would it be best for one to lubricate ones hands and bring it to a climax that way?'

I thought I'd wait till dinner to ask him that.

'Do you like adventure, Darn?'

'Damn tootin' I do . . . what you offering?'

'Do you really like gambling, Darn?'

'Yes! I really love gambling and casinos make me randy as hell.'

'Darn?'

'Yes?'

'I think you might be my perfect woman!'

And that was our first phone conversation. Well, that was most of the talking that I did. He did the rest and it went on for about half an hour. We arranged a date for the next time he was over and said we'd be in touch then.

This guy had more stories in his box than *Jackanory*. And they were good 'uns as well. Everything from owing the Mafia thousands of pounds to being held hostage in a luxury hotel room for three days, and almost losing his shirt in Vegas. He was in the early stages of setting up as a financial advisor and was building up a contact list of incredibly wealthy people. He was open about the fact that 'The millions are still to come' and something told me that his client recruitment methods were not entirely legit – brothels were mentioned a couple of times. Yet his stories were mostly incomplete so it was hard for me to understand what his involvement with these people actually was. He told his tales until the point where I was gripped, then stopped and started another one. Quite frustrating . . .

I'd like to record all of what he came out with but unfortunately, as soon as I told him I was a writer, he made me vow never to repeat a word of any of them – and from the many gunpoint scenarios he described, I think it would be best that I go along with his wishes. I'd hate to get blown up just for the sake of some extra material, so just take my word for it . . . this guy has seen some shit!

After that phone call they came in thick and fast. I was called every hour on the hour for the next two days. More stories of near death experiences were shot into my ear and constant declarations of joy about the fact that I was 'wonderful' were becoming regular listening. He had no qualms about admitting that the only problem he had with travelling the world on business was that he never had anyone to share his four-poster hotel beds with. He certainly wasn't shy, and I liked him. I appreciated his bluntness, I kind of figured that someone that open had nothing to hide, so I accepted his invitation to dinner and hoped that he wasn't as physically forthcoming as he was vocally.

Text Message From: Tash

Dawn, please will you tell me what your two favourite perfumes are.
Thanks.

Text Message From: Dawn

Obsession, Calvin Klein. Would never wear anything else x

We arranged to meet outside the Six and Thirteen, a Kosher restaurant on Wigmore Street – one of those funny roads where the numbering goes up on one side and down on the other, so one million is opposite number one but it takes you eight full lengths to work it out. Obviously I was late so I called him a few times and he didn't hide his lack of patience, yet it was excited impatience: he just couldn't wait to meet me.

'What are you wearing, Darn? I want to know which one is you walking down the street,' he said as I called him for the fifth time saying that I think I could see the place.

'I see you, Darn, my Goddess, all in black, I love the way you walk.'

I hung up and greeted him.

He was so hairy. I hadn't imagined him to be hairy at all. For some reason I thought he'd be bald, with a cigar hanging off his face like a third lip, like a giant sized version of the grown up baby in *Who Framed Roger Rabbit?* But no, he was big, with an incredible amount of facial hair which he promptly rubbed on each of my cheeks. He squeezed my upper arms so tight I thought my head was going to be expelled from my body like some sort of ballistic missile. He then pushed me away and gripped me so tight that my elbows swelled up like knees, then looked into my face like he'd just created me and was over the moon with how I'd turned out. It felt like the kind of thing that relatives do when they haven't seen a child for years. He was celebrating my arrival so much I half expected someone else to appear out of the restaurant and present me with a medal. I managed to shrink out of his grasp and relocate my lungs enough to breathe a wasted smile and rub the circulation back into my biceps before following his arm inside.

We were seated at our table; it was early, about 7.30, so the place was pretty empty. There was one very old Jewish couple dining together across from us. They didn't say a word to each other but spoke merrily to the waiters. She appeared to have problems with keeping the soup on the spoon and he couldn't eat his fast enough. She didn't have time to finish before he clicked his fingers for his main course, and when the plates were taken the spoon fell off hers and sloshed cold soup all over her lap. Luckily her napkin caught it so she was pleased about that. The old man tutted and rested his chin in his hand.

I observed all this while he sat opposite me staring at the painting on the wall behind my head. I thought that if he was allowed to eyeball everything else in the room then so would I. It seemed a little strange though. He had been all over me until we sat down. I wasn't quite sure how to bring his focus back to me; he seemed to be in some sort of trance. I smiled and leaned towards his gaze. And he smiled back adoringly, but his eyes didn't move. Then a storm ran up my back as I realised what I was faced with. He was the most cross-eyed person I have ever encountered. All this time he had been staring right at me. The guy was so boss-eyed that while one eye rested happily on the picture, the other lasered at my head. It was the freakiest fucking thing I have ever seen and suddenly my eyes were flipping from side to side like I was watching a tennis match. It was impossible to know where to look.

Mention it, mention it, I willed. It would be so much easier if he acknowledged it.

Maybe *I* should mention it, I thought. But I knew that would be rude.

So, after looking down for a brief moment, I gathered myself, commented on the cutlery, raised my head and homed in on his nose. It was small and flat and shining with grease.

'You are the most beautiful girl I've ever seen,' he said as he revealed his perfectly straight yet harshly stained teeth.

How do you know? I thought, you can only see half of me!

Physically I didn't fancy him at all. But I didn't rule out the chances of something sexual happening between us. Mostly because he was so bizarre and I was intrigued to know what he would be like in bed – I just wished that it didn't have to be me that had to find out. The ideal scenario would have been someone else having sex with him and telling me about it . . . but no, this was my set up, I couldn't pass the fuck . . . sorry, buck.

I was gasping for a drink, but he just ordered water. I panicked. I couldn't face the prospect of a sober evening with him; I needed an ice breaker. Luckily when we ordered some food he asked me which wine I would like. Thinking I was ordering a bottle I was devastated when he only ordered a glass. I seem to have a real problem with people who only order a glass over a meal. I don't know what it is. I always feel a bit like we might be in a hurry, and because I tend to drink quite quickly I feel a little on show, or rude for ordering more. And as expected, I quaffed it within minutes and sat with an empty glass until our food came.

While we were ordering his incessant sniffing was driving me bonkers. He was obviously attempting to control a very insistent stream of something mucoid from breaking for freedom. Yet rather than pop off to the gents to get a tissue he kept squashing his left nostril with his index finger and it really was making me feel quite sick. I excused myself and went for a wee, hoping he would take this moment to get rid of it. When I returned he had, thank God! There was no way I could have eaten my sushi with that shit going on.

'What are you thinking, Darn?' He kept asking. At first I said things like 'How lovely it is to meet you', or 'This food is divine', but after the 76 millionth time I was finding it quite invasive and just smiled, tight toothed, and didn't bother looking up.

He did most of the talking, as I had expected. It was hard to stay focused on him as his inflection wasn't capturing. He spoke slowly, not like he had on the phone, and after every phrase came a pause and a change of position, so a story that could have taken five minutes took twenty.

He seemed to have forgotten all of the phone conversations we'd had, as he told me all the same yarns all over again. And although they were fascinating it was hard to retain my expression of amazement. Made me wish I had never grown my eyebrows back from when I was sixteen. I overplucked them to the point where they looked like barely visible miniature boomerangs that had landed on my forehead. I thought I looked like Audrey Hepburn; my family said I looked like I was about to be run over. Startled was the word I think they used. Yet, somehow that would have been perfect for my meal with Tash.

The guy appeared to adore me, but it was all aesthetic. He didn't ask me where I was from, what I was into, what I wanted to be, do, think, own, drive, listen to or even talk about. It didn't seem to matter to him. I got the impression that he was doing his best to impress but there was something very unresponsive about him. Like it didn't matter if I'd heard him or not. I think he just needed some female company.

One story he never seemed to tell was that of any love in his life . . . ever! Everything he told me involved him in places with various nutters but never with a lady. Maybe he was a virgin? No, I imagine that he had women in his bed sometimes, you know . . . women of the night . . .

He was one of those men whose head is always onto the next subject so he wouldn't remember anything I told him anyway.

That just makes me not bother to waste my breath. If I truly believe that the person opposite is interested for all the little things that make me me, and not just because they think I'm good looking, then looks and nervousness can go unnoticed. As much as I don't want to talk about myself all night, I also don't want to sit and listen to them – it's dull, and stops me getting drunk! More importantly, I find it hard to believe that a guy who can't focus on my chat would be responsive to my needs in bed. I don't like sex where the man just has sex; I like sex when a man has sex with me. They have to respond to the way that my body works, moves, feels, rather than sticking to a tried and tested routine. I got the distinct impression that Tash would do the latter.

He ate very quickly so I felt obliged to keep up, which was hard as I had ordered two huge rolls of rice and fish which deserved to be handled with care, else there would be some serious spillage. He had lamb medallions, and to avoid any slopping sauce he launched his navy tie over his left shoulder. This unfortunately revealed that one of his shirt buttons was undone, the gap was being forced open by what looked like two grizzly bears. It would seem that his hair didn't stop at his neck; it went all the way down. As he looked down to his food I snuck little peeks at his chest and could see that the whole shirt sat on fur and not skin. He was so hirsute he could have been wearing a hair suit. It was *not* a pretty sight!

I don't have a problem with hairy men. Actually, yes I do, I don't like them. But I wouldn't stop myself sleeping with someone who was hairy if I really liked them – just for the record . . .

Dinner was over quite quickly. After dessert I lit a cigarette and he lit a cigar. By this time a small hen party had seated themselves on the table next to us: a granny who looked like a battered up wicker basket; a couple of aunties with proper old-school hair dos; a mum in a twin set with an unnaturally correct posture; a pair of ugly sisters and a bride to be with huge upper arms. She annoyed me from the minute she walked in. I had observed her well. She wanted this that and the other and was hassling the waiting staff for everything from a clean napkin to a higher chair. Her poor future husband, I thought to myself.

When Tash lit his cigar the women went into fits. He remained blissfully unaware. I couldn't understand how he hadn't noticed the seven sisters next to us who were talking about nothing but ways of asking him to put it out, and playing musical chairs with the bride to save her from having stinking hair on her wedding day.

They were really irritating me. I can't abide it when people hint like that. They sat and huffed and puffed about the smoke, when all they had to do was nudge us and ask politely if he would put it out. I started to quite like him then – he was irritating these women and I enjoyed that. They finally got off their high horses and one of the aunties twisted her neck to say:

'Excuse me, but the smell of your cigar is turning us off our food. Would you mind putting it out while we eat?'

To which Tash replied:

'So I'm smoking, what'ya gonna do?'

It was hilarious; he was totally out of order. The smell of his cigar was revolting. It was stinking the entire restaurant out and everyone was looking over at us, but he saw no reason why he should put it out. No wonder this guy was single; he was selfish through and through. He did what he wanted when he wanted and didn't give a toss what the consequences where.

The aunty turned back to her group of twittering ladies who were stumped from the audacity and decided to move tables.

After that all he could think about was getting the bill. I could tell that he was uncomfortable in his chair. His legs had been flapping about since the main course. God knows how his impatience deals with all the long haul flying he does. The waiters kept forgetting to take the bill and his temper was rising. Mild cusses were being emitted and I dared not say a word until we had left the building. On the way out I gave a small smirk to the bride to be, whom I still thought was a knob, even though I wasn't particularly impressed with Tash's behaviour either.

Outside he gave me my bottle of Obsession. It was huge and I really appreciated it. I'd just run out and for the first time that night he actually fed off my reaction. He smiled and said, 'I'm so glad you like it, you deserve it.' I leaned towards him and gave him a kiss. It was then I noticed his smell – I hadn't during our greeting, the hug had prevented me from breathing. He smelled of a fusion of dirty hair and hot suits. It wasn't an unclean smell, just a warm smell, his smell, there was no aftershave and no over-powering BO it was just the smell of him and I didn't like it.

'There is a park near here, Darn. I would be honoured if you'd take a walk with me before you have to leave.'

'The parks are closed at night,' I cried in a second, there was not a hope in hell of me entering a park at 10 p.m. with some crazy boss-eyed hairy dude who clearly has the attitude that what he says goes. So I agreed to walk with him for a while, but said that it wouldn't be long before I had to go home.

His arms were flung around me and, as we walked, he pulled me so close that my body was almost at a right angle to my hips. It was not a comfortable stroll. But he led me regardless of my stiffness.

When we reached New Bond Street he managed to slip into the conversation that we were heading towards his hotel. How con-venient for you, I thought.

As I window-shopped and tried to turn his attention to any-thing other than me, his head remained in my direction until, just outside Fenwick's, he pulled me round and kissed me square on the lips. It was hideous. He pushed his closed lips onto mine, which were jammed shut and motionless, and kissed me like they did in the old black and white movies – no tongues but a whole load of head movement. His beard stank but I was glued to it. Then, out of nowhere, a scrawny little tongue appeared to be emerging. It probed my lips like a determined little sperm pes-tering an unresponsive egg. I couldn't believe its force. I did my best to keep it out but it defeated me and was soon licking my teeth. It didn't seem to fatten, it remained long and thin like a dog's willy.

Meanwhile his beard was chaffing my face and his nose was push-ing mine back into my skull. I couldn't breathe. Small snippets of air made their way up my nose but they were so filled with the stench of his face that it did me more harm than good. I worked hard to force him out of my mouth but he was adamant to see it through, so I remained motionless and turning purple until he broke away and said, 'You have the softest lips I have ever kissed.'

Whhhhaaaaaaattttt? I'd had my lips pursed so tight I'm surprised he didn't cut himself. What was he thinking? How could he think that was right? That it was nice? That I had responded? It was madness, but before I had a chance to run away he'd grappled my arms again and was hoisting me down New Bond Street.

I had to do something; this guy seriously thought we were going to get it on. I had no idea how to get out of it. I turned to him, determined to make him stop, but he seemed to take this as a come on and I had to go through the whole ordeal again – with the added bonus of his hands gripping my bottom. His penis was so hard in his trousers that it was hurting my pelvic bone. I tried to wiggle away, but obviously he saw this as a sign of some sort of sexual pleasure. He held me tighter and rubbed his hard-on from side to side on my pubis, skewering my face with his rancid dog's cock of a tongue and making exclamations like 'Ooerr' and 'Oogrrr'.

I found the strength from deep within – I feared I'd lose the power of my urethra from excess external pressure – and pushed him back and away from me. He fell against a shop window and wiped his mouth on his sleeve, his crazy, hungry eyes glistening with excitement, his teeth on display.

'You are one horny man!' Were the first words that left my bruised lips. 'But you must respect me when I say that I'm not the kind of girl that does this kind of thing on the first night. I'm going to go home and think about what a fantastic evening we've had, then tomorrow I'll call you and we can spend your last night in the UK together, at your hotel. OK?'

'But I want you tonight, Darn.'

'I want you too, but not tonight. I want it to be special, so tomorrow. OK?'

He eventually gave in after I managed to convince him that he was going to be shagged like a king in less than 24 hours. Then I ran. I literally ran all the way up New Bond Street, along Oxford Street and up the Edgware Road to my house, desperately trying to blow his smell off me. When I got home I showered for half an hour and spent the next 24 ignoring his calls.

Gross!

TUESDAY 22 FEBRUARY

Plato: Part Two
I know we hardly know each other but . . . .

The Date

It wasn't until about a month later that Plato and I got round to seeing each other again. I had been really excited about it. We'd had quite a few text messages and many funny phone calls. Occasionally he emailed me his crazy stories of drunken nights out, all of which I read in stitches. So we had got to know each other a little better.

We met in Itsu on Wardour Street. Apparently on our first date I'd banged on about my love for sushi so he insisted we had a quick meal before we went on to get absolutely blasted. I arrived early so took a seat and dribbled over the sashimi until he walked in. When he did our greeting was excitable to say the least. We were both so happy to see each other.

He had a suit on again as he had come from work and looked very smart. His smile was still huge and he had obviously recently had a haircut as there wasn't as much grey on display as last time. Apart from that he was just as I remembered and I was over the moon to be with him again.

He wasn't really eating as he'd had a huge steak at lunch. I'd also had a massive lunch but, as per usual, I was ravenous, so I soon had a pile of little plates in front of me.

'Wow, where the hell do you put it, hollow legs?' He said. It was the first time he'd experienced the full wrath of my appetite.

'Oh my God, I'm such a pig. I'm so sorry, how rude.'

He insisted that he didn't think it was rude but actually quite wonderful that I enjoyed my food so much. It wasn't long before he too was taking plates of yumminess off the rotator table for me, adamant that I ate the lot. Eventually I admitted defeat and sat back, allowing my belly to hang to one side. He laughed at me.

'Anyway, thanks for the show, Dawn, now it's time for your prize.'

'My prize?' I perked up. I thought he was going to buy me a shot of some Japanese liquor or something. But he didn't. He reached down to under the table and pulled out the plastic bag that he had arrived with. I suddenly got all nervous.

'Here's your birthday present. I'm sorry it's late but it's taken us ages to sort out another night out so it's a little belated, I'm afraid.'

My birthday had been on the 23rd of January, a couple of weeks after our first date. He'd remembered and called me on the day to say hi.

'Oh my God, you didn't have to do that.'

I was so excited to see what it was. I knew it wouldn't be anything special but even a box of chocolates is nice when you're not expecting them. I shook the package and smiled at him.

It was a box of chocolates.

I said 'Yummy' and 'Thank you' as I took the box out of the bag, and then almost threw up my sushi when I saw what it really was.

It was an itsy bitsy digital Dictaphone.

'I can't believe you . . .'

'Well I remember telling you about my friend who had one and how much you said you could do with one for your writing.'

It was a conversation that had lasted about three minutes in the early stages of our first meal together. I had indeed mentioned that I could really do with one but I could hardly remember it and I couldn't believe that he had.

I wriggled out from the table, went round to him and kissed his cheeks like a maniac. He smiled and nodded and insisted it was a pleasure.

'So . . . if you think you've had enough sushi, I think we should get out of here and go get plastered.'

What I liked about going out with Plato was the way that he

pre-planned our dates. There was none of this going for dinner then not knowing what to do malarkey. Like the last time when he had booked a table in Milk and Honey for us, he'd done the same at Trader Vic's, the cocktail bar below the Park Lane Hilton.

We ordered two JD/DCs and sipped away on them, chatting about all the places we liked to go out in London. His job was very sociable so he knew all the best places to go and promised to take me to them.

I cared for him more and more throughout the evening. He was a class 'A' gentleman. Not smooth like The Gentleman, but honest, kind and undoubtedly genuine. His nerves where always going to be there but I got used to them quite quickly, and wouldn't have changed him for the world.

The people on a table next to us had a huge plate of French fries. I must have been eyeing them up because next time the waitress came near us he ordered me a plate of them. I rolled my eyes and said he didn't need to do that, but still managed to eat every single one. He didn't touch them.

After the lard was gone he told me to drink up as we were going upstairs. My heart sunk as he clearly wasn't the person I thought he was. I had never imagined him to be so forward, part of the reason I liked him so much was because of how polite he was.

I slumped and he quickly jumped to his defence.

'No, No, not upstairs upstairs. I mean to the 28th floor. Windows on the World. It's the bar on the top floor.'

I was so embarrassed, as was he, but we promptly saw the funny side.

When we got upstairs I was blown away. Windows on the World was beautiful. It had glass walls so you have panoramic views of the whole of London. I must have walked in there with my mouth wide open, like I'd never seen a view before. It was stunning.

'You have just introduced me to my favourite place in the world,' I said.

He was chuffed. We took a seat and ordered some drinks.

'This is what I imagine New York bars to be like,' I said.

'You've never been to New York?'

'Nope, never. But I plan to move there next year for a while. I know that I'll love it.'

'You would love it. I'll take you to New York.'

I laughed and I think I mumbled 'I wish!'

'Seriously, thinking about it I'd love to go back. I also really need a holiday and seeing as all my mates are either married or mad I would be honoured if you'd come with me.'

We chatted about it a little more and, when he'd convinced me he was serious about it, I agreed; I'd have been stupid not to. We adored each other's company and, even though I was unsure of whether anything further would develop, I couldn't think of anyone better to take up on that offer. So I accepted. And we drank to our forthcoming trip.

At about 1 a.m. we made our way down to the lobby where we sat on a sofa and had a little snog. It was a nice kiss, I enjoyed it but I think I had already established in my head that our relationship wasn't going to be about that. This was a friend, and one who I wanted in my life forever. However, being the type of person who has slept with most of her friends, there is always hope!

I walked home alone that night, talking into my Dictaphone the whole way. I knew I had done the right thing by accepting his offer, and I was stupidly overexcited about it.

WEDNESDAY 30 MARCH

Plato: Part Three
New York – Fighting the Horn . . .

The Trip

A couple of days after our second date he called me and said, 'Dawn, it's all booked. We're staying at the Avalon, which is just by the Empire State Building. I've got you your own room, so please don't worry about that.'

Actually I hadn't worried about it. I liked him so much that I could have easily shared a room with him, whether we had sex or not. But I was grateful as five days is a long time to spend with someone you hardly know; there was a risk that we might have driven each other nuts by the end of it.

We arranged to meet by the Paddington Bear stand in Paddington Station, which is literally a five minute walk from my house, so I pulled my suitcase there without a problem and arrived on time. He was already there. I threw my arms around him in my usual way.

He looked so different. I tried to work out what it was that had changed – and no it wasn't just because there wasn't alcohol involved. It was because he wasn't wearing a suit. His jackets had hidden his slightly protrusive belly well enough for it to have been totally unnoticed before. I didn't mind though; a belly is the inevitable consequence of a good social life, and a common feature on a skinny forty-year-old's body. I quite liked it.

A pale blue anorak had been teamed up with a pair of navy cords and a pair of tan leather loafers. I would describe the look as 'Uncle going shopping'. Not good, not bad, just practical.

We were both extremely excited, talking over each other and

being a bit manic. On the train to Heathrow we got through about four bottles of water because we were so dehydrated from yapping so much. When we got to the airport and checked in we promptly found a pub where we could get two strong Bloody Marys to calm us down.

We were flying with Virgin and had Premium Economy seats so were in the cool upstairs bit. Plato also managed to get us at the front so we had lots of legroom, which was great as I could experiment with levels. When things got a little uncomfortable in my chair I could sit on the floor for a while.

The flight was fun. We didn't sleep at all but we did some reading, some talking and we watched *Closer*. It was such a brilliant movie, though I have to say when they started doing that bit where they chat over the Internet I got a little bit embarrassed. Not sure why . . .

I was like a kid at a party when I found my in-flight goody bag. Plato helped me pull off my boots and I put on my bright green fluffy flight socks. I was so overjoyed with them that I went downstairs and walked all the way to the rear of the plane and back again. They were very comfy and much better than wearing my big stupid boots. He didn't put his on though, so I stuffed them in my bag for my sister. I liked them so much my sister never seemed to receive them. In fact, I have just got the giggles because I realise that I'm actually sitting here wearing them now.

At the end of the flight we were both a little delirious, but still managed to lose ourselves in fits of cackles while I tried to get my boots back on but couldn't because my feet had swollen. I had forgotten that happened and was initially a little frightened by the sudden expansion of my ankles. I thought I had caught a disease.

After passport control, baggage reclaim and the short train journey from the airport to Manhattan we were finally there. Exhausted but seriously excited we emerged from Penn Station and my eyes twinkled. I was in New York and it was as fantastic as I had imagined. Instantly I sensed the city's energy. Everything looked like a movie set, slightly unreal. The yellow taxis were everywhere, the buildings were huge and the streets were all so straight that you could see for miles down them. It was incredible.

I couldn't speak for the whole walk to the hotel. Plato thought it was because I was unhappy about something, but I was so happy I was dumbstruck. I couldn't wait to see more.

At the hotel we checked in and dumped our stuff in our rooms. We were starving so met straightaway again to go and get some food. We both wanted sushi and as luck would have it our hotel happened to be on a street smothered with sushi bars. We went into the first one we could find and ordered a giant shared platter of all our favourites.

It was only about 8 p.m. but we were so tired it was pointless us pretending that we could go out. We struggled to eat all that we ordered and sat opposite each other for an hour speaking utter shite. All our words were coming out in the wrong order and our eyes were like little black dots in the snow because we were so pale. It wasn't uncomfortable though. The flight had given us the chance to relax with each other and got us tuned in with each other's moods so our disorientation was mutual and actually very funny. We admitted defeat and, rather than jeopardise the next day, went back to the hotel and said good night.

I had a bath, which was bliss. The tub was short but deep, I could immerse myself in it entirely so just my eyes peered out over the bubbles. It was just what I needed. Then I pranced around in my dressing gown for a while, unpacking all my clothes and planning my outfit for the next day. After that I gazed out the window and watched all the New Yorkers on the street outside, feeling like I was the luckiest girl in the world. Then I fell asleep at about 10.30 and dreamed about sex.

That must have been what set me off, because at approximately 2 a.m. I woke up with the most intense feeling of horniness I have ever had. I was so randy I was almost purring. I could hear people on the street outside and there was an orange light coming through the curtains. I could see my reflection in the television screen that was at the end of my bed, so I watched myself while I made the most of the state that I was in. I felt so sexy. My fantasies didn't involve anyone else. I thought about me and where I was and what I was doing. I didn't need to imagine that anyone else was there for it to feel amazing. I did it again and again until

8 a.m., when I immersed myself in the bath in preparation to meet Plato for breakfast. I thought I would look knackered but my cheeks were unquestionably rosy. He even commented on how perky I looked. I wanted to say: 'Yeah you would too if you'd had a six hour wankathon and approximately eight orgasms.' But I thought he might have choked on his bagel.

After breakfast we headed straight for Central Park. It was so beautiful. We walked and walked and walked. There were lots of couples and, even though I felt very comfortable with Plato, I did wonder what he was thinking at that point. I knew that we were going to be just friends. I liked him so much but a physical connection simply wasn't there. When we were walking in the park I suddenly thought, shit, are we here as a couple on a date, or just mates? Was he actually walking around with me thinking that we should be holding hands and sharing ice creams?

I panicked a little bit, but was determined for it not to show. At that moment I realised that a conversation was going to have to happen at some point to establish how I felt, but in the meanwhile we continued to wander around, and I have to say we were getting on famously holding hands or not.

After two hours of sauntering around the park we headed back down 5th Avenue to get a bite to eat. I'd warned Plato before we left about my rather abnormal appetite and he was fine with it, but he couldn't help but express his amazement at my conspicuous consumption of food. However, I must say that he was very sympathetic towards it and made sure that every three to four hours we were in a position to eat, even though he couldn't bear to fit another morsel in his tummy most of the time. That was a bit of an eye opener; eating approximately three times as much as a forty-year-old man. I should seriously look at my dietary habits!

After some lunch he left it up to me to decide what we were to do in the afternoon. I suggested the Sex Museum. Not to fill my head with porn for my next early morning session but because I love erotica and find its history interesting . . . OK!

We headed down there with our full tummies and had a good look around. Downstairs is simply a display of how pornography has developed through the decades. I have always been a fan of the Cheesecake era. Lovely voluptuous sexy ladies with big boobs and luscious lips. There is one particular series that I like. It's called the 'Ooo Series' and they had it on display there. It's where the photographer apparently caught the model unaware so she is pulling an overly exaggerated surprised expression, and possibly exposing a little more buttock than necessary. It's subtle, more suggestive than overtly sexy and I think the women look amazing. I stood there saying things like 'This makes me feel OK with being a comfy size twelve. I'm not going to try to lose weight ever again.' Of course about an hour later I was insisting that we walked faster to burn off lunch.

Upstairs at the Sex Museum, however, was a different story. There was screen after screen of pornographic films being shown. It was driving me wild. After the night I'd just had I needed to be locked away from that kind of thing for fear of doing myself some damage. But I was transfixed. I watched bottom after bottom bounce up and down, saw women give the most wonderful fellatio imaginable and was faced with more images of cocks than my poor little clitoris could handle.

In my rampant state I forgot about poor Plato, who is maybe not as comfortable in those sorts of environments as I am. I turned to find him and he was standing very still – well that is apart from one knee that was shaking violently – watching one of the softer movies. I called him over and we tried to have a normal conversation next to a movie where a very well endowed gentleman was incessantly ramming his schlong up a young lady's arse. A bead of sweat ran down Plato's forehead, so I suggested that we leave. I felt terrible about exposing him to that, when I knew at some point in the next few days I'd be telling him that he'd be getting no such action.

It was about 3.30 when we went back to the hotel for a sleep. As we were building up to our big night out on Friday we agreed to have some rest, find somewhere simple for dinner and have a relatively quiet night so that we felt superb for partying the next day.

When I got to my room I instantly sunk myself into the bath again. Unfortunately this woke me up, so when I got into bed to get a few hours shut-eye it wasn't happening. Although I knew that I needed to sleep, my insistent horn was taking over my body again. It must be what it's like to have voices in your head and trying not to hear them. I lay there squeezing my eyes shut, trying frantically to ignore the twitching in my knickers, but it was no good. The images that had been fed into my brain at the Sex Museum were filling the room and there was no fighting it. I gave in and spent the next few hours writhing around on my bed like a horny cat.

I dressed moderately casual that night but covered myself in lots of glittery jewellery so I felt special. We met in the lobby as arranged and walked towards Times Square. We weren't too fussed about going to touristy places but I knew I had to see it, and Plato insisted that it was best to do so at night.

We found a little bar right in the middle of it all and I gazed out the window in amazement. I had a Bloody Mary that totally knocked my socks off so we hurried to finish our drinks and went to get some food.

In Gallagher's Steak House I filmed him with my video camera as he ate his food. I was laughing so much that the camera was shaking. He was such a geek, but a great geek. A hilarious geek who was cool on the inside. He said such silly things just to make me happy and he found himself as funny as I did. There might not have been a sexual desire for me but I couldn't get enough of him. I was more than happy to tell him that he had fast become one of my most favourite people in the world, and he took the compliment gracefully, as I think he trusted that it was true.

We finished dinner at around 11 p.m. and I was absolutely exhausted. We strolled back to the hotel and went to bed. I found that a little awkward. We were a bit drunk and getting on so well that I wasn't sure if we were supposed to have a kiss before we went to our rooms or not. After all, I had to keep remembering that the last date we had been on we had kissed. I knew that we were building up to a big night out on Friday which is maybe when he expected something to happen. But before then were we supposed to be snogging in the lift?

I had got to sleep quickly, but surprise, surprise I woke up at five feeling like someone had thrown a bucket of water on my bed. I felt even more sexual than I had been the night before.

As I strummed away at myself I racked my brains for how I could finally get satisfied. I even went so far as to text The Gentleman to see if he could come and help. It was his English mobile so I knew he probably wouldn't get it, which is undoubtedly a good thing. I mean, what would I have said if he'd have responded? 'Oh hi, it's me. I'm in New York with a guy I met on the Internet. I don't actually want to meet you for a drink but would you mind popping over to my hotel room for a few hours so I could borrow your cock and calm myself down a bit . . . oh, and by the way . . . are we actually talking?' I don't think so!

I also texted an ex-boyfriend who lives on 5th Avenue to see if he could quickly stop by, and I had a feeble attempt at phone sex with a friend of mine in London who really wasn't feeling it as he was on his way home from work. So after those few unsuccessful attempts at sexual companionship I was still stranded in a strange city, hornier than I had ever been in my life with not so much as a foot long hot dog to play with.

Just before I climbed up the wall and pulled all of my hair out, it occurred to me that three floors above me there was Plato, who if I called his room and explained my state would undoubtedly come down and given me all the male attention that I needed. I picked up the phone and went to dial. But I couldn't do it. I just couldn't. It wasn't there. No matter how randy I was I couldn't think of him in that way. It would have been wrong and cruel to use him, as I knew that once satisfied the need would go and I would just want friendship again. It wasn't an option. I hung up the phone and immersed myself in the bath, wishing that the feeling would go away so I could just get some sleep.

We met for breakfast and the colour in my cheeks was fading. Plato commented on how tired I looked, but I insisted that I was determined to walk and walk and walk and enjoy my time in New York. The horn was not going to beat me.

As you can probably imagine I was starving, and, feeling like I had probably burned off over 2,000 calories through the night, I was happy to indulge in a breakfast of two bagels with cream cheese, three chocolate doughnuts, two slices of wholemeal toast with jam and peanut butter, a bowl of cereal, two apples a banana and a croissant. Because that's what you do when your body rejects wheat, you fill it full of bleached flour and spend the next 24 hours in absolute agony. But it was kind of worth it. Plato looked on in amazement as he munched on his bowl of fresh fruit.

We left the hotel by ten and our chat wasn't really flowing. He was very understanding to my situation and our silence was comfortable. We walked at a steady pace all the way to Greenwich Village.

My heart was constantly a beat faster than usual from the fear of bumping into The Gentleman. I know Manhattan has a population of about 2 million, but essentially it's not far off the size of Guernsey and the possibility of bumping into someone that you know can't be that unheard of. I had no idea what I would have said. How I would have explained Plato, and how I would have dealt with the emotions that seeing him again would no doubt bring back to the surface?

By the time we got there my breakfast had moved so I was a little more at ease with myself, and my sense of humour slowly began to re-emerge. I apologised to him for my low energy start to the day and he put his arm around me and told me not to be so silly and that it was totally understandable.

At around 12.30 we stopped at Katz's Delicatessen for lunch. Plato had had a small breakfast so that he could accommodate one of their famous pastrami on rye sandwiches. And by some miracle of the Lord I was absolutely starving by the time we got there.

We ordered sodas, sandwiches, two portions of chips and some pickles and worked our way through our hillock of food with utter commitment. That sandwich was so delicious that I couldn't speak. Every mouthful was savoured and the grease that ran down my chin was left to drip until I had sucked my fingers clean. We made a lot of noises throughout the devouring process but didn't actually talk. Inaudible statements like 'Ommgo' and 'Thsssogoo' were fast and few between. When all was gone we sat back and nodded at each other for about five minutes before we could actually find the impetus to speak.

'I have never been so full in my life,' he said.

'Nor me, but something's telling me to have another one while I'm here.'

'Maybe it's the rhinoceros you have hidden in your stomach?' I burst out laughing, but not for long; it hurt too much.

We walked for another three hours, until I felt satisfied that at least a doughnut and a few chips had been burned off. He was so sweet, we chatted about silly things like our school days and he taught me things about New York that I didn't know. Along Canal Street we tried on daft hats and big sunglasses, two pairs of which he bought for me.

I liked to watch him because he made me laugh. As we walked he told me some more of his crazy stories; my favourite being the time he was at a wedding in Pakistan. A Drag Queen, who was the entertainer, picked him out from the audience and made him the brunt of the jokes throughout the entire show. Obviously there was no booze involved, so Plato was finding it hard to see the funny side of the jibes. He was further distressed to get a sudden burst of diarrhoea. Knowing that the nearest toilet was about a mile away he began to make his way there as fast as he could, his buttocks tightly clenched. But this didn't escape the Drag Queen's attention, who instructed the entire wedding party of a hundred guests to follow him in convoy. Horrified, he went into the toilet and was mortified when he re-emerged half an hour later to see that they had all been outside waiting for him. They waved and cheered when they saw him.

The poor bloke, I really felt sorry for him. But as I watched him that day it all made sense. He was all tall and lanky and looked a little uncomfortable in himself. If a marching band was to come down a street you can guarantee that Plato would get stuck in the middle of it, and would be swept away until he finally got free in the middle of nowhere with no money, no phone and no idea where he was.

Our day was chilled and easy but by 3 p.m. I was so exhausted I had to go back to the hotel. I stopped off on the way to buy some extra strong painkillers to kill the throb in my gut – payback for the wheat party I'd had at breakfast – and when I got into my room my legs gave way and I fell flat on the bed, where I remained motionless and in the deepest sleep until he called me to wake me up at seven.

I woke up feeling fabulous and because of all the walking surprisingly not bloated. I jumped straight into a big bubble bath and sang show tunes to myself as I shaved my legs and washed my hair. I was so excited. My first proper night out in New York, I'd been looking forward to this for weeks and I was so happy that I finally felt normal again.

I got dressed in my most sparkly of outfits, put on my high heels and covered myself in jewellery. I was ready to party!

'Dawn, you look absolutely stunning,' he said as I came out of the lift. I did a little twirl posing for him and the doorman, who said I looked pretty too.

After a superb meal in Greenwich Village we found a cool downstairs bar to drink in. (You will have to accept my apologies for not remembering the names of these places, I had rather a lot to take in). This is where we had the chat, the conversation that had been pending since we arrived. The big 'We won't!'

I took a seat at the only table left in the place while he went to the bar to get the drinks. I wasn't nervous but I wasn't entirely sure how I was going to bring it up. When he came back I went for it.

'I'm having so much fun.'

'Me too, Dawn, you're great company.'

'And I couldn't have chosen a better friend to come with.'

'Nor me.'

'And thanks so much for getting me my own room. That was really sweet.'

'No problem. I didn't want to you feel like I was just bringing you here to get you into bed. I'm not like that.'

'I know, and I appreciate that so much. But look, I have to say this. I'm having such an amazing time with you and I'm so happy but I do think that we should keep it as it is. I adore you but if I slept with you it would be because I felt obliged, you know?

You've brought me here and I really don't want to mess up our relationship by doing that.'

'Dawn, I fancy the pants off you and if something was to happen I would jump at the chance, but I won't push it and I don't expect it. If all we ever are is friends then I'm more than happy with that. Let's just have fun.'

And that was it: job done. He really was as kind and gentle as I thought he was. He had full right there to say 'Well, why the hell did you come all the way to New York with a guy you met on a website who you snogged the face off last time you saw him if you didn't intend to get into bed with him?' But no, he didn't and I know a lot of guys that would, so I gave him a huge kiss and toasted to a most amazing weekend.

As we walked we stumbled across a café where people were singing. I insisted we went in. It was a karaoke place and that filled me with excitement. Within seconds I had the microphone in my hand and was singing all my favourite songs to Plato. Some people in the bar liked my voice so much that they were giving me requests. When I wasn't singing I was sitting on Plato's lap drinking JD/DCs and shots of tequila. I was in heaven until it closed. That was so sad; I could have stayed there all night. Plato promised me that we would go back there the next night but neither of us did the sensible thing of taking note of where it was.

Back at the hotel I gave him a huge cuddle and a big kiss on the cheek, feeling much more comfortable with leaving him than I had done before. I felt a bit guilty that I cut the evening short, it was only about 1.30 but I simply couldn't continue. So, holding my shoes, I said goodnight and went to my room, still singing to myself and smiling like a mad woman.

Just before I nodded off I called his room to say thanks, but there was no answer. He'd gone back out. I couldn't believe it. The first thing I thought was that he'd gone out to get some sex now that he knew he wasn't getting any from me. So I went to sleep feeling a touch confused and moderately upset.

I woke up at 8 a.m. after having a horrible dream that Plato had been really nasty to me when I told him that I didn't want to sleep with him. It made me feel sick so I called him straightaway to hear his voice. He sounded exhausted but he was as sweet as ever and told me how he had gone back out for a few drinks before coming in at about three in the morning, drunk as a skunk. We gave each other a few more hours in bed and met in the lobby at eleven.

This was probably one of the funniest days so far. We weren't so much hungover as still incredibly drunk. Rather than deal with more bagels and doughnuts we went to a small diner over the road where we had tubs of porridge and some vegetable juice as a healthy alternative. I had my huge sunglasses on and my hair was bigger than normal; he looked crazy and his glasses were wonky. We couldn't stop giggling at the state that we were in. Every single word that came out of our mouths was utter rubbish. We were taking the piss out of each other, being rude to each other and insulting our every move, but it was all done in very good taste. Finally we were best of friends. I felt like a huge weight had been lifted off my shoulders, and now I could be as friendly as I wanted to be without worrying that he was getting the wrong idea. I was having a ball, yet I was so drunk I could hardly see him – and I know that he could hardly see me because his glasses kept falling off. He must have slept in them.

We shouldn't have done it really, but we decided to go shopping. There is nothing worse than being in crowded places when you feel like that, but we set ourselves the challenge nevertheless.

On 34th Street we went in and out of all the high street shops. I picked up various items that I liked but vomited at the thought of trying them on, so put them straight back. I think it was just outside H & M when he said it. A simple line that caused me to lose the power of my urethra.

'So . . . um, Dawn. Where do you stand on Gap?'

My legs collapsed, my hand flew between my legs to hold myself and I fell against a wall as the most intense fit of laughter took over my being. I was out of control. My eyes were streaming and I was totally unable to contain myself. I was so loud that people were gathering round me and watching. Neither Plato nor myself could work out what it was that had had this effect on me, so he didn't know what to say when people asked him what was so funny. He told one woman: 'She's just drunk!'

Which didn't help me at all.

It must have been around twenty minutes before I could use my legs again. I managed to make it to Macy's, stopping occasionally to crack up and push my hand back between my legs to stop me weeing myself. I must have looked totally insane, especially because Plato wasn't laughing at all. He just got used to it and walked alongside me as if all was perfectly normal.

The crowds in Macy's shut me up. It was so busy and we both got the fear. Determined to get round it once so I could say that I had, we clung onto each other as we charged from floor to floor. Half an hour later and I couldn't get out quick enough. We were on the ground floor but I was stopped when I caught a glimpse of a beautiful necklace that actually took my breath away. It was a huge chunky piece that covers your whole chest in polished wooden beads. I stood staring at it in a drunken haze until I eventually walked away. It was about $200: I couldn't afford it.

Lunch was much needed so we had some huge salad bowls and then found a really nice coffee shop where we stared into space and talked about nothing.

'I think we should go back to the hotel and have a sleep or we'll never survive tonight,' I said.

He agreed so we headed back, but as the two strong coffees that I'd just consumed kicked in I had a second wind and decided to stay out and do my own thing for a few hours.

'You go back; I'm going to be in and out of girlie shops. You don't want to bother with that.'

So we parted. I had no intention of clothes shopping but I had seen a place near our hotel that did waxing and nails, I fancied a bit of pampering.

I went in and asked for a bikini wax. The beauty therapist came through to get me. She was Latino and didn't speak any English, so I had to tell the man at the till that I wanted a Brazilian and he passed the message on.

She took me to the end of the salon where there was a raised platform with a bed on it. She pulled across a curtain that I'm sure people could see through and I took off my jeans and knickers.

Going for a bikini wax was a stupid thing to do when I was

feeling as horny as I'd been since being in New York. For the past three days simply crossing my legs was bringing me close to climax, let alone having someone touching me down there. I know, I know, she was ripping hair out of my body, that's not erotic, but it was what she did after every strip that drove me wild.

Every time she waxed she blew on it. Not only did she blow on it but she looked me in the eye and blew on it. Let God be my witness, I'm telling you it's true. She looked me in the eye and gently blew on my fanny. There was a language barrier so no words were uttered. I could see who I presumed to be her husband through the curtains. Were we sharing a moment, or was I imagining this was happening? I didn't know what to do with myself. My legs starting twitching, I tried to break eye contact but I couldn't. She worked slowly and carefully to ensure that I got the smoothest line possible and she blew on my bits until they glistened back at her.

Finally it was done. I had the landing strip I had gone in for and I was utterly turned on. She put some finishing cream on some cotton wool and dabbed it on the waxed areas to sooth me. That felt nice. But not as nice as when she whipped it um . . . up the middle? On the bit that she never waxed. The saucy little minx new exactly what she was doing to me. However, when a new customer walked in and her husband shouted something to her that I didn't understand, she finished up quickly and clapped her hands.

I didn't want to leave, but I didn't know what I would do if I stayed. The only thing I could think of was to ask her if she would do my nails next and see if the situation developed. But it didn't. As she did my nails next to her husband, we sat in silence and she didn't make eye contact with me once. I left half an hour later practically running back to the hotel so I could make the most of the memory while it was still fresh. However, when I got back to my room my mission to the bed was interrupted as there was a box on it with a note saying: 'To Dawn, from her boyfriend.'

The Gentleman? Had he got my message and left me details of how to contact him? I was nervous as I opened it. I was regretting contacting him now and couldn't bear the thought of explaining that I wouldn't be able to see him.

But it wasn't from The Gentleman, it was from Plato. It was the wooden necklace that I'd seen in Macy's. I was so happy I cried. The effort, the thought, the surprise, it all got me. I put it on and called his room to thank him. He said I deserved it.

That night I wore it with pride. We went for a steak at Angie's Steak House and people on nearby tables were complimenting me on it. I felt gorgeous.

'It suits you so much, Dawn,' he kept saying.

I must have said thank you over a million times that night.

After a chilled out meal, some drinks on a bed in Duvet Bar and watching some excellent comedy at The Gotham Comedy Club we had had another fabulous evening. Back at the hotel we sat on a sofa in the lobby and hugged each other like crazy before we went to bed. I was so sad that it was our last night. We are both patient people but we had taken a huge risk going away together like that; it could have been a disaster, but it was perfect.

After a quick lunch on the Sunday we were ready to leave. In the taxi on the way to the airport I was gutted. I new I was going to miss New York like hell and my mind was ticking over as to when I could next get there. I knew it had to be soon.

As far as the date goes, I don't think I need to say anymore. I didn't fall in love with Plato but I fell madly in love with the city and made a friend for life. Well, I hoped I had. The one thing I hadn't managed to do while we were there was tell him that I'd just got a book deal for the journal and that he was heavily featured in it. So it wasn't until the next time we met that I found out what his reaction would be . . .

WEDNESDAY 13 APRIL

The Big Bumbino
One Hungry Hippo!

Post C

11/04/2005   16.44
From: The Big Bumbino
To: Dawn
Subject: An Italian?

Hi there,
That's a nice intriguing ad you've put up. Plus something
about it makes you sound genuine and sexy too, even if you don't
say that much about yourself. So, if you're a tall, fit, educated,
classy, sophisticated, sexy guy with Italian looks — well, me in
fact—, then it's pretty hard not to respond!
About me: I'm sane, sincere, not seeking a loving relationship; but I
adore the company of women, and the feeling appears to be
mutual. I enjoy a good time and a laugh; but also know that
nothing's better than an intense sexual encounter, even (or
sometimes especially) between strangers.
I'm 46, just generally a sort of tall (6'2), dark , and a pretty
handsome guy; I think.
Interested? Or like to know more? I hope so. Would love to hear
back from you and see your picture too.
Ciao bella x

12/04/2005   18.51
From: Dawn
To: The Big Bumbino
Subject: An Italian?

Well this does all sound very appealing . . .
I'm tall, elegant and sophisticated (well I think so anyway but my
friends might disagree!) I appreciate fine wine, good food, excellent
company and learning about new things.
I'm 26, mature for my age, I enjoy laughing more than anything else
in the world and I'm open and easy to talk to.
I like writing, I find the process very rewarding.
There is a large age gap here but I'm not put off by that if your not.
A picture is attached, I hope you like it.
It would be nice to meet up for dinner . . . where were you thinking?
Looking forward to hearing from you
Dx

12/04/2005   19.35
From: The Big Bumbino
To: Dawn
Subject: An Italian?

Hi D,
Yes, this all does sound extremely appealing — to me for
sure. Glad to read you're thinking the same.
It's true that I'm not interested I suppose in traditional old-fashioned
'dating', which is such a yawn, but on the other hand, I don't really
have an agenda or schedule either. Just want to meet an
interesting, open-minded woman and take it from there. It's enough
that I know you're thinking along the same lines and open to the
possibility . . . no commitments, no pressure; it'll happen naturally or
not; any other way wouldn't suit either of us. And, again, as you say,
there is the age diff, but I think that won't matter to us and might be
a true benefit. Again, for trad dating, you might think differently; but
for establishing a casual relationship, especially one that develops
over time, this should work fine . . . at least I'm convinced.
So . . .pwhew, after all that prelude you're probably thinking 'what a
long-winded blow-hard!' No, not really! I just wanted to be clear and
put you, I hope, at ease. Though you already sound quite self-
confident and laid-back. Traits I like to think I have as well.

Can't believe it's taken me this far into this email also to say the following: I love your picture! You're just adorable. I'm sure I'll be pleased to meet you soon. . . so, yes, let's have dinner instantly. Tomorrow evening is good for me. What part of London are you in?
Looking forward to hearing from you,
a presto,

12/04/2005   19.42
From: Dawn
To: The Big Bumbino
Subject: An Italian?

blimey that was an epic
You seem really great, I feel secure in meeting up with you for dinner and then seeing if we want to see each other again
I live just off the Edgware Road
How exciting x

12/04/2005   19.53
From: The Big Bumbino
To: Dawn
Subject: An Italian?

. . . how exciting indeed . . . domani per certo!! don't think I need to translate 'tomorrow 4 sure', but don't want to risk not meeting you for dinner tomorrow after all this . . . after all, I risked everything by already revealing to you my worst character flaw (tendency to write way too long emails), but, still, once you discover that's truly the worst thing about me (gave up being a serial killer years ago), then maybe you'll agree that's not too bad.
OK – The Bridge House, 13, Westbourne Terrace Rd How about on the early side (7:30? 8pm?) as it tends to get crowded later. . .
Looking forward lots to tomorrow — and thereafter, of course, too –

12/04/2005   23.10
From: Dawn
To: The Big Bumbino
Subject: An Italian?

Great see you there . . . 7.30

XX

The Date

I got there early after enjoying a lovely stroll along the canal and was really looking forward to meeting him; he came across as very articulate in his emails. He seemed confident and open, charismatic, and although he was 46, maybe a touch old for me, I quite fancied the idea of him as a lover. Especially because I have slept with an Italian before and they know exactly where to stick their salami, if you know what I mean . . .

I stood on a bench outside so I could see over the wall onto the canal as I waited for him. It was beautiful. I knew it was him as soon as I saw him bumble over the bridge. I'd seen his photos and, while they hadn't impressed me much, this was something of a surprise. The dark Italian locks that I had so enjoyed were now grey and twisted – either this was a serious case of someone needing to retouch their Just for Men or he had sent me some very old snaps.

He walked like a hungry baby, head in front of his legs, as if running towards the last slice of birthday cake. His feet trailed behind him, struggling to keep up with his belly's determination.

He saw me standing on my bench and kick-started his turbo engine which resulted in a few trip ups and a near death experience with a pram that crossed his path. If I knew then what I know now I might have presumed that he was trying to get in it.

'I wanted to get here before you to find us a nice table,' he said as he kissed me delicately on each cheek. His voice was very soft and quiet with a nondescript British accent. I told him not to feel bad about it and we went inside.

I was surprised he made a point of saying he was handsome, because he wasn't. It's quite a bold thing to say about yourself. 'Reasonably attractive', 'Never had any complaints', or 'I do all right' are better ways of letting someone know that you don't look like a trout that got its face stuck in a high speed propeller. But to say you're handsome is too much, like a girl saying she is beautiful: expectations are likely to be disappointed.

We took a seat in the corner of the pub and he took off his jacket. Underneath was an orange shirt, open to the third button exposing a few sporadic shoots of grey hair. It wasn't offensive but I might have preferred just one more button to be closed, I find it quite hard to keep my eyes off things like that and staring at someone's chest can often give the wrong impression.

As he studied the wine list I was excited to hear his choice. I like being educated about wine and his emails had suggested that he might know a little on the subject, but after staring at it for around three minutes he snapped the menu shut and ordered a bottle of house red. His head flopped towards his left ear, swooped backwards and then to upright again, he smiled and admitted he knew nothing about wine. Fair enough . . .

He was right about saying that he could hold his own in conversation, he was educated and cultured and passionate, a successful art buyer. He had travelled the world and was totally in love with his work. This was not only clear from his experience but also from how his eyes widened and glazed when he spoke about it.

The wine arrived and, being more a pub than a bar, we weren't offered the opportunity to try it, so he poured two glasses. It wasn't the best but it was certainly drinkable, however he didn't think so. He could have been right – it wasn't so long ago that I was a struggling drama student and drinking bottles of vinegar with dinner – I'm quite forgiving of most house wines. He took it back to the bar and that's when I saw it. A sight that had incredibly managed to skip my attention when he had approached me outside. A sight so hard to bear that I took a few more sneaky sips out of the wine from my glass before it was taken away. He had the biggest, most fattest and totally disproportional bottom you could ever imagine. It was huge. His shoulders were narrow, his waist was large but his bottom was titanic. He looked like Humpty Dumpty. No wonder the photos he'd sent me were head shots. To get that bottom in the frame he would have to be a couple of miles away from the lens. It was immense, and I couldn't take my eyes off it.

Embarrassingly he turned his head and caught my glare. I didn't mean to make him feel uncomfortable. In an awkward shuffle he turned his pelvis and stood side on to the bar, one hand perched on his hip. When I raised my head and saw his face, instead of a pair of blushing cheeks I saw a cheeky grin. Now I'm no body language expert but to me that wasn't someone hiding their arse, it was someone presenting their crotch.

I asked for that I suppose . . .

He came back with another bottle of house red and poured it into fresh glasses. We toasted again and took swigs, but before I had even had a chance to taste it he took it out of my hand and disappeared back to the bar, crotch proudly aiming itself at me again.

A slightly perplexed barmaid fetched him another bottle, which he tasted, then turned to look at me, this time blushing and not knowing what to do before he said that it was corked as well and to change the type. Finally I got the drink that I was absolutely gasping for, but that was only after he realised that it wasn't corked at all; he just didn't like it.

We kicked off the conversation by talking about New York. He had lived there for some time when he was in his twenties. He used words like 'magical' and 'breathtaking' which suited his gentle voice. He spoke slowly and always like he was thinking. Like when someone raises their head upwards and squints their eyes as if trying to remember a basic piece of information. It's not a stressed face, not like he has forgotten something important, just as if he is sniffing the air for possible words to make up the sentences. When he found them he dropped his chin and made momentary eye contact, then up he went again.

The first story was a bit of a shocker. He said that the night he arrived there he was sitting alone in a bar and a woman approached him.

She said 'I just saw you all alone and thought we could spend the weekend together.'

And they did. He spent three days with her, going to bars, exhibitions . . . bed. Then he never saw her again. It's obviously where he got his taste for random encounters with strangers; he had no shame in admitting that he had done 'pretty well' out of the website.

He was a very nice man, but, despite being educated and easy to talk to, he was boring. His voice was so soft it was often hard to hear and he didn't make me laugh once. He told me funny stories, like the one about the lady in New York and another one about a friend of his that thought her boyfriend's name was Tom instead of Tim for three months before he had the guts to tell her. Apparently he dropped every hint he could, left his ID everywhere that she would see it, even got his friends to make a point of saying his name loudly in her presence, but she never picked up on it. It could have made me howl but I was so exhausted by the time he had finished that all I could manage was the 'Oooo' face.

I watched him closely as he spoke. His features seemed to be confused about his age. His complexion was as pure as a baby's and his cheeks had a radiant pink glow, but his small green eyes were compressed by heavy hanging skin with dark pockets of flesh beneath. His nose was a small hook, which suited his possibly wizard like appearance, and his thin lips were surrounded by the occasional sore, which I presumed to be recovering shaving cuts.

He wasn't well groomed. His clothes were basic; his trousers thin corduroy and slightly too short – that could have been because they had to cover his rump – and his bright orange shirt was aggressive compared to his personality. Somehow it seemed inappropriate. As afore mentioned, his hair was too long and tangled, and his hands were dry with bitten nails.

He sat upright with both feet on the floor and his fists clasped between his thighs, occasionally raising his hands to rub his eyes – a frighteningly childlike move which took me back to his walk. I then realised that his mannerisms were very unusual. His clenched fists let free both his pinkies and his thumbs as he rubbed, like a baby would do after crying or waking up. He also affected a gentle rocking motion. With his feet still flat on the floor he shifted his big fat bottom backwards and forwards on his chair. I thought he was going to break it.

While I was taking my time to choose what I wanted to eat I sensed his impatience.

'Are you not eating?' I asked, as he wasn't looking at the menu.

'Yes,' he nodded frantically, 'I'm having the sausage and mash. It's my favourite thing on the menu, and I've eaten everything on it.'

Yes, twice by the looks of things!

'I like women,' he said as I asked him why he was Internet dating, 'but I don't want to get into a relationship. I have lots of younger female friends, but I've never hit it off well with men.'

This didn't surprise me. He was very simple. Childlike. His successful career didn't match his character. He wasn't forthcoming or bold and he was so low energy that I wanted to shake him. I wondered if these young lady friends took on motherly type roles with him. He said things like:

'My friend Sally is kind enough to do my washing for me. She picks it up every Friday and drops it off on Monday.'

And:

'I have a great and dear friend Caroline who reads to me by the canal. It's very relaxing.'

Maybe he goes online looking for cooks and cleaners or possibly people to change his nappies? It was at that point that flashbacks from an episode of Jerry Springer I once saw came flooding into my head. Adult babies . . . dark!

Throughout the evening this personality trait became more and more prevalent. He cut his sausage up into tiny slices before he ate one mouthful. It was quite an erratic process. The guy was starving but he couldn't start 'til all was sliced, then he lay down his knife and ate with just his fork. And he ate fast – very fast. I half expected him to tuck his napkin into his collar, but the years must have at least taught him not to. Actually he didn't even put his napkin on his lap; he didn't need to. He leaned right over his bowl so there was no gap between him and the table for the food to fall through.

I was glad my portion was small (for the first time in my life) as otherwise I might have been left eating alone for ages.

When we finished I said that I was going for a wee. I was really quick but when I came back he was sitting reading a book. It was very strange, like he couldn't not be entertained for any length of time. It seemed pointless; he must have got to read about half a page.

'The waitress came over and has offered us either another bottle of wine or two desserts on the house because they took so long with our food. What would you like?'

I said wine and the sides of his mouth plummeted, as he glared longingly at the chocolate mousse being demolished on a neighbouring table. Before the water works started I quickly added, 'Actually, let's have more food.' His smile was colossal.

We ordered an apple crumble and a cheese plate, which we devoured while discussing our favourite foods. It was a conversation that I was happy to have – I can talk about food all day long. In front of me was the crumble and in front of him was the cheese yet we seemed to go for the other one first, so I tucked into the cheese. Then we swapped and I finished the crumble . . . or so I thought. When the cheese had gone, and he had made numerous comments about there not being enough, he leaned back over me again and started to manically scrape the last bits of crumble that were firmly glued to the plate. He was possessed, uncontrollable. There was only a few crumbs but by hell or high water he was going to eat them.

It was irritating. Not only was I jealous when he managed to dislodge the last crusts, but his elbow kept rubbing against my nipple and on top of all that the spoon screeching on the plate was making my teeth itch.

After a nauseating few minutes he eventually put the spoon down and sat back. Christ I was relieved.

I was sobering up now, and I knew I didn't fancy him so I saw no point in staying. We put on our coats and left.

Outside he offered to walk me home. I had actually been looking forward to my stroll through Little Venice alone, but it was late, so I did the right thing for my safety and accepted. There was a path that led down to the canal, we took it rather than walk along the road. It was beautiful, so peaceful and all the barges were boasting an array of flowers and plants. He was stumbling again, head miles ahead of his big bottom, hands hanging straight down from his shoulders therefore in front of his body, quite like a primate, slightly unevolved.

It wasn't long before we came to the end of the path and to a locked gate that prevented us from getting back onto the road. There was of course the option of turning back, but I was finding conversation tough and just wanted to get home, so I suggested that we jumped the fence.

He tried first. He put his foot on a stone that was on the ground and held on to two of the large spikes that made the top of the gate. It was a frightening sight, this rather large bottom trying to get over a fence. I leaned forward to help him – I didn't want to touch his arse but I thought maybe I could support his back or something. Yet as I moved in I was forced away as an aggressive jet of toxic gas shot down his colon. It stank! It was so loud, but he didn't even acknowledge it. And not even in a way that he was trying to avoid it, he seemed totally unaffected by it. I was numb. The air was still and the smell wasn't moving, I was trapped in a fart pocket while fatty continued to try to hoist himself over the gate. I felt sick. He was really struggling and the farts kept coming. None as voluminous as the first but short, sharp bursts of putrid air were being pumped into my face and I was angered that he continued to do it.

He eventually gave up and I grabbed the opportunity to move in front of him and out of the firing line. I put my leg on the stone, flew my other leg over, used the strength in my arms to lift myself and jumped over the fence in one swift move. Then it was his turn. I was more relaxed this time round as I had room for manoeuvre.

He copied my move exactly and managed to land with a clump on my side. Finally we could carry on walking.

He had gone quiet and was breathing heavily. I looked at him and he began to hum in a very high pitched tone as he held his scarf with one hand and patted it onto the opposite palm. He looked like he was creating a beat, but then he turned to look at me, stopped, extended his left hand and revealed an inch-long wound that was pouring with blood.

'Oh bloody hell, why didn't you say anything?' I asked.

'I'm all right, I'll be all right,' he squeaked, holding eye contact with me as if trying to focus on not fainting.

His scarf was soaking and the blood flow wasn't slowing down. We needed to get some antiseptic on it straightaway. I made him walk faster to the Edgware Road so I could find him some disinfectant. He was being very pathetic and whimpering a lot. I wanted to just direct him to A & E but I worried he wouldn't make it on his own. He seemed to need me to look after him.

We went in and out of numerous shops asking for TCP. He trailed behind me as I charged about, but he didn't actually seem to know what antiseptic was. He had no idea how to look after himself. He repeated 'Thanks for looking after me, thanks for looking after me.' I felt like his bloody mother. All my observations of him being childlike were being reinforced. I was surprised by how a grown man could be so inept. I know he was in pain but there was no need to act dumb and stick his bottom lip out.

I came out of a shop and he was bent double on the pavement sucking the blood out and spitting it out on the ground. He stood up and had trails of it dribbling down his chin. All I could think was: thank God for this, it gives me an easy way out of having to kiss him goodbye.

I was panicking. TCP need to rethink their distribution methods as it would seem that nowhere in NW1 stocks it. We were getting closer to my house, and the last thing I wanted was for him to see where I lived, or ask to come in to run his hand under my tap. So I ran back to the first shop I'd gone into and purchased a bottle of Dettol. I poured it over the gash. He squealed and yelped but he knew it was doing him good. I stood and watched him dance around, stamping his feet and repeating long 'Ahhhhhs' until he finally stood still and admitted it didn't hurt anymore.

The bleeding had stopped but it was still a deep cut. I saw him into a taxi and sent him off to A & E, where someone else could take over the responsibility. Clearly I'm not ready for children.

Mamma Mia!

The Couple: Five

15/04/2005   **12.08**
From: Dawn
To: Gillian

Hi Gillian
I'm so sorry I haven't been in touch, I feel really rude about that.
Life just went a little bonkers for a while, all starting to settle now
though.
Happy to resume talks if you are
What do you say? Still interested?
Hope you're very well x

15/04/2005   **14.06**
From: Gillian
To: Dawn

Hi Dawn,
Great to hear from you. Hope it hasn't been anything bad that has
made life
so hectic.
I would be very happy to resume talks, yes still interested.
Let me know what your schedule is and we can arrange a date to
meet up.
Look forward to hearing from you again
Gill
x

15/04/2005   **14.13**
From: Dawn
To: Gillian

No nothing bad at all. Just a few work commitments and a big
house move. I have been settling into a new world. But nothing bad
– in fact all very very good.
I might be planning a holiday in the not to distant future so probably
best to meet up after that.
I will be gorgeously brown and desperate to show it of . . . in its
entirety!!!
It's great to be back in contact – let's keep it this way.
Sorry again and glad to see you still have interest in the idea x x

15/04/2005   **16.13**
From: Gillian
To: Dawn

Your holiday indeed sounds like a good idea. Have spoken to
Gavin, and he's very excited to hear you are back in contact too.
We have been trying to organize something for quite a long time,
but have had so many hoaxes. People pretending to be something
they aren't. It is really good to find someone genuine.
Very exciting, I can't wait! x

15/04/2005   **16.16**
From: Dawn
To: Gillian

I can imagine, don't worry honey I'm genuine, you guys just seem
so open and honest, I feel really safe about it . . .
I will be in touch, glad Gavin is excited to x x x

17/04/2005   **19.20**
From: Gillian
To: Dawn

That's good to hear. We always thought you were genuine, but then
we didn't hear from you, we thought it was another hoax. It is good
to know it was only temporary and we are now back on track, so to
speak! We'll look forward to seeing your tan then! I'll be as white as
ever unfortunately. With my colouring I very rarely tan. I'd love to
find out a bit more about you. I have so many questions. Obviously I
know what you look like, but it is difficult to know anything more
without asking. Tell me if I'm being nosey, I'd like to call it inquisitive
of course! Are you English? How old are you? What is your job? I'll
leave it at that for the meantime; I don't want to bombard you. I can
ask more next time. Gavin is 33, I have recently turned 27 – I am a
PA and Gavin works in storage. Feel free to ask anything about us.
Speak soon
x x

17/04/2005   19.37
From: Dawn
To: Gillian

Hey – what do you mean by a hoax? Just people leading you on and not turning up or what?
Don't worry about being nosey, we are going to get to know each other pretty well I think, knowing more about who I am is nothing! I'm English, born in Scotland, raised in Guernsey, now I live in London but work from home. I do bits and bobs of PR for an online gambling company but primarily I'm half way through my first book – I will tell you all about that when we meet.
I'm 26 – 5ft 10, size 12, confident, happy to experiment, all that kind of stuff!
I think you guys are really brave doing this and I think you are doing it in exactly the right way. It could be sordid but you come across so eloquently . . . I kind of feel that it would be rude not to . . .

17/04/2005   20.33
From: Gillian
To: Dawn

Well, we've had quite a lot of emails with people, and we exchange photos, they sound keen to meet and then they just stop the contact. Not sure what happens really. Either they get cold feet or the photos they send aren't actually them, I'm not sure really. Other times we've had replies from single guys, and that isn't what we've asked for. It just gets frustrating.
Basically we had an experience with one of my girlfriends over a year ago. We both enjoyed it a lot, and ever since have wanted to either repeat the experience or experiment more. We have been looking for another couple or a single girl. I'm not too sure how I'd feel about just 2 blokes at the moment. Maybe one day, but I don't really feel comfortable with it at the moment.
Wow, a book? I can't wait to read it!
Think you could probably tell my size from the photos, but if not, I'm size 10 if I'm lucky, but mostly a size 12 and 5ft 4. Happy to experiment too, as you can probably tell. Gavin seems to have brought out a side in me that I hadn't really shared with any previous boyfriends. He is 6ft 2, toned and has a nice big cock!
Thanks, I was beginning to wonder if we were going the right way about it. This makes it so much easier. I don't know how people

would react if we asked them in a bar or something? We'd probably end up with a drink poured over us! I know to a lot of people it could be seen as sordid, but I think if all involved are comfortable with it, then it is fine. Everyone is different and have different sexual preferences. I don't think anyone's choices are wrong, some people just choose to experiment more than others.

So how much experience have you had with this kind of situation? I know you had said before you have boyfriends but like to have the occasional night with a girl. Have you had a relationship with a girl before? Are you single at the moment? If not, does your boyfriend mind you doing this?

xx

MONDAY 18 APRIL

The Gopher
Never Trust a Man With a Cat . . . Let Alone Three!

Post A

11/04/2005   13.50
From: The Gopher
To: Dawn

Hello There,
Saw your advert online, I'm **** from London a professional male of 36 years. Would love the idea of taking a pretty lady for dinner, what is your favourite food? If you are interested please get in touch.

11/04/2005   13.52
From: Dawn
To: The Gopher

Ooo, sushi . . . all the way!

**** is an interesting name . . . where are you from?

04/11/2005   14.43
From: The Gopher
To: Dawn

Hi There, I'm from England but ancestors are South American. I have attached a picture so you can see whether you like a date or not after the picture was taken I have started wearing glasses due to working on PC's! I don't waste time and I expect the same.
Best wishes

15/04/2005   11.42
From: Dawn
To: The Gopher

Wow, I can't believe that is you in that photo, it looks like a picture
of a movie star . . .
What do you mean by wasting time?
Have you had many online experiences then?

15/04/2005   13.22
From: The Gopher
To: Dawn

Hi There,
Thanks for the message. Well, I have had bad experiences online
as people simply waste time. However, if you are free one
afternoon next week we can meet and go for a nice Japanese meal
or maybe one evening if you are free.
So take care and do write when you have some time. Thanks for
your compliment. I'm not a movie star! But a very happy normal
human being.

15/04/2005   13.26
From: Dawn
To: The Gopher

One afternoon next week, or evening would be delightful . . .

15/04/2005   14.34
From: The Gopher
To: Dawn

If you are free Monday next week we can go to a Japanese
restaurant in Kew Garden. We can meet at 11.30. Just near the
Tube station there is a nice one. Do you drive? Please may I have a
picture so I can recognise you.
Let me know . . . Thanks

15/04/2005   **14.37**
From: Dawn
To: The Gopher

I don't drive no but I will get there . . . Monday is perfect!

15/04/2005   **15.00**
From: The Gopher
To: Dawn

Thank you and you look very cute I must say! Please tell me more about yourself. What do you do and where you from? May I also know your name? Do you work or are you a lady at leisure?

15/04/2005   **15.03**
From: Dawn
To: The Gopher

My name is Dawn
I work from home as I'm a writer.
I'm 26, 5ft 10, very confident and love socialising – what else would you like to know my friend?

15/04/2005   **15.07**
From: The Gopher
To: Dawn

Hello My Friend!
I like ladies who are creative and I think you sound very creative. By the way I started wearing glasses about three months ago, this is due to lot of computer work, Glaring at the PC is bad for the eyes.

15/04/2005   **15.13**
From: Dawn
To: The Gopher

You told me that . . . ha ha you obviously are still adjusting.
Tell me more about you.

15/04/2005   15.23
From: The Gopher
To: Dawn

About myself, I have my own Diamond company. I travel a lot and have travelled around the world a great deal and have met interesting people. I enjoy the company of nice creative ladies as I like fashion and all things nice. But I also have very high morals and values in the way I conduct my business with great ethics. These nice qualities have honoured me in everything I do, because I treat people with utmost respect and dignity the way I wish to be treated. By the way, you have a lovely smile and a tasty set of white teeth! ha.ha.ha.
My star sign is Aquarius and may I know yours? I believe in Astrology and the planets as I feel it has an influence on us and sometimes they can reveal many things about our behaviours and how our lives unfold.

15/04/2005   15.37
From: Dawn
To: The Gopher

I'm also Aquarius . . . what does that mean then?

15/04/2005   15.44
From: The Gopher
To: Dawn

You and I will have so much to talk. We will both learn a lot from each other and that's the way it should be. I'm honoured I met you! Thanks to the Internet xx

15/04/2005   15.46
From: Dawn
To: The Gopher

Hurrah to the Internet
And thanks to whoever set up such a brilliant website . . .
I must be off now – my kitten needs some attention from Mummy – see you Monday x

15/04/2005   15.54
From: The Gopher
To: Dawn

Ah, you have cats? I have three, Max, Louis and Oli – Maybe one day they can meet yours?
OK, 11.30 at Kew Gardens on Monday. This suits me fine if you are OK with this. I will look forward to our date on Monday at 11.30 outside Kew Garden Tube Station. Please get off the Tube and come out and I will be parked just outside the Station. x

15/04/2005   15.55
From: Dawn
To: The Gopher

That's it! No need to reply – this is confirmed . . . 11.30 am . . . see you then x x x

The Date

I couldn't work out if I was excited about this one or not. His emails were extremely friendly and in his picture he looked just like David Hasselhoff. Both hands on his hips, standing like a dude, with luscious curly hair, in front of a blurred background with a slightly sepia-tone to it. But there was something in his modulation that suggested the possibility of him maybe being quite square. Also, David Hasselhoff look-alikes aren't my usual aim, but for the sake of an afternoon of burning passion I was happy to go along with it.

His talk of star signs was quite cute. I'm not really into all that but a lot of my girlfriends are and I like the fact that it exists. I do have a tendency to buy the *Sun* every day just to see what Mystic Meg has to say, but I pay no real attention if it's not what I want to hear. But it does make me laugh when people say things like:

'Are you a Virgo?'

'No, I'm an Aquarius.'

'Ah yes, you are a typical Aquarius!'

'But you thought I was a . . . oh forget it!'

I think that just makes people look silly. But I liked this guy's temperate tone so was happy to allow him to convince me that it isn't all moonshine.

I got the train to Kew Gardens and saw his car as soon as I alighted. It didn't look like there was anyone sitting in the driver's seat at first but as I walked closer a small white dot got bigger and bigger until I identified it as a set of teeth. They were huge and continued to grow as I got nearer to the vehicle. The lump in my throat, which I have become so accustomed to, parked itself in my gullet as I bent to great him at the driver's side window.

'Wow, great car.' Were the only words I could muster.

'It is my pride and it is my joy,' he replied and suggested that I got in. I walked around the front of it looking like a stroke victim, my face stuck in a grotesquely disappointed expression.

It wasn't him. It was not the sexy looking hunk of spunk from the picture. I couldn't believe it. The picture was why I met him. Usually I go by the emails and although his were very sweet, I was essentially wooed by the thought of a hot Latino lover caressing my naked body in one of Kew's flowerbeds. But no, he couldn't have been further from my fantasy.

I couldn't look at him. I stared forward with my hands clasped and squashed between my thighs, which I was squeezing together tightly. My bottom lip was still trying to make contact with the floor and my forehead was so wrinkled I looked like a Chinese Shar-pei.

He drove off like a grandpa on a Sunday and parked about ten minutes down the road. During the journey all we talked about was where we were going to park. I didn't know the area, but as we were going to a place right by the station, I wanted to suggest that we stayed where we were. However, keen not to have to look at him or make any other sort of chat, I went with it and expressed much annoyance about the amount of double yellow lines and selfishness of 'Permit parking only' areas. None of which I actually give a toss about.

When he parked the car, a painfully disjointed and OAP style manoeuvre, we got out and began the walk back to the station. It was now that I had to take him in, come to terms with what I had and deal with it appropriately.

'Wow, Kew is really beautiful. I've never been here before,' I said.

'Yes, it is. So why are you Internet dating?'

Oh Jesus, he doesn't mess about . . .

'Um, to meet friends,' I answered, hoping that my words really conveyed 'Not lovers!'

We started to walk. I sensed religion so I didn't want to talk too much of my naughty adventures. I merely said that I had met a few people, some good, some bad.

'Yes, there are lots of people who are just online for one night stands. I do not understand that attitude. I mean . . . why?' he raised both his hands in total disgust.

'Yes, I know . . . terrible! Don't understand it either,' says she who had spent the morning pruning her shrubbery with the intention of rolling around in some grass . . .

It was only 11.30 but I was starving, so I was very happy when he suggested an early lunch before a walk around Kew Gardens. Looking forward to the nice sushi restaurant by the station that he'd mentioned, my taste buds began to roll. But no, once again, he didn't quite provide what he had described and we sat in the conservatory of a little café which served pies, quiches and jacket potatoes. I had no problem with that, it was very nice, but when I realised that there was no sushi restaurant at the station I wondered why on earth he'd said there was.

It was apparent that this guy's tactic was just to get you on the date. A deceiving picture and the offer of fabulous food were good, but when I asked him about the diamond business that he 'owned' I wasn't particularly surprised to learn that he didn't own it at all, but that one of his clients owned it and he did their accounts. Not quite the same methinks!

We ordered our food from the counter. I had a huge slice of pie, naughty because of my wheat intolerance, but I felt like I deserved it. He had a jacket potato with prawns. We took a seat and I looked at him. I was over my disappointment, now I was just annoyed.

He was more like a Gordon the Gopher than David Hasselhoff. His teeth were long and strong, while the incisors were crooked and there were two indentations on his bottom lip where his two front teeth rested.

When my appetite was satisfied I began to feel a little sorry for him and wondered why he felt the need to lie so much. He wasn't hideous looking and was obviously reasonably successful – he drove a nice car, was kind hearted, intelligent, knew how to use a knife and fork etc. I made a point of giving him the benefit of the doubt and tried to get to know him a bit, so I asked him about his experiences with Internet dating. He'd got one.

It was a woman that he met through an American site. They got talking, they had a lot in common; he liked the sound of her, she liked the sound of him. They talked for months, exchanged pictures, had phone conversations and fell in love with each other as much as you possibly can when you haven't even smelled, met or touched each other. Eventually they decided to organise a meeting.

It was her that came to him. He arranged a long weekend of fun for them. He made up the bed in his spare room in case she wasn't comfortable sleeping with him. He was excited and stocked the fridge up, got some good DVDs in, got his hair cut etc., etc. They had become so close he really thought that a lasting relationship was likely to occur.

On the day that she was supposed to arrive he went to pick her up from Heathrow. The flight was delayed, so his anticipation was intense as he waited in Arrivals for the love of his life to walk through the door. The flight eventually landed. His nerves rocketed while the passengers collected their luggage. The doors opened and people started to come towards him. He tried to remain calm as he stood on tippy toes, peering over everyone's heads to catch the first glimpse of his love in the flesh. And then he saw her, the face that he had been waiting for. Just a dot in the distance getting bigger and bigger as she approached him. Her smile beaming as her pace – and her size – increased. That distant dot grew and grew and grew until, standing just inches away from him, was the beautiful head he had been expecting, but with about 280lbs of lard and blubber hanging off the end of it.

He looked down.

'She'd lied to me. I'd seen photos of her in swimsuits and she was nowhere near as large as that. I felt totally humiliated and betrayed.'

Now I ain't no genius but ain't this the guy who sent me a picture of someone ten years his junior, with more hair than his follicles could ever handle and a totally different dental configuration?

I had no idea how to respond. Was I supposed not to have noticed the extreme physical differences between him in person and his alter ego that emails across the globe? Or did he really believe that I would convince myself that the photographer was some sort of genius, and that through miraculous camera trickery the fruity looking Latino dream boat was indeed him, just photographed from a particularly flattering angle?

'So what did you do?' Seemed the best thing to say.

'I kissed her on each cheek and drove to a hotel. I went in, booked her a room and left her there for the rest of her stay.'

'You mean you didn't even spend the weekend with her?'

'No! Where I come from it is not acceptable to lie and deceive people that way.'

OK, now my head was really up my arse. What the hell was this guy's game?

'And what did she say? Was she not hurt?'

'She didn't really say anything. I think she knew why I was so upset. She actually took it really well.'

I'm not surprised, the poor woman thought she'd pulled David Hasselhoff . . .

We finished our lunch and went over to Kew Gardens for a walk. I'd never been so, even though I'm not particularly interested in botany, I was happy to see what all the fuss was about. He didn't want to join me in getting a school's activity pack and carrying out all the exercises in it. I was a little upset about that; the kids looked like they were having a ball.

It was a very pleasant day and I was grateful of the walk as that humungous piece of pie was already weighing me down.

'I love to walk, it's such good exercise,' he said.

I agreed, I walk everywhere I can. It's very good exercise but not when you creep along at a snail's pace. That burns about as many calories as eating a cake. I'm a stomper, but I did understand that I wasn't there to work out so I managed to keep my steps small and infrequent enough not to leave him behind. I was bored though and the further and further we got from the entrance filled me with dread, as it meant we had further and further to walk back. I'd told him everything about my life that I was willing to share with someone I was pretty sure I was never going to see again, but he kept on saying 'So . . . what else?'

It got really irritating. I chatted away about things like Guernsey, London life, drama school, my cat. The conversation wasn't riveting but it was fluid and coherent to the surroundings and pace of the motion.

But he kept on saying it. I found it galling. Rather like when you're walking down a road alone, carrying lots of things but feeling pretty happy because you've just been shopping and some irksome bloke takes it upon himself to say 'Smile!' or 'Cheer up love, it might never happen!' Instantly I get catapulted into an abhorrent mood and want to scream 'What the fuck am I supposed to do? Walk around like a clown with a big fat smile on my face like I've necked a load of happy pills and just won a million quid?' Urgh, drives me crazy. His constant 'What elses' had a very similar effect. I hadn't stopped talking and telling him all about my life, but when there was even the slightest gap in conversation he made me feel like I was dull as hell. I wanted to shake him and tell him to enjoy the silences, because I sure as hell did.

I turned it around to focus on him. I wasn't really listening but I'd lost all impetus to speak. I drifted in and out of the conversation, but I think he was telling me at one point that he kept birds, and that every now and then he enjoyed a brandy on ice. All pretty mundane chat that failed to change my mind about him.

'There's a bench, let's sit and rest.'

Rest? Rest? We'd only walked ten feet and it had taken us half an hour to get there! I wanted to go home. But, I didn't want to be rude so I sat with him for a moment.

'So, what else?'

'What else what? What do you want to know?'

'Tell me about the other kinds of men you've met online?'

OK, seeing as I was there I might as well have had a conversation and at least he had got me onto something I was passionate about. I looked forward to telling him some funny stories. Open his mind a little.

'Well, there are lots of guys out there who just need someone to talk to. I've found myself taking on the role of counselor many times. A guy takes me out and all he can talk about is his difficult divorce. I want to shake them and say "That's not the kind of stuff I want to talk about on our first date!"'

I laughed.

'So people just tell you all about how much they have been hurt in the past?'

'Yup. In gross detail. Bad idea!'

He took a few moments where he positioned himself comfortably on the edge of a picnic table, and went on to tell me a blow-by-blow account of how his wife of fifteen years came home from work one day and announced that she was leaving him and how she totally destroyed his life. I couldn't believe he was saying it. I'd just told him how unappealing this was and he went full throttle into a heart-wrenching account of his emotional anguish. It was sad and I was sorry for him, but I just couldn't be the sympathetic ear he wanted.

My eyelids were giving in and I thought it would be ruder to fall asleep than it would be to make my excuses and leave. But my delirium had kicked in and coming up with a good escape plan was tricky. I got all my words tied up and said,

'Oh, shit. I've just remembered. I have to go home to feed my cleaner.'

I realised what I'd said and repeated myself, but for some reason I just kept on saying it. This made me laugh. Which was hugely inappropriate in light of the circumstances. He didn't see the funny side, and I felt awful, but I insisted that we had to leave immediately as my cleaner needed her food.

The pace was turbo on the way back compared to the ambling of before. I couldn't get away fast enough. Bless him, he'd obviously been hurt and was trying to get his life in order, but I couldn't be the one to help him and I thought it best to leave promptly before I gave any wrong impressions.

He walked me to the train station and I said goodbye. A kiss on one cheek was our farewell and I couldn't have been happier to get away. It wasn't what I was expecting at all. No David Hasselhoff in sight and if we were both typical Aquarians then there must be some serious leverage in the zodiac rule book!

TUESDAY 19 APRIL

Herr Fingers
This Little Piggy . . .

Post C

12/04/2005   17.16
From: Herr Fingers
To: Dawn

Hi there. I did a similar thing three weeks ago. Had to be in New York for business and decided to stay the weekend just for fun. Combining business and pleasure and all those good things. Anyway I placed an ad to see if anybody wanted to show me around, have dinner, go out and have fun. I met somebody really nice, had a top weekend and savor some happy memories. To cut a very long story short, I would love to repeat the experience and see if this really works or if I just had bags of beginners luck. I'm German, 34 – 6ft6 – well built – open minded – easy going etc etc. Let me know if you want to hook up . . .

12/04/2005   18.19
From: Dawn
To: Herr Fingers

Wow, 6"6 – that's huge!!! If I went out with you I could wear my stilettos with pride – I'm about 5"10, or maybe 5"9 not quite sure, but I'm definitely tall!
Nice to meet you, I'm Dawn x

13/04/2005   09.07
From: Herr Fingers
To: Dawn

Hey . . . and I always thought size didn't matter . . . .!
If I can ever persuade you to come on an adventure with me you
would get away with high heels easily. You are making me curious
now. Talking about curious, what is with the lack of picture, cheeky?
Now don't tell me you are shy!
Where in London are you?

13/04/2005   09.14
From: Dawn
To: Herr Fingers

Oh, sorry about the lack of picture . . . here you go . . . I live in the
West End
Now, what's this adventure you plan to take me on?

13/04/2005   09.27
From: Herr Fingers
To: Dawn

Wow you are seriously cute . . .
I'm German, but have been in London for about 7 years.
OK adventures! That is tricky. Not sure what you like. First attempt.
Spice things up right? Here is the scenario. We meet for a drink
and a bite to eat. We have an amazing time, a really good laugh
and feel very comfortable together. So comfortable that we decide
to drive to an airport, book a flight to Ireland in the spur of the
moment, spend the night in a beautiful room in a castle, there is
Champagne, candles . . . . The next morning we go for a walk in
the fresh air in the beautiful surrounding countryside before we fly
back late afternoon!
Any good?

13/04/2005   10.56
From: Dawn
To: Herr Fingers

I love that idea – very extreme.
Sounds like a proper adventure!
How could I possibly refuse an offer like that!

13/04/2005   11.10
From: Herr Fingers
To: Dawn

Obviously I need to think of something else now in order to keep it a surprise. Should not be too difficult. I'm quite creative . . . . or extreme as you put it.

13/04/2005   11.15
From: Dawn
To: Herr Fingers

Yeah, don't you just love meeting people on the Internet? It's kind of underground . . . I enjoy that!
Ooo, more ideas? keepum coming x x

13/04/2005   11.29
From: Herr Fingers
To: Dawn

Underground dating? Got a good ring to it. I know what you mean. The element of surprise tends to make things extra exciting. So what if the person you meet is a total nightmare. Rather a night out, even a bad one, than staying at home watching Eastenders. Got nothing to lose, right?
I'll keep the ideas to myself for now. Adds to the spice!
So how am I going to tempt you to actually meet me . . . . . . ?

13/04/2005   11.33
From: Dawn
To: Herr Fingers

ha ha . . . don't ask me to do your job for you MR!
Come on . . . give it your best shot!

13/04/2005   11.45
From: Herr Fingers
To: Dawn

That's not how it works cheeky!
Meet me in a lounge type sort of bar anywhere in London and
leave the rest to me. Bring your passport just in case . . . . and a
toothbrush. I will arrange everything else!

OK how about Tue 19/4, 6:30 bar Soho . . . . Old Compton Street?

13/04/2005   12.12
From: Dawn
To: Herr Fingers

Done!

13/04/2005   12.15
From: Herr Fingers
To: Dawn

So to recap . . . what do you need to bring?

13/04/2005   12.17
From: Dawn
To: Herr Fingers

Myself?
My passport and my toothbrush . . .

13/04/2005   12.19
From: Herr Fingers
To: Dawn

Cool see you there . . . for drinks, drinks and conversation x

13/04/2005   12.45
From: Dawn
To: Herr Fingers

Yeah . . . and the rest!

13/04/2005   12.50
From: Herr Fingers
To: Dawn

It's 'the rest' I'm looking forward to . . .

The Date

It was a nice idea but I didn't bother taking my passport; I was pretty sure that he wasn't serious about that. And anyway, I only live up the road from Soho; if he was for real I could just pop home and get it. Along with my toothbrush, a spare pair of knickers and a truck load of condoms.

Mind you, I didn't have particularly high hopes for the evening. I was hideously premenstrual. Not that I was being moody, I just felt like I was about to give birth to a five-year-old and my boobs were so sensitive it hurt to run to the fridge, which I seemed to be doing every three minutes. I was hoping that the effects of alcohol would numb the pain and allow me to forget about the curse that was due to strike in about two days time. So I went along anyway – for some bizarre reason I get incredibly horny when I'm in that state.

There was no mistaking when I walked in which one he was. He made everyone else at the bar look like an Oompa Loompa. The dude was like Goliath!

He seemed a little nervous in his mannerisms. For example he kept putting his bottle to his lips but not taking a sip, and while we were waiting to be served he struggled with whether or not to rest his elbows on the bar or stand straight. Occasionally he experimented with leaning his bottom against the bar and trying to get their attention by looking over his right shoulder. This position really wasn't right. It was actually quite hard to watch and the barmaid was in no hurry to serve us, so I flicked out my arm and waved my hand around insisting that we were next to be served. Finally we were. He got a bottle of white and we found a seat in the corner of the pub.

'Zis is zi best seat in za house,' boomed a voice which was as deep as could be expected from someone whose lungs were twenty feet away from their mouth. I was dealing with some serious resonance here. If this guy hummed on your bits you'd come harder than Ron Jeremy.

Actually it was a rubbish seat. All the cushions were coming off it and the lights were too bright, but it was secluded and that was blatantly what he liked about it. He had no qualms with being sexual with me. I was asked seriously what I would like for breakfast and he was suggesting bra removal within minutes of sitting down.

I was wearing a baby doll boob-tube with a knee-length denim skirt and cowgirl stilettos. I had a strapless bra on, which was giving me jip. I subtly tried to pull it up, but nothing escaped his attention and within seconds of my sly manoeuvre his hand was down my back and he was trying to undo it. Some rigorous wriggling took place and I managed to get it out before the clasp was opened, but he didn't half give it his best shot. His hands had minds of their own. As he sat still and talked about work stuff they were running all over my body like rats scurrying in and out of every crevice.

When I did manage to shake him off, his disappointment wasn't well hidden and his eyes were glued to my boobs. There's always that joke about guys who speak to girls chests; well he was the ultimate at this. On numerous occasions he openly mentioned how lovely he thought they were. I wasn't complaining: it's a nice thing to hear.

I told him I was a writer and he suggested that I should write a book for men about dating. I agreed that would be a marvellous idea and he said he would definitely read it. I agreed that also would be a very good idea . . .

I really liked him. His company was very easy and he was funny. Yeah sure he was being quite full on with his come ons but we were on a date after all and it was pretty unthreatening. His determination was mildly admirable. I appreciated his honesty that he loved sex and wanted it. Jesus, how could I give someone grief for that?

He wasn't good looking. But he wasn't ugly. Hard to place really. The only reason I would probably notice him was because of his height, and even then I'm not sure I would pay much attention. He had one of those faces that just makes up a crowd. No distinguishing features. He didn't have fantastic eyes, or kissable lips, a big nose or a good hair do. He just had hugeness. I'm not underestimating that, I think it's a superb quality, but that alone isn't a particularly stimulating feature. That is of course apart from his fingers. Bloody hell they added a whole new meaning to the phrase 'finger fuck'. Each one was like a little penis that I would have happily accepted at the age of sixteen. Long and nimble with fat bulbs at the end. All wriggly and pokey and eager to please.

Sometimes I see things like cartoons when I stare at them for too long. It's just something that happens and, as he bellowed on about Frankfurt, I was seeing these ten hungry cocks racing all over my body playing a very imaginative game of hide the German sausage.

I know I say I didn't find him very attractive, (Let me just reiterate that he wasn't by any means unattractive, but he didn't have any depth of sexiness to him. No sex appeal – even though he clearly loved sex and was very confident – and he lacked a sensuality which is more important to me than looks). But I was happy to flirt with him thinking the night may well turn horny.

He got drunk very quickly. Actually it might not have been that quickly as we did manage to put away four bottles of wine in about two hours. It's all a bit of a blur. All I can really remember is him saying:

'I'm not zo goot on vine,' and then letting out what from an average lung would be a hiccup, but from his it was more of a belch.

We didn't move from our secluded seat and I think we were involved in some serious snogging by bottle three. The lights had been dimmed so we felt even more private and our little love nest was serving its purpose well.

There was a table opposite us that had full view of our antics, but when the people on it left, he jumped at the chance to run five horny willies up my leg and nestle them all in my pants like suckling piglets.

Each one had a go inside me, occasionally two sneaked in together which was a little tricky but I did my best to accommodate in the position I was in. Getting fingered in a pub after drinking too much too quickly and by someone that I didn't particularly fancy – it was like being sixteen again. But it was fun for that reason, it felt naughty and I quite enjoyed that.

However, he was drunk and wasn't focusing on pleasuring me, more just about stuffing me as full of his digits as possible and licking my face like he was cleaning it. I tried to keep the kissing minimal. Just small tongueless, slightly open mouthed ones, because every time he opened his mouth I almost lost my head in it. It was a cavernous, gaping black hole of which I was keen to avoid, lest I might be lost forever.

I certainly wasn't as drunk as him so after about ten minutes of being manhandled by this horny oaf I broke the contact by removing his hand from my knickers. It was a relief I have to say. I had been right about his lack of sensuality. He was one of those guys that just sees a fanny as a hole and thinks that you can work it by just shoving things up it. Believe me if that were the case I would be strapping springs to my feet and bouncing up and down motorways landing carefully on the traffic cones. But, alas, it takes a little more than mere entry to get my juices flowing.

As I prised him off me a loud noise echoed in my head. A rhythmic sound that increased with pace and mood as our heads became unstuck. I recognised the sound as that of achievement or celebration. When he moved out of my way and back to my side I was faced with the perpetrators of this racket. It was the new residency at the table opposite, who had obviously been watching us for some time.

I laughed and hid my face behind my hand. I truly did feel sixteen again. I wasn't embarrassed though, I was loving it. Not in a sexy, exhibitionistic way – which would have been hard anyway seeing as I'd found the experience particularly unerotic – but just because it was mischievous and ridiculous and made me feel fun.

He was blissfully unaware and sat by my side with both elbows resting on a shelf behind him and his head hanging pitiably from his neck. It was time to leave. I finished the remainder of the wine and pulled him up to standing, but he kept falling back down. So I sat down again, not really knowing what to do next.

'Wake up, come on let's go and get some food. Sober us up a bit.'

'I vill be fine here. Get some more vine.'

'No, come on, we need to leave here before we get kicked out.'

I stood again and tried to pull him to standing, but I had no luck. That is until one of the men from the audience came over to help me and we managed to get him to standing.

'Thanks,' I said, not being able to look him in the eye.

'No problem,' he laughed, 'looks like you're going to have a fun evening.'

Yeah, like shizzer I was!

I slung his arm over my shoulder and led my date out onto Old Compton Street.

He flopped back against a door and pulled me towards him.

'You are zo zexy. Let's go back to your house and fuck.'

Now, I have had sex in some pretty drunken states, but this guy couldn't sustain his bipedal ability let alone an erection.

'Why don't we get something to eat and see how we feel?'

He agreed and I led him up Dean Street to a cute little Chinese café, where the staff shook their heads at us and the tables were too small for his legs.

He sat with a banana shaped torso, his knees above table level and his arms hanging down by his sides. His head still flopped down yet with the left cheek facing up towards the ceiling.

'What do you want to eat?'

'You,' he said, trying desperately to act sober. A stoned smile stretched across his face as he battled with the impossibility of lifting his head. His eyes remained 90 per cent closed throughout the process.

'So you like rice or noodles?'

I obviously excited him with that as he jerked up straight and grabbed the menu off me. Squinting his eyes as he worked hard to make sense of the squiggles on the page.

The waitress came over and practically snarled at my dinner

partner. I apologised to her for his state and assured her he would be fine after some food. I ordered him some beef noodles and he roared, 'Rice!'

'I think he would prefer the rice,' said the waitress realising that it was impossible not to laugh at him.

'Yes, I think we better get the man some rice. And can I have the garlic chicken but with extra garlic. Not cooked, just two cloves of garlic crushed raw onto the top of the dish, thanks.'

What can I say? My body was in a pregnant state; I had to give it what it wanted.

I made another grave attempt to make chat with my drunken comrade. 'Jesus, I'm going to stink of garlic after that!'

'You already do. You stink of it,' he unexpectedly replied in perfect English before erupting in hysterical and thunderous laughter.

'I do?' I asked in a quiet voice with a hand over my mouth.

'Yar, it vas the first thing I noticed. You smell like garlic sauce.'

His booming amusement continued to fill the café. I ordered a bottle of wine and began to plough my way through it alone. Bastard!

Our food came and he managed to shovel every last bit of it into his mouth. I was starting to hate him. He hadn't only covered my face in his spit, prodded my fanny like he was stuffing a chicken and sprained my shoulder from the weight of having to carry him but now he had told me I stank.

I'd drunk the best part of three bottles of wine yet had somehow remained virtually sober. My belly was starting to throb from the delights of a looming period and by this time I really did stink of garlic. There was no way we were having sex.

'Finished?' I asked sarcastically as he pressed one of his cock fingers onto the last grain of rice on his plate and lifted it into his mouth.

'Yar. Now let's go back and fuck.'

I didn't break the news there and then. We got the bill, paid up and went outside. Me walking quickly with my arms across my chest and a face like thunder, him bouncing off every surface and knocking over every chair within a three feet radius.

He fell against another door and pulled me towards him. I

kissed him, knowing that my breath must have honked but not really caring at all.

'Zo . . . where is your place?'

'Not far, but I'm going to go home alone tonight. No offence, but I think I'm about to get my period.'

'I don't mind.'

'Yeah, well I do, sorry.'

'Hey, ve can put a towel down.'

Jesus, what is it with Germans and towels?

'No, I want to go home alone tonight. Next time.'

'I can vait!'

I kissed him again and walked away. Every time I turned back he was in the same position. Flopped against the door, hands in his pockets, watching me walk away. Trying to look adoring but clearly just too pissed to move. God knows how he got home. Actually he could even still be there – it didn't look like he was going anywhere soon.

I made my way up Oxford Street leaving a trail of garlic behind me; one hand resting on the bottom of my back, the other feeling the way in front of me like a nine-months pregnant woman.

I was so relieved to get away. The premenstrual horn didn't get me that night that's for sure. I got in, made a hot water bottle, got into bed and slagged off boys in my head until I fell asleep. Next morning I woke up, got my period and felt absolutely fabulous.

Ah the joys of womanhood!

The Couple: Six

23/04/2005   **18.29**
From: Dawn
To: Gillian

Hey gorgeous

Thanks so much for your email. I have been writing all weekend
and I was drunk every night last week so have been struggling
today. Feel a bit like I'm made of vinegar . . . out again for a biggun
tonight so trying to feel normal again . . .
I need to answer some other questions don't I?
Yes, I do think you are doing this the right way, it's not right to
cruise in bars looking for this type of thing. I know that sounds
ridiculous, like doing it on some dodgy website is better but at least
you can filter and find someone you like. And someone totally
disconnected. You guys obviously have a strong relationship, an
encounter like this needs to be kept separate from that, so it can be
enjoyed. So although I think it's probably fun doing it with a friend, it
does run possibilities of maybe getting tricky!! Me? I'm so single its
amazing . . . he he, couldn't be more single if I tried. Its a choice I
have to say – with the book I just couldn't fit a boyfriend in at the
moment
I would be lying if I said I didn't have 'lovers', but no ties . . . it just
works at the moment.
And yes I have done this before, but like you, just with friends. Very
sexy experiences but it will be nice to have one that is more
genuine than a drunken romp. It's fun to play around every now and
then. And playing with a girl is a real treat but I don't consider
myself to be 'bisexual.' I have no desire to have a relationship with a
woman but a lot of my fantasies are about me and other girls. But I
love nothing more than a nice fat cock and a cuddle from someone
who is bigger than me.
Blimey!

XX

24/04/2005　　　**20.18**
From: Gillian
To: Dawn

Hey sexy,
Yeah, I know what you mean. I was a little worried about the
relationship with my friend after the threesome, but thankfully we've
both been fine about it and there is no awkwardness. I know she
enjoyed it, but wouldn't want to repeat it as her relationship with her
boyfriend has got a bit more serious.
I have been asked if I was bi sexual, and strangely enough I gave a
very similar answer to yours. Although, I guess I haven't really had
enough experiences to make up my mind completely. I don't want a
full on relationship with a girl. I'm the same as you I find women
physically attractive, and think it is just a sexual preference to
experiment. I could never live without blokes though.
I just wish it was as easy to find a girl as it is to find a bloke. I've
wanted a repeat of last year's threesome for ages. Gavin and I talk
about it lots, and I think we just drive each other crazy with our
fantasies about it. You've become part of our sex chat now, so he
talks about what we would be doing if you were there. It turns me
on so much, I can't wait to meet you. He's been texting me today
teasing me with naughty messages as we aren't together. He said
"Would love to get the two of you facing each other, both face down
over a bed kissing each other while I got you both wet and ready
for my big hard cock. Would then get you both to play with
yourselves while you take turns to suck my cock."
He's quite dominant in bed (or wherever!) and we've experimented
with most things. Is there anything you don't like to do, we wouldn't
want to offend you? We have a few pairs of handcuffs, blindfolds, a
collar and leash, nurse's outfits, vibrators, and they regularly get
used. We'd like to use some of them with you, if you are willing?
Do you have anymore photos of yourself? I love the ones you've
sent through previously, but more is always good. I've attached a
more recent one of me on a night out with a few girlies. You should
be able to pick me out, I'm sitting being lazy at the front, while
everyone else stands!
Well I seem to have written quite a lot again! Sorry, it can be hard
to shut me up sometimes!
Hope you've had a good weekend.
Gill
xxx

TUESDAY 26 APRIL

Master Pendant
Oh yeah, go on then – Strangle me daddy!

I answered his post in the 'Men Looking for Women' section. It went something like this:

Perhaps you've just finished a long-term independence. Maybe you secretly like guys who are a bit older than you, but you don't want your friends to know. Perhaps you're bisexual & find it difficult to find guys who know you need to keep your girlfriends & boyfriends separate. Or maybe you've known for a while that there's more to human relationships & sexuality than the whole boring flowers-and-sofas-and-DVD thing?

. . . But you don't want to just go to the pub & pick some random bloke for a drunken shag. (Although you might want to occasionally, if you're in the mood, and not worry about someone else being jealous). If you're are intelligent, sexy, slim and 20–28,

Drop me a mail. Photos-can wait if you'd prefer.

I'm 38, English, smart, attractive, open-minded, very witty & sarcastic. I'm used to unusual and highly intelligent, sexually-open girls, and I'm very protective of my time and independence.

21/04/2005   14.15
From: Dawn
To: Master Pendant

I like the lack of desperation in your tone – quite a sexy post, a bit narky and straight to the point . . . nice!
I'm intelligent sexy and slim and I'm 26 . . .
I'm totally single and don't want that to
Change at all, but up for being slightly unconventional about things . . .
I think I might be a little unusual as well, in the way that I like my life to be a bit different
So um . . . .??

21/04/2005   14.47
From: Master Pendant
To: Dawn

Hmmm. Let's see . . . Unusual. Unconventional.
"Different".
Now, I wonder if you're trying to tell me something ;-) . . .
. . . Let me guess . . . . you're really not into "relationships" in the
normal sense . . . you like confident & interesting guys . . . . you're
possibly looking for "friends with benefits" . . . and you're also
maybe looking for someone who's going to make you push your
boundaries a little . . . .
Let's play a game. Tell me 3 more things about yourself. Interesting,
fun things. But one must be a lie . . . .
And if you've got a photo . . . .)

21/04/2005   14.52
From: Dawn
To: Master Pendant

Pretty much . . .
OK . . .

I'm a writer
I'm a voyeur
I enjoy pain

you?

21/04/2005   17.35
From: Master Pendant
To: Dawn

I reckon you're an exhibitionist, not a voyeur . . . .

My turn?

– I've had sex in public
– I'm never jealous
– I'm submissive

21/04/2005   17.37
From: Dawn
To: Master Pendant

I could be both . . .
I can't imagine you to be submissive for one minute . . .

22/04/2005   02.02
From: Master Pendant
To: Dawn

Well, in that case it seems rude not to give you an opportunity to
see how well your imagination stacks up against reality . . . .

I suggest we meet up for a coffee on Saturday
afternoon, or a drink next week on Tuesday . . . .

23/04/2005   13.01
From: Dawn
To: Master Pendant

You're going to have to tell me a bit more about you before I
arrange to meet you Mr!

23/04/2005   14.25
From: Master Pendant
To: Dawn

You want to know more about me. But you also like the mystery &
intrigue as well . . . .

23/04/2005   15.18
From: Dawn
To: Master Pendant

Can't deny that actually!

23/04/2005   15.41
From: Master Pendant
To: Dawn

Thought as much. Let's go with Tuesday afternoon. There's
something distinctly unconventional with meeting during the
day . . . . you can create your own little bubble of reality about

yourselves, while the rest of the world gets on with business as usual . . . .

What time are you free?

And do you want to stay anonymous, or are you going to tell me your name?

23/04/2005   15.45
From: Dawn
To: Master Pendant

I agree, all for a daytime meeting . . .

I'm free all afternoon – where you based, I'm in Marylebone x

And um . . . I might stay anon . . . because I know that the mystery is what is exciting you to.

23/04/2005   16.15
From: Master Pendant
To: Dawn

I've got dark hair & eyes, an evil grin, 5'11, 73kg
(That's 160lb if you're American).

The Globe Pub? Opposite Baker Street Tube? 2pm?

23/04/2005   16.51
From: Dawn
To: Master Pendant

Sounds perfect.

I'm 2ft with dark hair (all over) a forward thrust jaw line, big teeth, Black leathery fingers and a stripy bottom, which I think is really pretty . . .

You can't miss me.

23/04/2005   18.43
From: Master Pendant
To: Dawn

And I'll reserve judgment on the prettiness of your posterior until we meet . . . .

I'll probably be wearing grey jeans & a black jacket. Looking forward to it.

The Date

I was enjoying the mystery of this one; I hadn't even wanted to see a photo. He seemed very insightful, a bit shady and dark yet clever and intuitive. He was quite accurate in his descriptions of what I might be looking for and from his post, his listings of people's possible situations made him sound liberal and open minded. He was confident and I can't deny it, I found his emails very sexy.

The Globe is approximately a ten minute walk from my house. On the way there I wondered if we would be together back at mine in a few hours time. He had intrigued me and it was really turning me on.

When I walked into to the pub he was standing with his back to me at the bar. He was indeed wearing grey jeans and a black blazer jacket, but what he had failed to mention was the bright red picture that covered the back of it. It was most offensive, it wasn't a skull and cross bones but you get the idea.

I stopped and contemplated leaving; after all he had no idea what I looked like so he wouldn't know if he turned around. But I forced myself to stay; it was unfair to judge him by his grunge wear. I thought back to his emails and tapped him on the shoulder.

'Hello?'

He turned to greet me and I was momentarily blinded as the sun from outside reflected off a thick and round silver pendant which dangled from his neck.

Under his jacket was a black T-shirt with white writing on it. I couldn't make out what it said but for the sake of describing the look I would say that it was a band's logo. His lips were very plump and his skin was pale with rosy cheeks. His bulbous brown eyes stuck out like a rabbits with myxomatosis. His nose was large and unmistakably Jewish, his hair short and brown. He stood holding a large glass of white wine that didn't suit him at all.

'You look nothing like I imagined,' he said in a voice which I instantly compared to Mr Bean's. A very nasal and deep tone, no doubt a result of him constantly pressing his receding chin back into his neck.

I got myself a tomato juice and we took a seat in the corner of the pub.

We started off with the mandatory 'Have you had many Internet dating experiences?' question. He had had lots. He spoke of his 'female friends' whom he'd met this way. But something told me that they were more than just friends as even though he wasn't very attractive physically, he had a strong sexual aura about him.

He was upset that I was drinking a soft drink and made a comment that we wouldn't be having the afternoon of debauchery that he'd planned. His confidence, if not mild arrogance, was seeping through. I felt like I'd met a few of him before. Super intelligent grungy people who read a lot of philosophical books, devote themselves to bands like Pink Floyd, don't like anyone mainstream, famous or fashionable and insist that they are always right. Annoyingly they usually are because they won't allow themselves not to be.

He was well travelled; I'm not. He was into psychedelic rock; I'm not. He was into mathematics and science; I'm not. He didn't smoke; I do. He drank; I didn't. He liked the unconventional; I do too – which is why I stayed there, as maybe, just maybe, I would find a bonding point for us.

We were on our second drink after about 25 minutes. He had another large glass of white wine, which made his cheeks go even rosier, and I had another tomato juice. I was telling him about my flat and how I hadn't had the chance yet to stamp my identity on my bedroom.

'Yes, you need to get your hook in the ceiling.'

'I'm sorry?'

'For your swinging chair?'

I laughed uncomfortably and had some juice.

'Yeah, so I really want to get some nice pictures up and move the furniture round and stuff.'

'Yes and get a four-poster bed for your chains to hang from.'

He picked up his drink and gave me a knowing smile. I was very confused at the sudden talk of bondage.

'So, ha, like I need to ask. But which one of your three facts where you lying about?'

I was very surprised he needed to ask.

'That I enjoy pain?'

He choked on his wine and his entire disposition changed from laid back and casual to incredibly uneasy.

'Why, which one did you think it was?' I said

'That you were a voyeur?'

'And you still met me?'

He gulped the rest of his wine down. His cheeks now positively florescent.

'Excuse me.' He stood up quickly and stormed to the toilet, kicking over a chair on his way and requiring help from a waitress to straighten it again.

While he was in the loo I finished my drink and put on my coat. I was amazed by his inability to hide his disappointment that we wouldn't be spending the afternoon playing a game of 'Stick that spike up my hole.' He had clearly got himself quite excited about it.

When he came back I was standing ready to leave. He picked up our empty glasses, walked to the bar and put them down, then stood still and gestured for me to go out first.

Outside we had an awkward kiss on each cheek, said goodbye and went home. There was simply no point in pretending that it could work out.

WEDNESDAY 27 APRIL

Flash

So . . . He took you to Nobu? Did he Nob-U?

Post C

12/04/2005   **21.11**
From: Flash
To: Dawn

Hi, I'm a 40 year old guy who runs his own business in the City, I
have the opposite problem to you – always going to great
restaurants and bars just need some new and refreshing attractive
person to share it with. I'm pretty fit and no minger – happy to
provide a photo. Let's arrange a date and do cocktails and dinner –
my fav venues are blue bar, zeta bar, home house for drinks and
dinner Nobu, Zuma, Sketch, Hakkasan – you choose my treat.
Most of all you need to be entertaining and fun (oh and gorgeous of
course) – so how about it take the leap – you won't be disappointed

12/04/2005   **22.33**
From: Dawn
To: Flash

Well if you're going to be like that then I choose Nobu
But some ground work first if you please . . .
Send that pic, along with your vital statistics . . .
I have conditions too, you must be fun, open minded and easy
company . . . part from that I have no major rules
Oh, just one thing – apart from the nice places and the dashing
looks that you describe . . . why else should I go out with you?

13/04/2005   07.33
From: Flash
To: Dawn

Not sure if I should just rely on the photo to win you over or maybe better to give it the hard sell too! Given my lack of photogenic qualities I'd better play safe!
OK I'm 5ft 10 muscular build – aka no gut! No hairy back or other obvious turn offs (piercing aside – joking!). I work in the City as a sort of financier – but no massive ego – am intelligent and witty, but from a normal working class background so no snob like tendencies – just a beautiful and rich normal guy really!
So why a date with me – despite the obvious nice venue, great food and lashings of cocktails and wine, I guess my humour and charm will be appealing, it will be fun! Also if you like skiing or sunshine I own a bevy of holiday properties and am easily tapped for the odd break (which we all need). Oh and I drive a Masrerati but would not expect you to be swayed by such obvious showy stuff (happy to provide photos too!)
So let me switch it round what are you really after and what will I like most about you?

13/04/2005   10.45
From: Flash
To: Flash

Hey – nice pic!
You have a very friendly face I have to say and when a man with a friendly face offers me Nobu I find it hard to refuse . . . .
OK – I'm 5ft 10, possibly 5ft 9 and occasionally 6ft 1
I have shoulder length dark hair that I usually wear up, because I like BIG hair and I think it looks rubbish down.
I'm size 12 . . .
I'm confident and absolutely hilarious . . . see?
Um, I'm a freelance media type, I'm an actress, as in I studied it. I love cats (my Siamese Lilu is like a child to me), clothes and cars (Maserati's specifically)
So . . . dinner is definitely on the cards, although I would have to say that I am not, as a rule, a 'first night' kinda gal so keep your fingers on ya sushi if ya know what I mean . . .
Ha ha, sorry, that was a very odd thing to say – but don't want to give any false impressions at this point . . . don't ya think?

16/04/2005   **12.30**
From: Flash
To: Dawn

OK attached is my roaring love, though I only bring her out on special occasions! (Can't believe I'm trying to snare you with my car!).
You sound tall? Hope I don't have to wear my Cuban heels! At 5 10 1/2 I may be below you (now there is a thought!) Though stood on my wallet I'm much taller (joking!)
OK so the deal is dinner at Nobu – but first I need a pic – only fair and borne out of one bitter experience with a post op transsexual (cost me dinner but at least I sussed it in time!). So come on be brave!
Where do you work/live – I'm in Soho and live in Victoria so you don't get more central London than that!
No worries about first night nerves, I'm chilled as long as we are having fun, but if you do throw yourself at me then I promise will still respect you in the morning! Else I'm happy to settle for just the taste of sushi and cocktails!
OK where's that photo – alternatively if you give me the "I don't have one" line – how about meeting for a coffee during the day as a low risk option?
Your call
oh and what shall I call you?

18/04/2005   **11.03**
From: Dawn
To: Flash

My name is Dawn – hey . . . we should get a date in the diary.
How's about Wednesday 27th April?

20/04/2005   **13.03**
From: Flash
To: Dawn

OK babe Nobu booked for next Wednesday – so better get your party hat ready don't forget I want that tel no before the big day!
Wow I can almost taste that black miso cod!!

21/04/2005 **09.30**
From: Dawn
To: Flash

hey hey hey – this is so exciting
8pm is perfect – I will get all dressed up – but flat shoes. I don't want to
tower over you. Hee hee hee x x x
Oh, my number is ***********

22/04/2005 **07.22**
From: Flash
To: Dawn

Cheeky beast!
OK let's make it the Blue Bar at the Barclay Hotel – really great cocktails – lovely atmosphere and just sometimes you can see a top businessman fawning over a young hooker – pretending it's his niece or something!
Address is 1 Wilton Place SW1. Best to get a cab and I'll reimburse you – my treat.
Wow it is exciting just a week to go!

The Date

I hate to be so shallow, but I was definitely wooed by the Maserati. I'm no motor slut but you should have seen the picture of this thing. It spoke to me through my computer, it got into my head and I knew I had to meet its daddy.

I liked Flash because of his confidence and I thought he seemed chivalrous, playful and polite. He wasn't pushy, and something told me that this wasn't a man looking for a relationship but just fun, like me.

He spoke about his riches openly but didn't make any sloppy and sleazy sexual advances. He came across as a very wealthy man who likes to treat and spend time with pretty girls, and I can appreciate that. If I was a very wealthy woman I'd like to spend my money on, and spend my time with, pretty boys.

I had a good feeling about this guy, so I covered myself in fake tan and sorted out my bikini line just in case things went to plan.

He called me the morning of the date and I was very glad that he did. His gentle voice was friendly and conversation wasn't awkward or stunted. It relaxed me totally about the evening. I was nervous about him being a 'Key jiggler'. You know the type? Wanky rich people who wear linen suits and snakeskin loafers, who flash their gold teeth and jingle their car keys constantly. It is a trait most commonly adopted by the *nouveau riche* and one which I despise wholeheartedly. Although I couldn't see that he wasn't doing the above, he certainly didn't come across as arrogant or smarmy. When I asked him how glam I should go he told me that anything from jeans to a cocktail dress would be acceptable.

'Well, what will you be wearing?' I asked.

'Oh, I'll just be in my boring work suit.'

'That's rubbish!'

'Yeah, but don't worry. I'll look amazing!'

Love that!

I called him again when I arrived at the hotel. I was standing in the lobby, he opened the double doors that led into the Blue Bar with a huge smile on his face, and his arms extended to great me. His forthcoming welcome told me instantly that I was going to enjoy my evening.

'I love your legs,' were the first words he said to me as we kissed on each cheek. It was that black skirt again, the one with the split that exposes practically my entire right thigh.

'Ha ha, good line,' I replied and we sat down at our table.

I ordered a JD/DC. He had a cocktail.

He sat with one foot resting on the opposite knee, his arms spread out and supported by the seat back. His mannerisms were graceful, possibly camp, but not too camp. OK, I realise that is confusing. What I mean is that it would have suited him to limp his wrist, but he never did, and I would not have been surprised if he'd stuck a pinkie out when he picked up his glass, but he didn't do that either. He wasn't macho, but I liked that. I'm the type of girl who likes guys that sit with their legs crossed, men that are physically in touch with their feminine side – to an extent of course. I find nothing viler that extreme machismo. Big butch hunks who are so heavy-handed that they crush everything they touch. Or men with such huge muscles that their arms hang miles away from their bodies, like they are carrying invisible basketballs under them. Overly male males are not good. I like bodies that feel soft to touch, I don't like extreme definition and I have no desire to cuddle up to someone with a belly like an abacus. I liked his gentle physicality, his rounded middle, his fleshy chest. He was cuddly. I quite wanted to nestle up to him straightaway, but I realised that might be ever so slightly unappreciated by the rest of the bar's populace.

I marvelled in the way he kept staring at my thigh, and was even more jubilant about the way he kept touching it. It's great when you meet someone and not only is the conversation easy, but there are no inhibitions about being tactile with each other. Sometimes when someone you don't know very well touches you it feels invasive and uncomfortable, but every now and then you meet someone who you gel with and physical contact feels as natural as conversation. I enjoy the latter immensely.

I fancied him. Though it wasn't altogether a physical thing, I was merely enjoying the ease I felt. I wasn't overly keen on his grey hair, or his slightly upturned upper lip. I didn't care very much for his businessman's scent or his short and stubby fingers. But his chat, his humour and his smooth style won me over instantly. So, even though something about him screamed 'small cock', I was willing to work with it, and hope that my Cockdar had made a mistake on this one occasion.

It appears to be standard procedure with an Internet date, to spend a small amount of time discussing that you met on the Internet. It's best to get it out the way, open the subject up and see where the other person is at. Flash was very comfortable with it. He had met lots of people this way, made friends, lovers and had relationships. He was divorced, with two children, loved his kids more than anything, still had a fantastic relationship with his ex wife, had loads of friends, loads of money and wanted to enjoy life as much as possible. He actually made me feel a bit dull. He was always off on some extreme sports holiday or going to fun places. His life was made of bubbles and he was sparkling.

When it came to the dating thing he was so open. I didn't get the impression that he was promiscuous; he simply enjoyed good company because he was good company. This wasn't a guy who was meeting people on the Internet because he couldn't meet them any other way; it was a guy who was meeting people on the Internet so that he had as many people in his life as possible. Great attitude!

One thing I would say though is that he did expect to impress. When I told him I had been to New York on an Internet date he wanted to better it. I could see his mind ticking over as to where he could take me. He went quiet and told me to 'Shhh'. I laughed and suggested that maybe we should get through dinner before we arranged a weekend away.

We had two drinks at Blue Bar then walked over to Nobu. At our table he promptly ordered a bottle of wine and said that I could order the food. I was more than happy with this.

'I have to warn you I have a very healthy appetite.'

'Order everything on the menu if you like, might as well.'

I looked at him and laughed, as if to say to stop being ridiculous, then I gazed back at my menu willing him on to say he meant it.

He didn't, although I'm sure if I had he wouldn't have minded.

I ordered four starters, three main courses (one of which was the blackened cod. There is a reason why everyone who goes to Nobu raves about that . . . dear Lord!) A few sides like Edename, seaweed, Miso Soup, and two plates of mixed Sushi and Sashimi.

The waitress suggested that I stopped ordering as that was plenty. I looked up and Flash was looking at me as if to say: 'Fuck me, if you eat all that you deserve a medal!'

Needless to say I ate the lot. When it had all gone, the waitress came over to say that if we wanted anything else we had to order it then as the kitchen was closing. Immediately he saw the passion in my eyes and ordered another plate of mixed sushi and sashimi. I was most grateful, and got through that just as fast.

Dinner was fun. We played a little bit of 'I've been to the best restaurants' ping-pong. But I won when I told him that the week previously I had eaten at Hell's Kitchen, the reality TV show restaurant.

'Yeah . . . you might have the cash, but I've got the contacts!' I said. We laughed at what a couple of show offs we were and got back to our mound of food.

He was entertaining and absorbing, but the thing I liked most about him was his open mind. We didn't discuss things like drugs or our wayward teenage years, so I don't even know if he had any. I didn't really have any inclination to hear about his childhood, parental status or previous relationships, but we did spend most of our time discussing different ways of being with people.

Like me, he agreed that you can never say never on the way you would react to certain situations. Because timing, circumstance and the people involved decide your actions, not always your morals. I liked this as so many people are too quick to judge other people for the way they cope with difficult situations, when in their shoes they probably would do the same.

Flash was incredibly unjudgemental. I told him a few things to test him (and no, I'm not telling you!) and he was prudent and measured in each of his responses. Always willing to hear an explanation before casting judgement.

We also discussed fun. He didn't say cheesy things like 'Life is all about having fun' or soulless jargon like 'I always look on the bright side.' He was real, and we both agreed that no one can see the bright side of everything, but what you can do is make sure that you have enough people who care about you around if the dark side gets you. My philosophy exactly. Never expect to take the world on alone. We toasted to good friends, of which we both clearly had lots.

I also appreciated how open he was about his money. Wealthy people are often so cagey about their cash. I don't really get that, so it was refreshing to be with someone who wasn't ashamed to say 'I'm loaded because I do a job that pays me millions and that's just that!'

And why the hell not? Flash's money made no sense to him. He said many times how stupid it seems that he does the small amount of work that he does, but still gets paid so hugely. When he told me that he was quitting work to go travelling because he had all the money he was ever going to need and didn't want to spend his life in an office just to keep topping up the bank balance, I respected him all the more.

After a thoroughly enjoyable meal he suggested we go dancing at Annabelle's. Two hours previously I would have been all over that idea like sashimi on rice, but now, at full capacity, there was as much chance of me dancing as there was me eating a Big Mac. So I recommended Windows on the World, which was just next door at the Hilton. He'd never been there before so was more than happy to go.

The four minute walk there did wonders for me. That's the best thing about sushi, you can eat it and eat it and eat it but the fullness is comfortable. By the time we got into the lift to shoot us up to the 28th floor my energy levels were rising again, so the fervent snog we had when the doors pinged shut was not a problem.

I can't really be sure who made the first move. I'm pretty sure it was a mutual manoeuvre that seemed categorically inevitable, although my back was to the mirror and he was pushing me against it. He held my hands behind my back, which was quite sexy, yet the kiss didn't send any major shivers down my spine.

But I enjoyed it, I really did. His lips were soft and he was sensuous. Occasionally his tongue lashed out and headed for my stomach, leaving me with the responsibility of sucking it until he retracted. But lots of guys do that so I come to expect it. But I wasn't blown away. I hadn't expected to be, but I would have liked to have been. Yet like I said, it was a lovely snog and I was content to continue with it. And repeat it.

Coming out of the lift was fun. He had glittery lip gloss all over his mouth and mine was a little redder than normal. A member of staff on the door knew exactly what we had been up to so I shared a little simper with him. I love all that!

I ordered a glass of Shiraz. He complimented my choice and did the same.

'So . . . I'm still thinking about how I can better New York.'

'Oh don't be silly. You don't have to better it. Just match it.'

I laughed like a dickhead at my own joke, until he stopped me.

'OK, let's go to New York next week.'

That shut me up. Jesus, what is it with Windows on the World.

That's twice I've been there and got a trip to New York out of it. (Note to self . . . take all future dates there)

'But I'm not having any of this separate room, platonic shit,' he added, 'that guy must be mad.'

'No, he wasn't mad at all. He was wonderful.' I got a touch defensive.

'No, I know. I was only joking. I can understand it. I'm the same. It's just a pleasure for a guy like me to get to spend time with someone who is such great company. I imagine he went home very happy. Sex or not.'

'Yes, I think he did. We had an amazing time.'

'But still, if you come away with me there are no separate rooms . . .'

Fair enough. I knew I'd been lucky with Plato. The chances of most guys taking you away for four days and being OK with not getting any action are slim. It made me appreciate him all the more – and think twice about accepting another trip away.

We left the conversation that we would talk in the morning to arrange dates. I needed to sleep on it. I was in two minds.

He took me home in a taxi. On the back seat we snogged man-ically until we'd made the short journey up to Marylebone. I enjoyed that kiss much more, it was somewhat more erotic. But it wasn't enough for me to ask him in, although I don't think he would have done anyway as he had a meeting at 7 a.m. And to be honest, he was in his forties, incredibly wealthy, with houses in London, Surrey and Spain. It wouldn't feel right for him to come to my place for some sex, lovely as it is, with my two housemates and the possibility of people having a small but lively party until the early hours.

We had one final pash on the steps that lead to my front door and I went inside – happy after having a divine evening, yet con-fused as to where I wanted it to go from there.

THURSDAY 28 APRIL

BFG
The Big Fucking Ugly Giant!

Post E

26/04/2005   **11.57**
From: BFG
To: Dawn

Subject: The girl who seems to have everything is missing
something . . .

Perhaps I can be of assistance. Are you still hunting?

26/04/2005   **12.02**
From: Dawn
To: BFG

The hunt continues . . . .
Who are you?

26/04/2005   **13.06**
From: BFG
To: Dawn

44 White British, Amusing, educated, good company and very
socially-reliable! Manchester-born professional writer. 6'3, fit,
cropped head, clean shaven and, oh did I mention, hung like a
horse?
And you? Do you have a name?

26/04/2005   **13.08**
From: Dawn
To: BFG

Cropped head?

26/04/2005   **13.11**
From: BFG
To: Dawn

er . . . yes! Is that my undoing?

26/04/2005   **13.12**
From: Dawn
To: BFG

No, is it not cropped hair? Not a cropped head . . . that just sounds
a bit weird . . .

26/04/2005   **13.34**
From: BFG
To: Dawn

If there were hair there to crop, I would crop it, as it is, I crop the
head to keep myself amused

26/04/2005   **14.18**
From: Dawn
To: BFG

Sorry I was just being difficult
My name is Dawn, I'm 26, I'm writing a book . . . what do you write?
5ft 10, fit, socially educated, excitable and experienced . . .
Live in London

More on you??

26/04/2005   **14.21**
From: BFG
To: Dawn

Oooh Dawn- now you got me hooked. Another writer. Enigmatic
and literate!
It's almost too good to be true. Next thing you will be telling me is
that you are brunette and curvy and a great kisser too.
I write everything.
Borough area
You?

26/04/2005   **14.24**
From: Dawn
To: BFG

I'm brunette and curvy and my kissing wins prizes!
Live in the West End
Photo?
I will if you will x x x
So why you do Internet dating?

26/04/2005   **14.32**
From: BFG
To: Dawn

Trying to find a curvy 26 year old brunette novelist who lives in the west end, and can kiss like it's the only thing in the world, and this was the first place I tried. Just my luck, eh?

26/04/2005   **17.34**
From: Dawn
To: BFG

Yeah – ha ha, looks like you have found just what you're looking for!

26/04/2005   **17.37**
From: BFG
To: Dawn

Anyone gazing into your eyes over lunch today? Shall I?
Feel an overwhelming urge to see you! Or at least hear your voice.
How about tea? 3/4 o'clock in Soho?
Valerie Patisserie Old Compton Street

27/04/2005   **10.07**
From: Dawn
To: BFG

Perfect. What's your number?
Will call you now x

The Date

He answered the phone and I nearly got blown off my chair as the most ridiculously posh voice came soaring out of the receiver.

'Oh dahhhhhling, Dawn. You called me that's diviiiiiiiiiiiiiiiiiiiiiiine.'

I thought surely he must be joking. But it continued.

'I have a certain concentrated powerlessness for the inferiority I feel when my path crosses that of a beast so bravura as yourself.'

'You what?'

'For a female that can have such a hold on me after a mere handful of redolent emails.'

'Who?'

'There are so few young writers who hold beauty in so many forms as physical and within their intellectuality also. This quite accurately is a stupefying sensation.'

'Oh right, so um . . . do you wanna go eat some cake?'

I mean really! There was no need for all that claptrap was there? OK the dude's a writer but I am too, and you don't catch me trying to get every word in the Oxford English Dictionary into every sentence do you? That would be preposterous *in extremis* and a profligate misuse of our bodies corporeal endeavours, not to mention our minds neurological processes.

Our phone call went on for around five minutes. I said very little but everything I did say he followed with a pause, then a long statement about how fabulous I was and then some more words that I'm sure he was making up.

His voice was very deep and his drawn out words were exaggerated and entirely monotone. He was so posh I could hardly understand what he was saying. The end of his sentences tapered off in a quick downward and throaty way, until they were mere gurgles by the time he finished.

So why did I agree to meet him when he was ugly (I knew this as I'd seen a picture) and spoke in a jargon which I had more chance of breaking Governmental codes than understanding? No, it wasn't because he told me he was hung like a horse. It was because he was a writer and I found that quite enchanting, so, although he was blatantly mad, I quite fancied the idea of humping a literati toff.

I walked to Valerie Patisserie extra fast so I could indulge in a big cream cake when I got there. He was sitting upstairs as arranged. I know I'd seen a picture but nothing had prepared me for what I saw. He was ugly beyond ugly, and I don't feel mean saying this because it was a self-confessed fact. He was on the phone and gestured an apologetic 'Two minutes', so I sat opposite him and tried to get used to this vision of hideousness that sat in front of me.

He was huge. He sat with his back against the wall, his right arm resting on the table that the rest of his body stretched alongside of. Every feature of his that was in view was colossal. His nose was so huge I'm surprised it didn't topple him. I know that it is not uncommon to describe a large conk as a ski slope, and I have racked my literary mind to come up with something more original but I can't, because that is exactly what it looked like. But I'm not talking about no black run here, this neverending chunk of cartilage seemed specifically designed for the 'Never skied before and possibly very elderly' demographic in that it moseyed on for ages. A long and gradual decline, stretching under miles and miles of lumpy snow before it came to a feeble and uneventful end. I imagined miniature people climbing up it with hiking sticks and backpacks, exhausted, hoping that one day they may finally reach the brow line.

Despite the vastness of the slope, there was still plenty of room left on his face to accommodate his eyes, which were permanently half shut due to the weight of his multi-layered eyelids. His short and dead-straight lashes pointed directly down following the same inclination as his nose; his pale, speckly green irises were bordered with grimy yellow slop and the skin encasing the eye was purple and infused with broken veins.

Before I go on I must add at this point that when he mouthed 'Do you want anything to eat?' There was no question that my answer was no.

His phone call continued. I got the impression he wanted me to listen to what he was saying, but I was transfixed so didn't take in a word.

His ears were like big wooden spoons stuck to the side of his head and with possibly the longest lobes I have ever seen. All fleshy and floppy and totally pointless. A small black dot suggested that once there had been a ring there and he fiddled with them continuously.

His bald head had small patches of bristle on it that shared the space with itchy looking blemishes and pubescent spots. His lips were thin, the top one also parallel to the nose so all his features headed for the floor in perfect succession. His slow movements and dreary voice were devoid of any energy, and, as I watched him, I saw his aura pouring into the ground. It was taking me with it.

He got off the phone and stood up. His huge hands pressed into the table as he pushed himself to standing. I remained seated and watched this giant grow and grow and grow. He moved into the gangway and beckoned me towards him. I obliged and he squeezed me to his chest, my arms hung behind him. His torso was paper thin and I could feel his ribs through our clothes. He pushed me away and held my arms then kissed me on each cheek. He smelled of joss sticks.

'You really are the vision I thought you'd be.'

'Thank you. Excuse me, can I get a peppermint tea please?' I called to the waitress; anything milky might have induced vomit.

He never held eye contact with me and didn't really respond to my answers to his questions. It was as if he wanted to talk at me, not with me. It was hard to make out if he liked me or not. Yes, I know he was hugely complimentary about me physically but we certainly were not gelling mentally. I didn't like him; it was as simple as that. I didn't think he seemed like a very nice person and I couldn't see how anyone would.

'I'm from Guernsey,' I said, bored of listening to him drone on.

He made a face that patronised me and took a sip of his coffee.

'I have a Siamese cat called Lilu who inspires me when I feel down.'

'I despise felines,' he said as he stirred his coffee, 'and Siamese are particularly offensive. They make me sneeze.'

Christ, I would want to be in the room when that hooter exploded.

'I went to drama school.'

He piped up again.

'Oh Dahhhling, another thespian, this is just too good to be true.'

'Are you an actor?'

'Yes, I have trod the boards for yars. I have just finished a play. Marvellous piece. I feel lost without it.'

'I gave up acting because I thought the people were wankers.'

We took sips of our drinks.

I was almost falling asleep. He was so unstimulating and so negative that I was struggling with keeping my head above neck level. I couldn't be bothered to listen. Too good to be true? Was it? And what was? He wasn't flirtatious, inquisitive and didn't appear to give a flying toss about anything I said, so what the hell had he met me for?

'You must have a cake'

'No, really I couldn't.'

'Oh you're not trying to lose weight are you?' he said in a judgemental voice. When a lady refuses something calorific because she doesn't fancy it and men jump down their throats about them being vain or fanatical, it makes me so angry. It's a bad thing to say. Has the same effect as 'Ooo, time of the month' when you make the slightest overreaction. I wanted to say 'Sometimes, just sometimes, women don't eat cake you know!'

'I went for a lovely walk in Hyde Park yesterday. It's a great place to find inspiration in the mornings.'

'Yes. Good exercise too. Better than the Nazi that comes to my house once a week to pull my girlfriend and me around for ninety minutes.'

OK, I didn't fancy this guy at all – in fact I never wanted to see him again in my life – but the way he mentioned his girlfriend so easily threw me. I had no idea up until then what he was meeting me for and then I got it. He wanted a lover, didn't really care who it was and wasn't afraid to say it. It all made sense. The lack of interest in who I was, the adoration he felt before we had even spoken simply because I was female. I was a mere venue for his penis, location didn't matter.

I wondered what a relationship with someone like him would be like. He was so transparent. There was no sensuality, no feeling, no emotion. He was just words. I visualised his brain like the dome that's used for the final game of the TV show *The Crystal Maze*. A wind machine blowing around thousands of little bits of paper. But in his head they were not bank notes, they were words and they flew out of his mouth in random unison. They were not heartfelt or imparted with structure or meaning; they were simply expelled and received as utter shite.

When I had finished my tea I said I needed to leave. He paid for our drinks and we went outside.

He cuddled me like we were old friends and said, 'Shall I call you over the weekend?'

Surprised and mildly dumbstruck, I nodded and shook my head at the same time, then walked away. I was so confused. He made no sense to me at all. I turned and watched him walk in the opposite direction. This massive piece of nothingness that strides around the earth freaking people out. Very peculiar!

A few days later I received an email.

01/05/2005   09.49
From: BFG
To: Dawn

Happy Mayday, Comrade!!
I'm flattered that you would like to see me again. Perhaps late afternoon, or mid evening?
I have a few things I must do today, but it would be lovely to have Round Two with Dawn to look forward to!
Me x

I didn't reply

02/05/2005   05.37
From: BFG
To: Dawn

Hello my dear Dawn –
Did you get my garbled message yesterday? Today a bit busy-how
you fixed tomorrow to do something nice? Lunchtime or
something? Will you email me to let me know? (Prefer email today-
your call may not be appreciated by a certain
party!)

02/05/2005   10.38
From: Dawn
To: BFG

Hey
I'm not actually that comfortable with this so I'm going to end it here
Take care and good luck with all
Dawn x

See ya!

FRIDAY 6 MAY

The Gentleman: Part Three
Forgiven?

The Date

The Gentleman and I stayed in contact despite him telling me to sod off, but it wasn't particularly pleasant. We had sporadic bouts of email banter, but after a few polite and possibly sexual ones, the chat always got twisted. He would be snide about the journal and I'd end up writing yet another epic email defending myself, saying that every date I had been on was genuine, I do what everyone else does, I just happen to be writing about it at the same time. Blah blah blah . . .

When I got back from New York I told him that I'd gone there with someone I'd met online. He couldn't understand why I hadn't contacted him to tell him I was there. Truth was I had, I'd texted his mobile. I could have emailed, and I was going to, but something stopped me because I knew that if I'd have snuck out of my hotel to meet him he would have dissed me for being there with a date. So, even though my plan was to get in touch, when I got there and I was having such an unbelievable time with Plato, I knew that meeting The Gentleman would have been very disrespectful and hugely inappropriate. So I left it.

11/04/2005   18.27
From: Dawn
To: The Gentleman
Subject: I was in NY

I didn't have your email address on my web mail
I found that quite upsetting
I love New York though . . . it's super cool!
How you doing?

12/04/2005   00.38
From: The Gentleman
To: Dawn
Subject: Re: I was in NY

Oh come on. You didn't want to contact me. That's not fair. So when I'm in London should I not look you up?

12/04/2005   08.49
From: Dawn
To: The Gentleman
Subject: Re: I was in NY

No I wasn't going to contact you so I didn't email you before I went. Then I thought, oh this is ridiculous! And went to email you but your email wasn't in my web mail . . .
So . . . yes you should definitely look me up when your over, would be absolutely love to see you x x

Ps The only way I had to contact you was your English mobile. I text it but presumed you wouldn't get it, although I hoped you just might x x

12/04/2005   11.55
From: The Gentleman
To: Dawn
Subject: Re: I was in NY

I don't understand why you didn't contact me before you left, it's not like you just ended up in NY 1 day.

12/04/2005   12.11
From: Dawn
To: The Gentleman
Subject: Re: I was in NY

I was there with a friend, a man, platonic, but a man nevertheless
so it might have been strange and I didn't want it to be.
I know . . . I didn't think you would want to see me
It was stupid, I should have just thought bugger it!

12/04/2005   12.16
From: The Gentleman
To: Dawn
Subject: Re: I was in NY

You are odd.

12/04/2005   12.27
From: Dawn
To: The Gentleman
Subject: Re: I was in NY

You're odder
You do funny things I never know where I'm at with you
Odd bod!

12/04/2005   12.29
From: The Gentleman
To: Dawn
Subject: Re: I was in NY

Well, now I'm certain as to where you are at with me. You were
probably only a few blocks from me.
That's strange to me if you were truly here platonically with
someone.

12/04/2005   12.35
From: Dawn
To: The Gentleman
Subject: Re: I was in NY

Well it was!
I loved New York so much.
Where about do you live?
We stayed on 32 Street The Avalon, just by the empire state, but
then I suppose you would know that.
I just don't know how I would have explained to him that I was
going to meet you . . . as it happens when we got there I went for a
nap every afternoon as was slightly jet lagged, that's when I felt
pissed off as I could have seen you during that time but it was too
late and I hadn't contacted you. I could have done with your
assistance with a few things ;)

12/04/2005   12.45
From: The Gentleman
To: Dawn
Subject: Re: I was in NY

Wow, we were within walking distance.
This is really weird.
We seemed to get along great, but there has been nothing but
weirdness surrounded by things that have happened.

12/04/2005   12.29
From: Dawn
To: The Gentleman
Subject: Re: I was in NY

I know I just don't understand it. But I will tell you how I see things
. . . I was meeting people on the Internet – as you were. I also
happened to be keeping a journal of my experiences . . . I never in
a million years thought I would meet someone like you. I was just
looking for a bit of fun, not anyone that I might actually fall for! So,
we go out on a second date – because I wanted to so much. That
night, only the second time we met, I told you about the book. You
didn't like the idea. I understood that. You buggered off without
saying goodbye.

I had two more dates lined up, so I went on them. But if you hadn't thrown such a stupid paddy I might well have stopped there. I had only been doing it for two weeks and had no idea if anyone would ever want to publish it anyway. When I met you I kind of forgot all about keeping a journal.

But you were still angry

You started sending me filthy text messages which really confused me. Then you would say something snide about my book and tell me to get lost . . .

You go back to NY, you tell me you don't think we should talk anymore . . .

Then we start emailing again, but straightaway it's weird. You're all sexy and I have no idea if you have forgiven me or not. Then I mention the book and a few snide comments pop up again, making me feel so guilty.

The weird thing is about all this is that I can't let it go. I stopped the dating for a bit. But then I got a book deal and I'm so happy I want to scream, and that's how I should feel. But for some reason I still feel guilty which means that when I have contact with you I'm all defensive and it creates this weirdness.

I keep contacting you hoping that it will just be nice . . . .

12/04/2005   13.36
From: The Gentlemen
To: Dawn
Subject: Re: I was in NY

Well, I'm glad I brought a new rain coat because it looks like I'm going to need it.

I'm in London next week.

I wonder if I will call x

So he was coming back over to London. And even though he had started to really piss me off, I felt that I had to see him. The reason he'd pissed me off was because he would be rude to me, then send emails like 'Where is the love?' – I got about a million of those – or 'Where is the love in what you just said?' or 'I don't feel much love here.' I just wanted to scream 'There is no fucking love, you prick, you told me to bugger off!' but I didn't and when he arrived in London and invited me out for dinner I accepted, expecting some serious bickering and possibly a full-on row. I really did feel angry about the guilt trip he was always laying on me, but intrigue led me there. OK, I went there because I couldn't say no, but at the time I didn't know why.

I met him in Sumosan, on Albemarle Street, one of my favourite Japanese restaurants in London. He was sitting in the bar downstairs. I can't say I was nervous; the weird thing about it is that I'd only met him twice in my life but it had a huge impact on me. And because three months later it was still going on, I kind of felt like we were in a relationship as opposed to two people going on their third date. So I felt more charged than nervous. I was also sure that I was going to be doing a lot of sticking up for myself.

I had my defence sorted though. What The Gentleman didn't know is that he'd replied to many of the posts that I'd put onto the website since he'd left, not knowing that it was me. So if he dared tell me that he hadn't been active on it I was going to chuck his Nigri in his face and leave. Mind you, I have to be honest here and say that if I responded to him from a different email address and tried to get saucy he always pulled out . . . but that's not the point.

When I saw him I came over all funny. I fumbled about his face as I kissed him on each cheek and stuttered over most of my words. He looked gorgeous and was as cool and calm as he had ever been. This stunned me a bit. The atmosphere wasn't even slightly as awkward as I imagined, so I sipped happily on the JD/DC that he had already ordered me.

'I signed my contract today,' I said, trying to provoke the conversation just to get it out of the way.

'Well, congratulations,' he toasted. 'we shall have to have champagne later to celebrate.'

'Yes,' I replied looking rather confused. We drank our drinks, discussed his trip and he told me how well he thought I was looking.

'Have you been working out?'

'No,' was my coy response.

Nice touch!

We went upstairs to our table where I asked if I could sit with my back to the wall.

'Of course, the lady should always sit facing the room.' Still a Gentleman through and through. I was bemused.

He ordered a bottle of Frog's Leap. Our wine. It was the same one we had in The Ivy, the night I broke the devil news. We toasted again and he congratulated me for the second time.

'OK, now you're just confusing me,' I blurted, not able to hold it in any longer.

'Confused? Why?'

'Because for the last three months you've done little else but grumble about what I do and now you're acting like you're absolutely fine with it. Aren't you going to have a go at me, or be rude or bitchy or something?' I said. He looked straight at me.

'No, not at all. I was gutted in January, we got on great then you dropped the bombshell that I was just one in a long list of guys you were meeting. I felt like a bit of a dick to be honest, just one of a string of guys that you were writing about. Not good for the male ego.'

'It's not like that. And I told you on our second date, I didn't have to do that.'

I was preparing for attack.

'I know, but it doesn't matter. Now I've thought about it, I've realised why you did it and I think its fantastic news. I'm happy for you. After all this time I believe you're here tonight because you want to be.'

'I do.'

Wow, I wasn't expecting that. He held his smile and I almost slid off my chair. I said thank you and he nodded. End of! We were back to getting on famously and fancying the pants off each other.

While we were talking he ordered some oysters.

'Hmmm, sexy,' I said as the first one slid down the back of my throat.

He winked and tickled my right ankle with his left foot. I didn't even bother looking at the menu; he took control of that again.

'You like everything, right? Twice!' He laughed as he remembered that I could eat a hippo under the table, then eat the hippo.

'I'm just going to the loo.'

'Cool, I love this part,' he said and shifted his chair round so he could watch my arse as I walked away. I revelled in it.

The food was exceptional. The tenderest sashimi I've ever eaten. He knows his sushi and told me all about the best places to get it in New York, so I knew for next time.

'Of course, I could have taken you last time you were over but ... '

'Oi!'

We laughed.

We only had one bottle of wine and refused dessert so we could go somewhere else. I suggested Windows on the World. No, I wasn't gunning for another trip to New York, it's just because it's my favourite place to go for after dinner drinks . . . OK! We got the bill and jumped in a cab to the Hilton.

In the lift on the way up to the 28th floor I convinced myself that the bar was on the 18th. I have absolutely no idea why, apart from the fact that I'm clearly mad.

'How can the top floor bar at the Park Lane Hilton be on the 18th floor when there are 28 floors?' he asked.

'I don't know, it just is. I'm sure of it.'

Sure enough the doors opened and all we were faced with was a rather offensive carpet and a corridor of numbered doors.

He smirked. I blushed.

A hotel guest who got into the lift with us asked if we were getting out before they got in and The Gentleman said, 'No, we've just always really liked the doors on this floor and wanted to have a look.'

I literally lost control of my larynx and howled with laughter. He also held his belly with hysterical giggles as we shot up to the top floor where the bar indeed was.

We sat at a table that gave us a perfect view of west London and he looked at the wine list.

'Now, I think I offered you champagne didn't I?'

'Yes, I think you did, but it's cool, I'm happy with wine.'

'Shut up, we're having champagne.'

Right Oh!

I really wasn't bothered. I'd been at a party the night before where champagne had been flowing all evening and I actually got sick of it. (Hark at me 'Oh Dahhhling, I couldn't possibly have any more champagne . . .') But seriously the champers at this party was really sweet and by the end of it I felt like I was sipping syrup. So I told him that, but he had the solution and ordered a bottle of dry champagne. It was delicious.

'Ooo, I shall have to remember this one, what is it?'

I picked up the menu and had a look. No wonder it was so bloody delicious, it cost £300.

'You smooth bastard.'

He grinned, but stopped when I knocked my glass over. Whoops . . .

'You're wearing that bracelet again,' he said as he looked at my wrist. I looked at the bracelet then looked at him. He was smirking like a little schoolboy who's just seen his mate's sister's boobs.

It was a gift I had been given by a friend for Christmas. It has beads on it that hang so it makes a bit of noise when I move my wrist. As you can imagine this can be quite loud if I move my wrist continuously, which is why he remembered it from the last time he was over. His grin turned into a wide smile as he recalled the last morning we spent together. I had slept with it on.

We drank our champagne and decided to go downstairs to Trader Vic's. A raunchy snog in the lift relieved a little of the sexual tension that had been building up over the Brut. But it was only 11 p.m. so we had to be strong not to just head back to the hotel.

We ordered a big shell that was filled with cocktail. You get a huge straw each so that you can sit back and sip away. We were feeling a bit naughty by this point so, rather than be elegant about it, we sucked as hard as we could and had a race. Just as we got to the bottom I lifted up my straw, keeping my tongue over the end so that the drink remained in it and aimed it at his face.

He shook his head but did the same. Both of us sat still, holding eye contact, wondering who was going to give in first. It wasn't going to be me. I held my ground. He held his. Our eyes burned into the back of each others heads as we tried to hold the stare and not break with laughter. Time passed and passed, until he literally burst and blew the contents of his straw all over my face. Shocked, my tongue lost its place and my load trickled meekly back into the shell. He roared, and roared and roared.

I looked at him as if to ask what was so funny. He tossed his head back, shut his eyes and held his arms across his chest. It was my chance for revenge. I grabbed my straw, refilled it from the shell and spat the whole bloody lot all over him.

Brilliant!

Now we were both uproarious.

Vicious glares from our neighbouring tables forced us to compose ourselves and sit up straight. He cleared his throat through a few remaining giggles and picked up the cigar menu.

'Does the lady like fat ones or thin ones?'

'Either, she's not fussy.'

'If I gave the lady a fat one would she like it at first but then get sick of it and wish that I had provided a more slender version?'

'That is always a possibility. The lady hasn't had a fat one in a while so maybe she could have the thin one to get her in the mood?'

'OK, just have a little thin one now and wait till later when I'll give you a really long fat one.'

'Yes, that would be ideal, thank you.' Then in the most polite voice he ordered us two cigars and another shell of cocktail.

Meanwhile my eyes had fixed on the food menu, so he grabbed it and ordered five dishes for us to pick at. It was like he read my mind. I always love a man who lets me have a second dinner.

There was a group of people sitting next to us who were all really drunk. They weren't being rowdy but one of them was asleep, two of them were crying and one was sitting alone, arms crossed and in a mood because he wasn't getting any attention. As we sipped on our cocktail I heard a retch and the guy who was lying on the seat next to me puked all over himself. It was everywhere and stank. The Gentleman jumped up and moved me away, determined that I would not be touched by the encroaching vomit.

I was quite surprised The Gentleman didn't freak out about it.

He just laughed and moved away. He wasn't snobby at all and I suspected his past was filled with stories of drunken depravity. I knew he had a rebellious streak and that groups of lads getting pissed up and puking on themselves was not a sight to which he was unaccustomed.

I wanted to know more about him, to really talk. But it was late and we had started snogging so serious conversation was pretty much out the window. Now it was all about having one more shell, finishing the food and cigars and getting the hell out of there and back to the hotel.

Back in his room he went straight over to the TV and started to play around with it. 'What the hell are you doing?' I said.

He giggled and I went into the bathroom and took off all my clothes. I put on a robe and came back out. He was lying on the bed and there was some soft porn on the telly. He had a glass of red wine in his hand. I dropped the robe. He put his wine on the bedside table.

I crawled on top of him.

'Pornography? You're so naughty!'

'Naughty! I love the British accent, it's so sexy!'

I kissed him and he put his hands on my bottom and pulled me close. I couldn't stop smiling. I made my way down his body, undid his trousers, pulled them down.

'I think I will have my long fat one now.' He put his hand on the back of my head and a few moments later he breathed: 'I've never seen anyone gobble with such devotion.'

I almost swallowed his cock!

Next morning I woke up feeling very sexual. There's something about big hotel beds that make my hangover horn double what it would usually be.

He was already up, sitting at his laptop.

'Stop trying to pull other girls online and come back to bed,' I said. He came over. Jingle jingle went my bracelet.

The Couple: Seven

07/05/2005   **00.00**
From: Gillian
To: Dawn

Hey,
off to bed now. Just wanted to say . . .
I've been thinking about you lots, and I can't wait to spend the night
with you. Fancy you loads. Can't wait to get my hands, lips and
tongue on you.
Night, sweet dreams . . . .
xxxx

09/05/2005   **21.25**
From: Dawn
To: Gillian

Hey baby face
Loved that email – can't wait to get my chops on you either!!!
I didn't answer you a while ago when you asked me about 'what I
like.' Sorry, I didn't mean to avoid that question . . .
Despite my naughty mind I haven't actually ever used anything like
hand cuffs, collar, leashes all that kind of stuff . . . I just don't know if
it's my thing but hey, don't lock them away, I'm usually quite
experimental and in a situation like this I think I'm going to be
feeling extra naughty so lets just see what happens when I get
there . . . .
You know what . . . I don't feel nervous at all, I just know this is
going to be fun. Feel like I have known you for ages . . . funny!
We are probably looking at first week of June but let's confirm
nearer the time.
How do you want to set it up . . . I mean like, where? etc . . .
No pressure to decide this yet but it might be worth throwing some
ideas around
I hope Gavin is very well . . . looking forward to meeting him to . . .
Excited x

MONDAY 9 MAY

The Gentleman: Part Four
The Little Black Bag

The Date

When a non-Internet date stood me up on the Monday and The Gentleman texted me to go and join him at 9 p.m., I happily accepted. He was in that horrible Cheers bar on Regent Street again. He'd had dinner with a client so was pissed already. I walked there from home, which takes about half an hour so when I arrived I was warm and sweaty.

'You look hot,' he said as I flew into the bar.

'Thanks,' I thought I looked like shit.

'No, you look *hot*. Did you run here?'

Oh, so I did look like shit.

A large glass of iced water and a JD/DC were ordered immediately and I necked them both in less than three minutes. He looked really sexy in his suit. I told him he dressed well but he admitted it was because he only ever shops in Hugo Boss and buys whatever the mannequin is wearing.

'Oh, so it's not because you have a talent for outfit composition, then?'

'No it's because I'm 100 per cent colour blind and I have no idea what goes with what. I presume that the people in the shop don't dress the dolls in stupid colours so I just go with that. It makes shopping very easy.'

A hundred per cent colour blind. Bugger. Made me wish I hadn't spent so long applying my amazing green eye shadow. He wouldn't have a clue if I had it on or not.

'Let's get out of here. This place sucks,' I said as I pulled him away from the bar.

'No it doesn't, it's American.'

'Don't be such a spod, it's full of dickheads and slappers.'

'I like slappers.'

'Well I clearly like dickheads. Come on!'

He followed and the doorman made some joke about me being the boss. The Gentleman replied, 'You should see her in bed!' I turned back aghast; they were all laughing at me. I grabbed his hand and led him across the street to Destino.

'Hmmm, Swallow Street. How apt!'

'What is wrong with you? You're like a big kid tonight. All horny and naughty.'

'Ooo, keep saying naughty, I love it.'

I laughed at him, gave him a kiss and told him he was sexy. He was pretty chuffed with that and when I started to walk away he pulled me back and we had a disgracefully horny snog on the corner.

Destino was very quiet, which I was happy with because I wanted to talk to him. I wanted to know more about him, not just drunken stories but proper stuff. We ordered a couple of drinks and because he was so much drunker than I was he ordered me two tequilas so I could catch up. I caught up pretty quickly, but was still determined to talk.

'Are you Mafia?' Was my first question.

'Yes, and if you don't kiss me now I will kill you.'

'Urgh, stop it will you!'

'Stop what?'

'Acting like a horny schoolboy, I want a proper conversation.'

He apologised, sat up straight and took a few moments to wipe his stupid grin off his face. It was funny.

'No, but there is history of involvement in my family.'

'Seriously? You know if you are Mafia you can tell me, I've always wanted to be a gangster's moll.'

'No, I'm absolutely not Mafia so you can't be my moll. But you are more than welcome to be my bitch.'

Insatiable!

We ordered a calamari flatbread and ate it within seconds so we ordered another one which disappeared just as fast. Luckily that soaked up some of the alcohol and he managed to get serious for a while.

'Even though I'm not Mafia people always think I am because of my surname. In New York if I call a restaurant to make a reservation and they say they haven't got a table, I just tell them my surname and I get the best table in the house no matter what time it is.'

'Cool, bet you abuse that one?'

'Yup, I'm happy for everyone to think I have a gun in my pocket so that I get treated like royalty wherever I go.'

'So when did your dad die?'

'Fifteen years ago.'

'And your mother?'

This is where it got interesting, where I saw the side of him I had been wanting to see. His mother was very ill, with Alzheimer's. The Gentleman takes care of her and finds it hard because she has no idea who he is anymore. I understood this as my gran had died of it; I know what it's like when someone that you love literally loses their mind. He told me about how his brother disappeared after his mother's diagnosis and hasn't been in contact for two years. He was a junkie and apparently he's somewhere in Manhattan living in a crack den. It was hard to imagine that they were from the same breeding. The Gentleman seemed like such a diamond, but from the rest of his stories it seemed it wasn't always that way.

When they were children his brother was the golden boy and The Gentleman was the one that the family and schools were worried about. He was rebellious, not studious. The conversation took a welcome upbeat turn as he told me some of the things he used to get up to as a kid.

There were of course the tales of drunken nights out where he and his friends would end up in big fights and he kicked the shit out of everyone because he was so huge. And the many tales of high school expulsions and detentions that he received. But the story that really proved this guy had a wild side was one about a school bus.

He was picked up by the school bus as normal, but this day he was due to sit a big test. Being totally unprepared for it, he didn't see the point in going into the exam hall and he knew that if he got off the bus the teacher would see him and force him to go in. So, rather than get off the bus at the school gates, he pushed the driver off and stole it. He then proceeded to joyride it all over Manhattan until the police caught up with him and pulled him over.

I mean, that's quite a story from a guy whom I thought was made of marshmallows the first time I met him. It made him even sexier. Good boys are dull, bad boys are awesome!

We went back to his hotel in Piccadilly and had a drink in the bar, where we got more cigars. I seem to be developing a true love for cigars. Not only do I believe that I look very cool when I smoke them but I genuinely enjoy the taste. We puffed away but the bar closed so we went upstairs to the mezzanine to finish our drinks.

As we sat we watched a guy who was covered in tattoos.

'Christ, and I thought my tattoo was a statement,' I said.

'You have a tattoo?'

'You know I have a tattoo . . . you must have seen it.'

'I haven't, where is it?'

'It's on my bottom.'

He insisted that he'd definitely never seen it but I found this very hard to believe. He'd seen my bottom many times. I was very surprised.

'What is it of?'

Oh God. I took a big drag of my cigar, had a huge gulp of my drink and began to tell the tale of my arse tattoo.

When I was eighteen I was going out with this guy who worked on a building site. I used to call him at work and tell him I loved him but he could never say it back as all the lads would take the piss out of him. So he used to say, 'The first word has one letter, the second has four letters and the third has three letters.' So there it was, our little code, 143, meaning I Love You. We used to sneak it into conversations we were having when other people were around. Things like 'God I ate about 143 of those today,' or 'That must be the 143rd time I have done that this week.'

Anyway, it was his birthday and we went on a bit of a bender. If I remember rightly it was a Thursday and we were in the pub by 11 a.m. necking tequilas. By 12 noon I was slurring my words and declaring my undying love.

'I know what I can do to let you know how much I love you,' I garbled as I waltzed out the door and into the tattoo parlour next door.

'How much will it cost to have 143 tattooed on my bottom?'

A beast of a hairy biker dude emerged from behind a desk with a multi coloured face and so many bolts through his skin he looked like a game of Kerplunk.

'Four quid but I'm not doing it if you're drunk.'

'I'm not drunk, it's only 12 o'clock.'

How dare he!

Mortified, I returned to the pub and said 'I've got a tattoo, I've got a tattoo.' Plan being that everyone would tell me how stupid I was then I'd admit that I hadn't had it done at all. But they didn't. They all said 'Wow' and wanted to see it. I felt pretty stupid so, rather than admit the truth, I announced that I needed to go back to get some ointment and I ran back to the tattoo parlour.

'I'm not drunk and I'm insulted that you would even suggest such a thing. It is my boyfriend's birthday and I want 143 tattooed on my bottom to prove to him how much I love him. Do it!'

The big hairy biker dude was taken aback and agreed to give me this stupid bloody, permanent eyesore on my arse. I swanned over to the big dentist chair at the back of the shop, whipped down my jeans, and for some reason my knickers as well, and offered my right bum cheek to this rather menacing stranger. He did as he was told and branded me. I paid him and hobbled back to the pub where I received a rapturous round of applause for being such a devoted girlfriend. It was a fun day but when I woke up the next day the tears just fell out of my face.

'Nope, I've never seen it,' The Gentleman said as I finished my story, 'but I'll definitely be looking out for it. Let's go upstairs.'

Up in the hotel room I ran a bath. I love having baths with people. So sexy. But he refused to get in with me. He was well aware that it wouldn't accommodate us both – he'd obviously made that mistake before – so while I sloshed around in all the bubbles he sat on the edge of it and we talked about what amazing sex we had with each other. A totally self-indulgent conversation where we factually told each other how good we were in bed. It was very funny. I disappeared under the water many times to hide my blushing and he got even cockier as I nourished his ego.

During one of my duck downs I flipped over and reappeared bum first and on all fours. He ran a thumb over my tattoo and laughed.

'It looks like a prison stamp. But it's kind of sexy.'

Then he did something that I never thought was possible and linked his hands under my hips, lifted me out of the bath and through into the bedroom where he dropped me on the bed. After taking a moment to apply precautions, he stood on the floor, pulled my hips back and pummelled me like I have never been pummelled before. It was fucking amazing!

In the morning I woke up feeling randy as ever, sprawled myself across the bed and insisted that he go down on me before I left.

Bliss!

Slightly jaded from my early morning orgasm I went into the bathroom to find my clothes. 'Um . . . please tell me you have borrowed my handbag,' I said as I came back in. I couldn't find it anywhere.

We searched the whole room but it wasn't there. I was fuming. It had my keys, my phone (which was out of battery) and my diary in it. I called the lobby and asked them if a little black bag had been found in either the bar or the mezzanine in the early hours of the morning. They insisted it hadn't.

'It must be there,' said The Gentleman, 'you definitely had it in the hotel.'

'Well, it isn't there now, some fucker's nicked it.'

I was so upset that I left the room without really saying goodbye. Still half-pissed, I stumbled around the corridors banging off the walls, desperately trying to find the mezzanine to see if it was there. Lots of early morning coffee drinkers looked at me like I was a drug addict as I bolted in, with huge hair and stinking of sex.

It wasn't there.

I went down into the lobby and spoke to the man in reception.

'Hi, I left a little black bag in the bar last night, can I please collect it?'

'I'm sorry, Madame, but there was no little black bag left in the bar last night.'

'Um, yes there was. I know there was because I left it there.'

He went again to check. I was left looking like a hooker in the lobby. He returned and insisted it was not there. The manager came over.

'Look, I left my little black bag in the bar last night and now it isn't there so someone must have taken it. Please will you go and find it for me, it contains everything I own!'

I was acting very out of character. I'm the kind of person who would eat a meal with hair in it just to keep the peace. I hate complaining, but for some reason that morning I couldn't scream loud enough.

Off they went together to try to find my little black bag. But once again they came back empty handed.

'Well, I won't be coming here again and I certainly won't be advising my clients to stay here either.'

I know it was an odd thing to say and I don't know why I said it. I was trying to sound like a high profile businesswoman who had high profile clients over all the time. But I didn't, I sounded like a prostitute and there were hundreds of eyes on me. I looked crazed. My hair was huge and I was carrying my own shoes. There was no doubt about it, I looked like a pro.

'Fine!' I honked in a very high pitched voice as I swung round and left the building, leaving a haze of alcohol, sex and cigars behind me.

I strutted down Piccadilly absolutely livid, hissing at anyone who got in my way. That was until I ground to a halt and my memory jumped up and bit me on the arse. I hadn't even taken my little black bag out with me that night, I'd taken my purple one. I turned around slowly and began the walk of shame back up to the hotel.

I walked into the reception and everyone froze and went straight over to the manager.

'I'm ever so sorry I seem to have made a mistake. The bag that I misplaced last night was in fact purple . . . do you have it?'

He reached down and came back up holding my purple bag. I took it out of his hand, pivoted and left the building. My head buzzed with questions of woe. Why had I not used my brain? Why was The Gentleman colour blind? If he wasn't then he would have known about the black/purple thing. But most of all, and the biggest question was: why am I such a dick?

It wasn't until later that day that I realised through all the drama I hadn't actually said goodbye to The Gentleman. I called his mobile but it was too late. He'd already headed back to New York.

The Couple: Part Eight

11/05/2005   **23.41**
From: Gillian
To: Dawn

Hey sexy,
No worries about the handcuffs etc. As you say, we'll see how you
feel on the night. We won't do anything that you aren't comfortable
with. Everyone has different things that turn them on, and I quite
enjoy being tied up.
Gavin seems to enjoy doing it, and as our relationship has gone on,
we seem to be interested in new things. He likes uniforms, and I'm
not worried about dressing up for him. I get a lot of pleasure out of
seeing him get excited.
The handcuffs have moved onto collars and blindfolds. I think he
just likes to feel dominant. Sometimes I can be dominant with him,
but he doesn't really do submissive very well. He gets far too
excited and has to take control again.
Yeah, I think I'm more excited than nervous. I think I'll be relaxed
around you as I feel I've got to know a bit about you now.
I think it would be good to go for some drinks, and a meal if that is
OK with you? Then back to a hotel, for the fun!! Gav and I have
stayed in a hotel a few times that we like. It is in East London near
the Excel centre.
He likes it as it has a big mirror at the end of the bed, and he likes
to watch us having sex. It is good for when he is behind me, as we
can still have eye contact but be in a position that can sometimes
feel a little detached.
We can decide on something between the 3 of us, it'd be best if we
all did something we know we'll enjoy. Did you have any ideas?
Right off to bed now, sweet dreams, night gorgeous!
xxxx

16/05/2005   **17.02**
From: Dawn
To: Gillian

Hey baby
The hotel sounds great – it's a bit of a trek for me, I live in the west
end but I think it will be worth the travel!
Just going to go to Guernsey for a bit of a break and to see the
folks – so when I get back we can arrange a date.
You guys are great you know. I just love how you really enjoy sex
and each other. So many couples have so many inhibitions, I love
the way you two are so in tune with each other and accept each
others fantasies . . . and luckily usually have the same ones. It's
really amazing you know!
Ha ha, I have had boyfriends like Gavin, you try to take over every
now and then but the horny little fuckers just can't deal with it and
whip you on your back before you've had a chance to tell them how
naughty they've been!
Better than going out with a motionless length of rubber though aint
it!
Yeah get Gavin in on the emails that would be fun . . .
Big wet kiss to you my princess x x x x

16/05/2005   **23.21**
From: Gillian
To: Dawn
Cc: Gavin

Yeah there has always been a definite chemistry with him from day
one. Guess I'm lucky, although I don't get as much time with him as
I'd like, so maybe that is why things are still good. We don't live in
each others pockets, and have a lot of time to ourselves so it is
easier not to argue and get bored with each other.
A motionless length of rubber is not how I'd describe him, that is for
certain. He is a cheeky monkey sometimes, and I think we should
make it our mission to put him in his place for a while, what do you
think? Up for the challenge? You'd love that wouldn't you Gav?!!!!
Right I'm off to bed now. Speak to you soon.
Night sexy
Big kisses for you too . . . .

18/05/2005   17.59
From: Gavin
To: Gillian; Dawn

Right- before I start may I just add one observation: I'm NOT a "cheeky monkey". I'm indeed a "very cheeky bad monkey".
There's a difference.
Anyway, I had written an epic saga last night on e-mail to y'all which covered every aspect of life, death, sex and monkeys but my goddamned e-mail crashed as I tried sending it. Suffice to say I was highly un-amused as I invested an hour of my time trying to conjure up ways to impress you both: all that creativity lost now! Can't really remember specifically what was written but it seemed to revolve mainly around all things simian (I'm, after all, not called monkey boy for nothing) . . . .and I vaguely recollect discussing the merits of light bondage involving naughty girls being spanked. Then again, it may be that I have been daydreaming just now; something to do with Kylie in a cat suit being a particularly naughty little minx! Well, it is approaching 6 and I've been working like a fiend all day so reckon I can afford myself 5 minutes Kylie time. (Gill, please: no jealousy here – Kylies got a great bum as do you. Now, Liz Hurley on the other hand . . . . grrrrrrr!!)
So- again, I seem to have lost track of what I was saying! Ah, yes: Dawn . . . Hello!! S'ppose I'd better introduce myself albeit by e-mail. I think Gill has more or less covered all angles in terms of who we are, what we like etc but did she mention I do a mean Sean Connery accent?
I have to make this short as I'm running late again and haven't stopped for any munchies and getting a bad sugar low and can feel myself starting a weird turn, plus I've got footy to play now however suffice to say on a final note that everything Gill has said is 100% accurate: she is indeed an uber minx, a foxy foxlicious foxttastic fox and I'm . . . .well, judge for yourself, eh?
OK- gotta dash: food to eat, bananas to peel, people to shout at, balls to be kicked, tackles from behind to made (the boys love it from behind . . . apparently !?) Sorry, off on a tangent again.
Hope you're well – look forward to meeting you soon.
See ya , Gavin.

WEDNESDAY 18 MAY

Plato: Part Four
The Telling

The Date

I'm going to keep this one brief as I've already said so much about my relationship with Plato, but this date was so special that I feel I need to say a few words about it.

It had been a long time since New York and we had tried and failed many times to meet each other to catch up. I'd really missed him and when we eventually got a date in the diary I was so excited. Although the worry was overriding my enthusiasm as I knew I had to tell him about the book.

We met in Souk, a small but fun Moroccan place near Covent Garden. We sat in a little booth so were totally secluded from anyone else – the perfect place for him to throw dinner in my face when I told him my news.

When I saw him we kissed and hugged and talked over each other like we did on the way to New York. We had so much to catch up on, but unfortunately everything that I had been doing was related to writing my journal, so I didn't really give much personal information to the conversation. I wanted to be able to tell him but I just couldn't do it – which was stupid seeing as most of what he was saying was unbelievably supportive of the fact that I wanted to be a writer.

Polite as ever he asked me before making any choices on wine, food or water. I was asked about fifteen times if I was OK with the restaurant and he apologised profusely after talking for more than five minutes at any time. I kept telling him to 'Shut up apologising'. Eventually he did.

When our food came he took the things off my plate that I didn't like and I did the same to him. Then when I finished before him he swapped our plates over and let me finish his. I ate all of the dessert because I knew he wouldn't like it, and when he went to the loo and I was asked if we wanted anything else, I ordered a peppermint tea for myself and a black tea for him because I knew that he didn't like coffee. All this was done with fluidity because without realising it, we knew each other so well . . . it was very sweet.

After dinner we went onto The Player, a bar on Broadwick Street, where we drank two cocktails before I made my announcement.

'I've got something to tell you. I've lied to you and I need to tell you the truth because I love you so much.'

He didn't say anything but looked petrified and took a frantic sip of his drink after he pulled his straw out of his nostril.

'You know that I have met other guys online?'

'Yes.'

'And I know that you have met other women and we have always been cool with that?'

'Yup.'

'So how would you feel if I told you that I've met lots of other guys and I have been writing about my experiences and that I have a publishing deal and that the book comes out in February?'

I pressed my face against his cheek and waited for his answer.

'Ah bloody hell Dawn I thought you were going to tell me you were married or something. I would feel absolutely ecstatic and say that you deserve it and that I'm over the moon for you.'

And there it was, the truth was out and we were still friends. No drama, no slamming of doors, no guilt trip nor nastiness. He was everything I thought he was and now I knew that we would be friends forever.

For old times sake we went back to Milk and Honey where we sat in the Red Room upstairs. We drank JD/DCs, smoked big fat cigars and did impressions of New York gangsters until about 1 a.m.

We shared a taxi and he dropped me off at my house, up until which point we hugged continuously. When we said goodbye our cuddle was so strong I didn't want to let go. He kissed my hair and we told each other a million times that we loved each other.

I got into bed with a huge smile on my face that night, feeling so safe knowing that I had people like Plato in my life. I snuggled up close to Lilu and fell quickly into a very sound sleep.

19/05/2005   09.06
From: Dawn
To: Plato

Thank you for an amazing evening . . . again
Thanks so much for not flipping out about the book, I knew you wouldn't but I was so worried I would offend you . . . but you're right
. . . why would it?
You are amazing . . . I love you
BIG love
I'm off to the library
Love you still X X

19/05/2005   10.32
From: Plato
To: Dawn

Honey, I'm genuinely delighted for you – from first meeting you I could tell that you were destined for great things, I'm sure this book will be the first of many for you.
As I might have said before, I tried Internet dating without any preconceptions or game plan. I'm not desperately seeking someone, but if anything happened then that would be OK also.
What I'm definite about that if I was looking for an ideal partner then you, without a shadow of a doubt, would be that person – you're everything a guy could ever want and more.
Have a good day Miss P — yes, let's do it again soon.
xxx

The Couple: Nine

23/05/2005   **09.33**
From: Dawn
To: Gillian; Gavin

Hey babies, huge apologies for my silence. I hope you weren't thinking that all Gav's talk of monkeys put me off . . . not at all; I actually have a real penchant for monkeys. When I was at drama school we had to go to Chester Zoo and take on the mannerisms of an animal of our choice. I chose a Macaque. A particularly agile marsupial. Therefore I spent the next week with my legs bowed, my tongue wedged into the gap between my top lip and my top teeth, making very odd noises and banging the backs of my hands on random objects. So all this talk of monkeys actually makes me feel quite at home. In fact, it could be said that I'm also a very very cheeky monkey so looks like we may have quite an evening ahead of us!
OK, I'm off to practice my Sean Connery accent. There is no way I'm going to let yours top mine Gav. Actually – I might also practice my Donald duck . . . no one topples that one!
BIG kisses to both of you
Moi x x x

24/05/2005   **16.25**
From: Gavin
To: Gillian; Dawn

All right ladies?
Thanks for the e-mail Dawn: good to hear from ya. Especially good news that you are a lover of all things Simian. Trust me, there's nobody that can come close to my connection to monkeys. Godammit, I'm 99% chimp, 1% man! I once visited Perth zoo in Oz, reputed to have the best monkey enclosure in the world: I managed to cause a mini riot by calling out and mimicking those inside. Should have heard the noise: a cacophony of wails, shreaks and monkey chatter complete with stick throwing, tree hugging, random urinating, chest beating, flea biting nonsense! All because I did my "monkey turn" and went ballistic at the site of 50+ spider & vervet monkeys. But, as they say, that's another story -perhaps one to discuss over a glass of wine?

Anyway, I'm struggling to find how you think you could possibly even get close to my Sean accent. I have many a random female stop me in the street, pawing me and asking if I'm Mr Connery's son , lends me the assertion that I'm supremely skilled in the "yesh, Mish Moneypenny" department. So, in fact, you'll find on reflection that I'm actually 90% monkey, 1% man & 9 % Sean!! Cool ratio, eh? Then again . . . .

I've got to cut this one short as I need topping up with food again: have had another "mental, mental, radio rental" day so need to cut loose and get some munchies.

See y'all soon, Gav.

TUESDAY 24 MAY

Flash: Part Two
Shut up and have it!

The Date

I really liked Flash after our first date and felt really guilty about the journal that I was keeping. I had literally just got my book deal and now it was all official I knew that developing relationships with people would involve me telling them about it. But after The Gentleman's initial reaction I was somewhat hesitant to do so. So when Flash called me to arrange a weekend away I stalled him, and when he emailed me to invite me to dinner I told him that I wouldn't be able to see him again, even though that made me sad.

03/05/2005   **13.01**
From: Flash
To: Dawn

OK bit late notice, tried to get Hakkasan and Zuma, one fully booked the other had a table at 10.45! Was hoping to have you in bed by then so declined (sic!). Sketch is closed so we are going to Locanda Locattelli – a la Jean Christophe Novelli!
If not your thang – then let me know and I will try harder (other options would be Boxwood Cafe – Ramsay, or Cinnamon Club – French/Indian fusion – great food).
So what do you think??

03/05/2005   **13.36**
From: Dawn
To: Flash

Sweetheart something has come up in my life which means I'm going to have to put this on hold please don't ask me what just accept my apologies for messing you around
I will be in touch and I'm so sorry x

03/05/2005   13.45
From: Flash
To: Dawn

Hey no sweat – I really enjoyed our night out it was a great laugh –
like you I'm not looking for a serious relationship and like you am
very busy so anything would only be sporadic anyway.
Take your time and sort yourself out, and when you fancy a laugh
or just need to go to that expensive restaurant, or to get some rays
– you know where I'm.

03/05/2005   13.55
From: Dawn
To: Flash

You are such a great person, I shall certainly keep in touch x

I wasn't happy with doing that. I really wanted to see him again,
but I just couldn't be doing with any more guilt trips. However,
when he got in touch with me a few weeks later I thought 'Bugger
it' and suggested we met for dinner. Seeing as Plato had taken it
so well I had a new sense of security and I saw the benefits of
being truthful. I was excited to see him again and hopeful that his
reaction would be positive.

We met in Home House, a member's bar on Portman
Square. We were a little awkward with each other, which was
hardly surprising. Although he didn't, and I'm pretty sure
never would ask me why I had told him that we couldn't see
each other again, it was clearly on his mind, and mine too. I
wasn't sure at what moment to tell him about the journal. I
knew that if I told him straightaway then that would be all
we talked about all night. So I held off so we could catch up
on other things. I'd put some fake tan on that day so was
looking bronzed.

'You're very brown, you been on holiday?'

'No, I haven't. It's out of a bottle.'

'It looks very natural. Are you lying to me?'

He was very suspect of me and was trying to whittle things

down to work out what the drama was. I assured him I was telling the truth and wondered what he was thinking.

On our last date I was telling him about how I ate on the TV show *Hell's Kitchen*. I went there with my friend Richard Dunwoody, the twice Grand National winner. Recently I have started to write a column in a newsletter for a singles' club called *Racing Pulses*. It's specifically for people who are into horse racing and sporting events. Richard got me involved and half way through telling him about it he stopped me.

'So . . . the jockey? Has he become a thing?'

'No. not at all. We've just become very good friends.'

Again he was trying to get to the bottom of my drama. But I still didn't put him out of his misery.

We spent sometime talking about singles' clubs and things such like. Discussing how in the past they would have been considered sad or desperate, but now they are actually very trendy and a thriving way of meeting people. He mentioned a singles' weekend he was organising in Spain at the end of the month, and invited me along.

'That'll turn into one huge orgy,' I said.

'No, I can guarantee it won't.'

'Well I definitely won't be going then.' Sex in the sun sounded fun!

'And how is the novel going? Have you started to send it out to agents or publishers yet? I can't wait to read it.'

'Um, blah, fgueer, mallour, dtterr' I turned luminous then managed to squeeze out, 'I'm in negotiations but I don't want to talk about it in case I jinx it.'

'Fair enough,' he said

Flash was dressed in a light khaki linen suit. It was very cool and I complimented him on it. He seemed a little shorter this time than he had before, and possibly a touch fuller figured, but his tan was glowing. He still managed to look good, yet I still didn't know whether I fancied him. I was chickening out as well, looking for excuses. I thought that if I didn't fancy him, and didn't want to see him again, then I wouldn't need to tell him about the book, I could just have a pleasant evening then ignore his calls. But no, that wasn't a possibility because I certainly wanted to see him again. So it was a case of more Dutch courage and for me to just tell him.

After two slightly awkward drinks we got a taxi to Sumosan. When he told me that's where we were going I couldn't believe it. I was only there a week before with The Gentleman, but I was very happy about it.

We sat down at our table and I did everything I could to not hold eye contact with the waiter that had served me last time – Lord knows what he would have thought. Luckily we were assigned someone else to look after us for the evening.

We went straight onto wine and as we were both starving ordered very quickly. Knowing the menu quite well, and now being a pro-sushi eater, I made a few suggestions. He ordered three starters, two main courses and then he gave me control of the sushi and sashimi order.

'OK, that's all the main dishes, now this young lady is going to go ballistic on the sushi.'

The waiter smiled at me, I took a deep breath and rolled off as much deliciousness as I could. When I finished I looked at him as if to say 'Did I go too far?' and he looked up at the waiter and said:

'You'd better double up on a couple of those to make sure she gets enough.'

Yes!

We had relaxed a lot when we got to the restaurant. Chat was flowing more easily and I was gearing myself up to telling him about the book.

'I love Las Vegas, I was there on a work's trip last year and now I'm determined to go there for a few months and write a journal on my experiences.'

'That would be great. Have you kept any other journals?' It was a chance . . .

'Yes, one or two about various periods of my life.' . . . which I ignored.

'Oh right, I bet they would be a good read.' He said giving me chance number two . . .

'Yes, I think they are.' . . . Which I blew. Seed sown, opportunity not grabbed. Bollocks!

We carried on talking about Vegas. I told him about the four foot hippie that gave me over $500 to play on a blackjack table in The Pyramid Casino, and how after I had lost it for him we went up to his hotel room where I ordered over $150 worth of room service before taking magic mushrooms that were infused into chocolate discs, and smoking what was undoubtedly the strongest weed in the world.

He laughed but I wondered if I should have told him. I got the impression that he would never abuse his body in that way; despite drinking he seemed to take very good care of himself. I worried that he might think I was some sort of junkie as opposed to just someone who finds an opportunity for fun almost impossible to turn down.

'Wow. I've never smoked a joint or a cigarette in my life. When I was at college I was so into sport that I would never have even thought about it. My body was a temple.'

'That's very impressive. When I was a student my body was a tampon . . . it absorbed toxins.'

We laughed and he further demonstrated his open mind to other people's antics by calling the woman on the table next to us a 'wanker' when she looked at me like I was scum for lighting a fag. OK, it was no smoking . . . but still!

After we'd JCB'd our way through all the food and sunk the best part of three bottles of wine, he asked me if I wanted anything else. I said no, but, and I'm starting to realise that I must accidentally nod when I say no, he insisted I ordered one last thing. I was brought a menu.

When I'd eaten at Sumosan the previous year the person that I was with had ordered sea urchin. I remembered not particularly liking it but when offered the opportunity to see for sure I ordered two.

The waiter brought it over and it was impossible not to note the excitement on his face.

'Is there something you want to tell us?' I had to ask.

'This is the most expensive fish on the menu and I've never tried it – can I watch you eat it?'

Bit odd but OK . . .

Flash and I both dived in at the same time. Our excitement was stopped dead when the taste exploded in our mouths. It was as gross as I remembered.

'How is it?' asked the waiter.

'I feel like someone has just cum in my mouth,' answered Flash.

Mine almost came flying back out again as I lost myself in fits. The poor waiter, sure but unbelieving of what he'd heard, had no idea how to react and scuttled off with cheeks so pink it looked liked we'd pinched them. Flash sat motionless with a look of utter disgust on his face before adding:

'Not that I would know of course . . .'

We finished it though. It was a delicacy and although it tastes like freshly churned semen we felt obliged to see it through. In a strange way I quite enjoyed it. No further comment.

Food eaten and wine consumed, it was time to do what I had to do and tell him about the book. I took his hand.

'OK, so I have something to tell you.'

He looked really nervous. God knows what he thought I was going to say.

'The reason why I told you I couldn't see you again, and the reason that I refuse to talk about the "novel" that I'm writing is because I do have a publishing deal, and because my book will be on the shelves in February. But it isn't a novel.'

Pause.

'It's a journal of my experiences of meeting people on the Internet and you're in it.' I shut my eyes and clenched my teeth and waited for his hand to be pulled from underneath mine.

'Well that's great, isn't it?'

One eye opened.

'You want to be a writer and you are one. I think it's absolutely fantastic news'

My other eye popped open. He came to sit next to me and took my hand.

'You deserve it so much.' We kissed and I said thank you.

'But how the hell are you going to write it if your laptop won't work?' – I'd mentioned earlier how my laptop had packed in that day, and that I had lost over 10,000 words – 'I think we should meet first thing in the morning and go and get you a new one.'

'Oh don't be so silly, I'll sort something out.'

'How? You haven't got any money?'

'But . . . '

'Dawn listen, I earned 3 million quid last year, and I will probably make triple that this year. Me buying you a laptop would be a charitable donation and would not make the slightest difference to my bank balance.'

At which point the bill arrived. It was £302.

'You see? Just see it as a couple of dinners.'

I thought about it for a while and then accepted. Although I wasn't entirely comfortable with it, I . . . oh what does it matter why, I just said yes in the end.

We spent about another ten minutes in Sumosan snogging like teenagers before he got me a cab home.

The next morning he called at 10 a.m.

'I'm on Tottenham Court Road. Come meet me, we're going shopping.' I did as he said.

We walked into one of the computer shops, where he said to the shop assistant 'We will take that one.' Fifteen minutes later I was the proud owner of my very own Sony VGN-B3VP.

We went back to his flat to set it all up, which is when I thought that if he expected anything in return he was going to ask for it. But he didn't. He installed Word, taught me all about how to use my wireless connection and wished me all the luck in the world with my project. He was lovely.

So apart from the passionate snog – that I instigated – the laptop was given as a gesture of kindness that I appreciated wholeheartedly.

I took it home and got straight back to work. Writing about my evening with Flash and how lucky I am to have met yet another truly amazing person on the Internet.

The Couple: Ten

26/05/2005   **23.11**
From: Dawn
To: Gillian; Gavin

Hi Guys
I just got back from a few weeks holiday in Guernsey had such a
gorgeous time. I love it over there so much. Great people, great
pubs, great everything really! I wrote and partied . . . perfect!
No tan though . . . well that's a lie, I have a great tan but it isn't from
the sun!!!!
So . . . how you guys set for Friday 24th June??
Let me know, I can't wait
Dawn x

15/06/2005   **20.46**
From: Gillian
To: Dawn

Hey gorgeous,
I have spoken with Gav and he is fine for that Friday. I've booked
the hotel and hopefully a day off work beforehand so I feel more
relaxed and not rushing to meet after work. Just need to get my
bosses sign off tomorrow.
He wanted to make it the Friday as he also doesn't want to be
getting up at the crack of dawn the next day to go to work.
So it looks like we have lift off then! Looking forward to it very much.
Can't wait to meet you.
I'll be in touch again soon with more arrangements as to what we're
going to do.
Also I remember you writing that you like sexy music. This could
mean different things to everyone, so if you can give me an idea of
what you like then I can try to arrange this to get you in the right
mood . . . . I like virtually every music going, as I went to music
school for a few years when I was younger. I think it's made me
appreciate all types. Gavin likes quite a lot but isn't into commercial
pop music. I'm sure we can work out something that will please
all.

We'll need to exchange numbers before the night. Mine is **********.
I wouldn't want us to miss each other on the night.
I'm so excited!
See you soon
Gill
xxxx

19/06/2005   11.23
From: Dawn
To: Gillian

Brilliant – Oh my goodness this is so exciting!
Glad Gav can make it on the Friday . . . although he will be getting
up 'The Crack of Dawn' anyway . . . hahaha, sorry, couldn't resist!
Music wise, I will leave it with you. I like everything to . . . don't
worry I will definitely be in the right mood, even in G4 are blearing
out the radio . . . I have a sore bum today. Played Polo yesterday. It
was so much fun. I haven't ridden a horse in about 15 yrs so I was
really nervous at first. But I soon got used to having half a ton of
pulsing muscle between my legs and by the end of the day I was
really quite good.
I have so much to tell you. I got a part in a new Channel 4 comedy
and I have been filming it this week. It's a hidden camera show, I
play tricks on men in bars . . . very very funny . . . very apt!
Oh dear . . . must dash, my cat is knocking everything off my desk
because she wants my attention . . . sweet little pooky!
SO looking forward to Friday – can't believe it's actually happening
and I'm feeling surprisingly comfortable with it tell me how you
would like the evening to go . . .
Big kiss x x x

22/06/2005   23.03
From: Gillian
To: Dawn

Hey honey,
OK, we have spoken about Friday lots, and think we have a good
idea how things should go. As the hotel is near Docklands, we
thought we could meet at Canary Wharf? If we say just outside the
tube station, at 7pm? Let me know if you want to change the

times? Also not sure if you will have things with you, and maybe will want to leave them at the hotel? I know Gav and I are meeting there earlier and arranging the room!

We have said, we can go for some drinks, and play it by ear. If we're hungry we can go for a meal. Then back to the hotel. Gavin is convinced that I'm going to jump on you as soon as we get in there. Guess he'll just have to wait and see hey!

He wants me to bring lots of things, so there will be a couple of uniforms, vibrators, handcuffs, blindfolds and a collar. I think that just about covers it. Tell me now if you think you will have any problems with any of this.

We wouldn't want to make you uncomfortable.

I think once we get back to the hotel we'll let the passion lead the way.

Gavin has ideas about us being tied up, separately and together, and blindfolding us so we have to feel our way around each other. He is very excited. Just talking to him about it makes him aroused! God knows how long we'll be able to survive having drinks before he wants to go to the hotel.

So what do you want to happen? Any preferences we should know beforehand?

Loved your email by the way. Thought you'd make some comment on the "crack of Dawn" . . . .

Polo sounds like good preparation for Friday, you'll have a pulsing muscle between your legs then too!!

You'll have to tell us when this show will be on, we'll look out for you.

Sounds like you've been having lots of fun.

Well I better go to bed, otherwise Gavin will think I'm ignoring him. Can't wait for Friday.

Night sexy

22/06/2005   23.06
From: Dawn
To: Gillian

Holar little lady!

Yes, meeting at Canary Wharf is perfect . . . 7? That's fine!

I won't have stuff with me, just a bag so let's just get to the pub, have some ice breakers and take it from there

Sure, bring all that stuff. I'm not really a regular user of all things kinky, I'm a very sensual person, I find that bodies and senses are powerful enough without the use of inanimate objects, BUT then again, I don't meet strange couples off the Internet all that often either so hey ho . . . I'm up for a new experience! – Only thing I don't really care for is the collar - not sure that would do anything for me . . . but anything else is all fun and games! Bring it along – educate me!

He is a saucy little bugger isn't he? being tied up sounds kinda fun . . . not sure it should be us though! What happened to us taking the dominant role huh?

Pounce on me all you like sweetie, Friday . . . I'm yours! All my fantasies have been about girls recently – wonder why that is!!! yeah – we can see how we go with drinks and food – and we should also get a few bottles of wine for the hotel room . . . always nice to have a tipple between . . . .

I like the build up of going for drinks as well. I feel strangely close to you guys and am really looking forward to getting to know you better – I don't imagine we will be doing too much chatting in the bedroom.

I hope you like giggling by the way – I giggle a lot!

Ooo, can't wait to spank your cute little butt I really can't!

Give Gav a little attention from me tonight but don't wear yourselves out for Friday!

So excited . . . can almost taste you already

Sweet dreams x x

FRIDAY 24 JUNE

The Couple
. . . At Last!

I'd known that this was going to happen for six months, but I
never actually thought it was going to. It was always months away
and I was pretty sure that some sort of nuclear fallout or another
kind of national disaster would save me from it. But no, the day
had come and there was sweet FA I could do about it.

I woke up like I had been stung with a cattle prod. Bolts of elec-
tricity flying up from my groin, through my stomach and out of
my mouth, resulting in constant 'What the fuck am I doing?'s
being emitted.

I needed some moral support, so I called my best friend Louise
who always makes me see sense without trying to tame me.

'Dawn, get over yourself it's just sex, you've done it hundreds
of times.'

'Yes, but I have never met a strange couple off the Internet and
done it like this before.'

'Don't be so gay. How long have you been talking to these
people for?'

'Six months.'

'Do you like the look of them?'

'Yes.'

'Do you trust them?'

'Absolutely.'

'Then go and get yourself a Hollywood and stop panicking.
You'll be fine.'

She was right. I trusted Gillian implicitly. When I first started
meeting people this way doing something like this was the furthest
thing from my mind. But when I received her first email I was
intrigued and had to reply. As our relationship developed I

admired her for how formal she was about the whole thing. I had many offers from people who wanted threesomes, but none seemed so genuine. I didn't want to go and meet some wanky city couple who were having an affair and wanted to get dark and dirty on my arse, or a married couple desperately trying to revamp their love life, or a couple where the girl was doing it simply to keep her man happy. With Gillian and Gavin their desire to see this through was clearly mutual. The way that she approached me made me feel comfortable that she was equally as turned on at the idea as he was, and her polite emails made the whole scenario seem very legit.

That morning I went to have breakfast. Usually I have a big bowl of organic fruit, possibly some gluten free muesli and maybe a couple of slices of rye bread with half a squashed banana on it. All pretty fibrous food so I avoided the lot and just had a cup of peppermint tea. I didn't want anything that might bloat me.

I paced up and down the flat constantly between nine and ten trying to decide what to wear. Was I supposed to wear something revealing and sexy? Or casual and flirty? I really had no idea.

'Louise, what in God's name do you wear when you meet strangers for sex?'

'Wear your tiny black miniskirt.'

'Isn't that a bit suggestive?'

'Dawn you're meeting strangers for pre-organised sex . . . I think you've suggested enough already!'

Good point.

So miniskirt it was. That meant fake tan, so I jumped in the shower and exfoliated myself like I was trying to find treasure under my skin. Feeling like a peeled prawn, I took on the next challenge – home bikini waxing. I'd heard good reports so decided to opt for that rather than paying through the roof for a professional job. I put the tub of wax in the microwave, waited for the ping, then, in my impatience, scalded myself with the stuff.

After twenty minutes of rubbing ice on my bits I was ready to go again. I stood with one leg on the floor, the other on a chair and carefully applied the wax. It felt nice going on. Then I pressed the special strips on top and it took me about another half an hour to have the balls to pull it off.

It wasn't as bad as I thought it was going to be, so I whipped off another few quite confidently but stopped at a neat little triangle. The idea was to give myself a Hollywood (all off!), but there was no way I was stripping myself that close to the edge. I was having dark visions of me waxing off my clitoris and never feeling pleasure again. So I tidied it all up with some depilatory cream, gave it a trim and said job done.

Next was the fake tan. I slopped it on, ensuring that all was even to avoid streaks, and I put it in areas that I'm sure were not necessary but were worth doing anyway . . . just in case they were into that sort of thing . . .

Waxed, plucked and tanned all I had to do was wait. I wanted to do some work but my fingers wouldn't follow my brain's commands, I prayed that it would sort itself out for later. I just sat on my bed all afternoon and cuddled Lilu. It was the only thing I could muster.

God knows how it happened but it was suddenly 5 p.m. and nearly time to leave. I eventually decided on jeans tucked into knee length black boots with a black vest top and a little gold cardigan. Simple and sexy – perfect! I wore black lacy French knickers, which with the black vest top I had on made quite a cute outfit for bedtime.

Just before I left I did a final check of my body. All was fine but I couldn't resist having a final trim of my triangle just to make it as small as possible. A move I deeply regretted as I created a very noticeable bald patch just off the centre to the left. Livid with myself I called my housemate Tara for advice; she's always good in a crisis.

'Don't panic, baby, just fill it in with eye pencil.'

'Great idea.'

I took a moment to think.

'Hang on, what if I got all hot and sweaty and Gillian comes back up with a black nose?' We fell into mild hysterics.

'You're right, babe, just leave it. I have a feeling that your wonky muff will be the furthest thing from their minds tonight.'

She was right, I was being dramatic. I took a look at my comedy fanny, smiled at my efforts and got dressed again.

I strutted down the Edgware Road towards Marble Arch tube as confidently as possible, repeating things in my head like: You're powerful, you're sexual, and they're going to love you. But no matter how much I said it I wasn't convinced. It's amazing how all of this time my friends have been saying things like 'What the hell are you going to do if you don't fancy them?' and I too had considered that to be a terrible possibility. But now, as I made my way there, the only thing that was going through my mind was: what the hell am I going to do if they don't fancy *me*?'

They had depicted themselves as a very sound couple, who had a vibrant sex life and used toys and wanted to experiment further. This threesome meant a lot to them. I had built them up to it over six months; I had even become part of their sex chat. I felt almost like they had found the woman that they wanted to have their child and that their hopes were so high for the outcome of the arrangement that if I didn't perform well, or wasn't what they wanted, that I would be letting them down. I was a new toy for them to play with. If I was shit it would be the same as hurrying home from Ann Summers and realising that batteries are not included in your new vibrator.

I've never observed other women's bodies so much in my life as I did on the way to Canary Wharf. Anyone skinny gave me palpitations and every time I saw someone with a slight wobble I felt relieved and lightened up on myself, wondering why I thought that they would be expecting someone perfect to walk in the door.

I know I'm sexual, but nerves were insistent on telling me otherwise. I had to stay focused. Think back to all the times I've had men begging at my feet for more. All the times where I have stared someone in the eye while they cum from the pleasure I'm making them feel. Yes, I had to get those inhibitions out of my head and relocate the beast within. This was no time for acting the virgin; this was a call for Horny Dawn! I had this idea on the train and spent the rest of the journey designing my super hero outfit. That seemed to make the time go faster.

At Canary Wharf station Gillian texted me to say they would be ten minutes late. I was fine with that; it gave my thermostat a chance to get back to normal after the journey had caused me to sweat buckets. I caught a glimpse of myself in a mirrored window and regretted hugely not washing off my fake tan. Seven hours had passed since I had put it on and I was starting to look like I had been Tangoed.

I walked in circles waiting for them to come into the station. They must have walked in when my back was turned because suddenly they were just there, in the middle of the concourse looking at me as if to say, 'Is it you?'

I knew it was them straightaway. They looked just like their pictures and Gillian's blazing red head was instantly recognisable. We smiled at each other and walked closer.

'So sorry we're late,' she said.

'No problem, it happens,' I replied, trying desperately not to follow it by a dull comment about the weather. We kissed on each cheek and then I kissed Gav.

'Great to meet you. I think we need to go get a drink,' he said in a mild Scottish accent that really surprised me.

I know it sounds awful but when Gillian had said they were from Essex I had expected broad Essex accents. But I couldn't have been more wrong. His voice was gentle and hers was eloquent and well pronounced. I saw straightaway that they were highly intelligent and very cordial people.

Facially Gillian bore no surprises. She looked identical to her photos. Her pale skin was covered in cute freckles and her eyes were deep and spoke volumes about her sexuality. She had an intense stare, which was incredibly alluring. When she spoke to me she looked right into me, conveying a confidence that was undisputedly genuine. At a glance you might not have noticed this girl's charm. It would be easy to see her as a pale skinned redhead and let society tell you that she was unattractive for her colouring. But I didn't see that, I saw further and knew that I was in the presence of an exceptionally sexual young woman.

Gavin, on the other hand, did knock me slightly off balance, though not in a bad way. I hadn't expected to find him attractive. Even though his picture didn't suggest that he wasn't, I mainly went there to have the experience of being with Gill, so I was hugely pleased when I actually thought he was fit. He was tall and slim, with tanned skin. His nose was large but caused no offence and his eyes were kind and brown. A receding hairline gave him a look of maturity that complemented his instantly accessible personality, and his casual dress of a blazer, over a blue shirt with blue jeans was well coordinated and very stylish.

Considering the nature of the meeting, nerves seemed to be well controlled. We took a short walk to a nearby pub. While Gav went to the bar I had the chance to chat to Gillian about what we were going to do.

'I have to say that I think we are all really brave doing this. I actually feel quite proud of myself tonight.'

'Good. Gavin and I have been talking about nothing but for weeks. We can't wait.'

Oh God, pressure to perform well. Horny Dawn . . . where are you?

When Gavin came back from the bar we settled into some easy chat about our pasts and who we were. Gavin writes children's stories. He had a very fertile imagination and made me laugh a lot with his tales of how he spent most of his childhood pretending to be a monkey. He was funny and when he told me stupid things about himself he laughed, as did Gill whose adoring stare was a constant and clear declaration of what a close and secure relationship they had.

Gillian spoke of the bullying she suffered at school because of her hair colour. She seemed so strong and together that it was hard to imagine how she could ever have been a victim. It made me admire her even more. Her bad experiences had turned her into a very sound-minded lady.

We only had three drinks before I suggested that we went back to the hotel. It was 9.30 and still light, but there was no point in messing about. I hadn't met them for a night on the lash: drinking was simply wasting good sex time. So we got in a taxi and went to a hotel in Docklands.

It was a cool place, a huge moored yacht that had been converted into a hotel. A very unique venue that suited our very unique situation. Gillian went up to the room first so as not to attract attention from the receptionist, Gavin and I followed shortly after.

In the room, two nurses' outfits and a set of handcuffs were laid out on a table. I smiled at them and Gillian said that there was no pressure to use them. She winked at me afterwards and I told her to feel free to open my mind.

The bed was large, but it was two single ones that had been pushed together so there was a small gap down the middle. A large mirror at the foot of the bed was enough to make you feel horny as soon as you walked in, and a bottle of wine and a box of strawberries added a calming and sensual tone to what could have been a harsh and intimidating environment.

Gavin went down to the car to get a laptop which was to provide our soundtrack for the evening. So Gillian and I were left alone.

I looked at her and removed my jeans and boots. She did the same and revealed a black satin basque with black lace suspenders. An unexpected attire to appear from under her casual jeans. Saucy little minx!

'I suppose the easiest thing for us to do would be to kiss?' I said.

She nodded and moved towards me. We went straight into a passionate kiss that saw us down onto the bed. By the time Gavin came back up we were fully engrossed and my hand had somehow founds its way into her knickers.

I was instantly aroused. The situation was verging on ridiculous and that was what was turning me on. Horny Dawn was having a field day and couldn't wait to show everyone her super powers.

While Gillian and I kissed, stroked and caressed each other, Gavin saw to the music before joining us on the bed. I kissed him and it was lovely; kissing a man and a woman so close together highlighted the difference in sensation. There was no comparison in feeling. Gillian's softness was delicious but Gavin's strength was equally as desirable. Both exceptional in their own ways.

The three of us shared a gentle snog. Gavin lying on his back, Gill and I on either side of him. I reached down into his boxers and took hold of his perfectly ample cock. It was solid.

Gillian moved away and disappeared behind me. Reappearing seconds later with some handcuffs and a black blindfold with the words 'Tease me' on it. I had a little smirk to myself but went along with what she had in mind.

She put the cuffs onto Gav's wrists and attached them to a pole above his head, then she put the blindfold on him and led me down to his cock. We both licked it and sucked it in between kissing each other. Gav was starting to writhe uncontrollably. I was relishing in the power of having him unable to control us, or see us and having to give into what we were doing. I got more and more involved. Gillian could sense my enjoyment and left me alone to take it all. She moved behind me, stood on the floor and buried her face in between my legs. It was bliss and I fought hard not to collapse. I worked hard until Gav deposited varying sized droplets of creamy fluid onto his chest. We gave him a moment to recuperate.

'I think it's time we showed her what we can do,' she said when she eventually came back round to the other side of Gav.

'I think so too,' he replied as she removed his blindfold and handcuffs and transferred them over to me.

I was totally at their mercy and entirely comfortable with it. I lay back on the bed as they removed my top, applied the cuffs and blindfold. I took deep breaths in anticipation and waited for them to start.

Gav took one of my breasts into his mouth and circled my nipple with his tongue. I was so sensitive and amazed by how heightened my senses were from not being able to see or touch. The many times I had refused to be submissive were filling me with deep regret as Gillian's tongue circled my clitoris and caused my legs to twitch from almost unbearable pleasure. I was having to focus so as not to explode. I wanted it to last as long as possible but I couldn't hold off. Within minutes I had cum and my body was melting from their touch. I lay back with my legs together, bent and flopped over to one side while they both laughed and stroked me.

'Jesus, that was incredible,' I murmured.

'I think she enjoyed it, Gavin,' said Gill in a low and sexy voice.

She then pushed two fingers inside me and I almost shot off the bed as I was still pulsing from my orgasm.

They took the blindfold off me and allowed me to move. I felt pathetic. Like I had no strength in my body. Gillian lay back and I knew I had to be fair. It was her turn and she fully deserved it.

While Gavin attended to her upper body I went down. Her plump little fanny wore a cute ginger tuft that was similar in dimensions to mine. I felt nervy as I put my mouth onto her but that didn't last long. I have been in that position before, but never so close to a pussy as juicy as Gillian's. My anxious start soon moulded into a confident rhythm as I used my tongue to massage her to a jolting orgasm.

All three of us moved to lay down in a row, our hands linked in a chain and smiling with total satisfaction.

Gavin and I put towels on and went and had a cigarette and a glass of wine on the balcony. Gillian lay on the bed waiting for us, her curvaceous, white body draped effortlessly on the mattress. On her side, she had her palms together under her right cheek. Only one of her soft, pale pink nipples was on display, and her fleshy upper thigh was resting on the bed in front of the other one.

When I came back in she watched me as my gaze reverted to the outfits.

'Put one on,' I told her. She beamed with childlike excitement.

'I think we have a naughty girl here, Gavin,' she said.

I smiled, and passed her a uniform.

She put it on and I understood. It was clear to see how sexy she felt in it. Her mannerisms changed instantly. She moved like she was dancing and found it impossible not to take on the role of dominator. She straddled Gavin and they started to kiss. I stood back and eyed up the PVC one. I reached for it a few times but kept retracting until I thought 'Fuck it' and put it on.

As I did each of the poppers up, I relished in how perfectly it fitted. It pushed my boobs into a wonderful cleavage and finished just under my bottom. I couldn't stop posing in the mirror. I looked amazing. I know it sounds arrogant to say but I really did. I didn't look stupid or comical, I looked hot and, as a surge of power shot to my crotch, I got back onto the bed to enjoy even more fun.

Both in our outfits, Gillian and I lay next to each other on the bed. Gav blindfolded us then knelt in between us, one hand up each of our skirts. Gillian and I were left to kiss while he seemed to disappear for a while.

Moments later a low hum filled the room. I thought it was maybe a boat mooring next to us, but Gillian's squeak proved that the engine in question had a much closer position.

'Ooooo, I got the Rooster . . . that means you get the Rabbit.'

Not really understanding what she meant I continued to kiss her. Gav's hand had moved off me so I replaced it with mine, but he told me to take it away. Seconds later there was another hum, this one slightly higher than the first and I was shocked as it became muffled as it made its way inside me. She was right, I sure as hell got the Rabbit, and I'm telling you now that that thing has changed my life. It was 0 to 60 in about thirty seconds. Wow!

I had only had one condition of the night, and that was that I didn't want Gavin to penetrate me. Only because I didn't think it was necessary and I would have felt wrong about it. I don't think there is a heavy line between foreplay and full sex but on this occasion I wasn't willing to cross it.

When Gillian came shortly after me, Gavin turned her over and fucked her as hard as he could. There was no denying that she was loving every second of it. I was enjoying watching. She was very vocal (as I am, apparently). She squeezed my hand so tight I was being thrust up and down the bed with them. She repeated 'Come on, fill me up', while he rammed her faster and faster until he crumpled down onto her, exhausted.

It was now about 1.30 and we were all satisfied and tired. Gav and I had somehow polished off two bottles of wine and Gillian had drank three Smirnoff Ice. The three of us lay talking, kissing and stroking on the bed, euphoric about how lucky we were that there had been such a strong connection.

I lay talking to them while I gently tickled Gillian's bits. She was still dripping wet. Even after hours of action we were all still primed.

Gav's hand joined mine and we started to kiss over her. It was a slow kiss and our tongues were being super-adventurous. It was gorgeous. So gorgeous in fact that we forgot all about poor Gillian who had disappeared down the crack of the bed and was reaching up at us to get her out. Her barely audible voice eventually grabbed my attention and Gav and I broke contact to resurface her. We all held our bellies as we howled at the comedy.

This was the beginning of a crazy fifteen minutes where the alcohol we'd consumed seemed to hit us all at the same time. I pranced around in my newly found favourite outfit, striking sexy poses and screaming obscenities like 'cum in my eye you mumma!' While Gavin made a headdress out of a bath towel, did a Scottish skit and then feel asleep on the sofa. I eventually collapsed onto the bed where Gillian was expressing utmost amusement at our performances and we both shortly after lost consciousness.

At around 3 a.m. I heard movement.

'Shall I wake her, Gav?'

'Yes.'

'How you would like me to wake her?'

'Kiss her.'

Then Gillian's mouth made contact with mine and my light snooze was broken as I woke to accept more naughtiness. Gav went down and Gill stayed up, she kissed me and licked my nipples and while his face buried itself in me, her finger circled my clitoris bringing me to a fast and intense climax. I could have stopped there but that would have been unfair. So, when Gav moved behind Gill and took her from behind in the spoon position, I moved down the bed and licked her while she became entirely merciless to us. We timed it perfectly so they both came together and a three way spoon sent us all back into a deep and secure sleep.

Later I woke to the sound of them masturbating each other. I was so horny that the damp patch in between my thighs was shining in the light coming through the window. But what I wanted was a soft and close fuck from a man. I couldn't face the commitment of a three-way at that time in the morning. I wanted intimacy and intensity. I toyed with the notion of jumping up to fetch the rabbit, but that would have undoubtedly caused them to try to involve me in their play, so I lay there still, enjoying Gillian's groans with my hand hiding secretly in between my legs.

She came and I stretched with an overdramatic yawn. I patted her on the thigh and called her a good girl. Her eyes were glazed over but she managed to eek a smile. Our night was over, and it had been perfect. We all got up, laughing and joking about our antics, got dressed and tidied up the room.

Gillian and I stood at a mirror putting make-up on and talking about cosmetics while Gav put all the toys into a little suitcase. Soon we were ready to leave. A close hug between all three of us expressed exactly how happy we all were. No arrangements were made to do it again, but that wasn't awkward. We knew we would be in contact. Gillian and Gav shared a sensuous kiss while I waited for her to give me a lift to the station. I watched them in the wing mirror. They were so much in love.

In the car we talked normally about general life stuff. Families, jobs, that sort of thing. We were friends, and after what we'd just done together we had a deeper understanding of each other. I kissed her on the cheek and said goodbye. She thanked me and I insisted the pleasure was all mine.

On the train the smile on my face was my body's way of showing the world how I was feeling. Never have I had that sense of achievement before. That night was without a doubt the craziest most extreme thing I have ever done in my life. But to see it through, and experience the amount of gratification that I did, was the most liberating experience I could ever hope for.

What next I wonder!

FRIDAY 1 JULY

The Broad
Back on the Straight, Long,
Hard and Narrow

18/04/2005   **22.08**
From: Gigi
To: Dawn

Hi there,
I too am straight; however, I have enjoyed the company of women
only a few times, but long ago. Since I recently broke up with my
boyfriend, I'd like to try the experience again, as I find myself
fantasizing about women quite often these days. I'm originally from
New York but moved to London about four years ago. My last
experience with a woman was over five years ago – so I hope I still
remember how or at least will enjoy re-learning! I still consider my
last experience the most incredible sexual escapade I've ever
had . . .
Attached is my photo, please let me know you're interested by
replying with yours. If not, good luck with your search!

Gigi X

19/04/2005   **14.23**
From: Dawn
To: Gigi

Hey
it's so nice to know that other people harbour these desires
Yeah, I have had a few experiences and really enjoyed them, but
would love to do it again, with someone a little more random than
friends . . .
I live in London to, in the West end type area . . .
Attached is my photo, hope you like . . .

Would you be nervous?
Is this the reason you are on this site or do you go on dates with guys as well?
Dawn x

23/04/2005   17.36
From: Gigi
To: Dawn

Hello Dawn,
Thanks for your email! Apologies for the delayed reply, but my work life has been hellish this week and I have been working until midnight. I can't believe it's already Saturday and, unfortunately, I'm in the office! Things should calm down in another week or so, but for now, it's a bit crazy.
Yes, what a lovely photo! All of my photos are silly holiday and party photos, so it's always difficult for me to figure out which to send!
I live in central London too, but in the Kensington area.
I can't say that I'm a very nervous person and look forward to meeting new people. It's when I don't get on with someone, face to face, that I get a bit nervous – not before, but right in the middle of it!
I've not responded to any men's ads. After having just broken up with my boyfriend, I'm more craving women right now. Besides, I'm moving back to America before the end of the year and would hate to fall madly in love with a man, then have to move away. I've done it once before and don't want to go thru it again. Just looking for sensual fun with no strings attached. It would be nice to have a few more girl-friends, but raw sexual pleasure is okay, too!
Fancy meeting up soon?
Chat soon,
Gigi

19/06/2005   11.29
From: Dawn
To: Gigi

Hey Gigi
Bit of a sore bottom, was playing Polo yesterday and I think I bruised my hide! It was the first time I have been on a horse in years so walking like a weirdo today.

This week is looking good for me and I would love it if you were free for us to meet up?
Any night you can do is good with me . . . just let me know you're probably in another country, lucky thing!
Big Love x

24/06/2005   06.22
From: Gigi
To: Dawn

Hey Dawn
well, have been a travelling fool. Returned from Italy Monday night and now at Heathrow waiting to board a flight to Germany – but this time for business. Found myself stuck in Berlin for the weekend because I've to be in our office on Monday & Tuesday, so I contacted a friend in Munich and will now visit him for the weekend! I've FINALLY got my first weekend in London next week – it's my first since 14 may! So, would love to meet up, if you're free.
Polo, eh? Sore bum? I can relate, but I'll save that story for when we meet.
Looking forward to hearing from you and finally meeting!
Take care,
gigi XX

24/06/2005   10.32
From: Dawn
To: Gigi

Check you out, your like Gulliver!!
Can't wait to hear your travelling stories, and of course the tale of your sore bottom . . . which I presume was from Polo? Hmmm . . . I wonder!
I have been a busy chicken to . . . got a part in a new channel 4 comedy and filmed that last week which was very funny. Its the same show that squirted Tom Cruise in the face, so its getting lots of press . . . .good for us (maybe), not so good for my producer who is currently out on bail.
Anyhow
Next weekend would be AMAZING!!!!!
I will be free late on Friday or all evening Saturday or all day and night

Sunday – haven't booked anything yet so you say when and we can go from there?
Seriously can not wait to meet you girl
Big Love x

24/06/2005   17.31
From: Gigi
To: Dawn

Well, how about Friday 1st July? At least coffee & chat
for a bit to see if we have any mutual "interest".

29/06/2005   13.14
From: Dawn
To: Gigi

Oh sod the tea and biscuits lets just go for dinner and take the risk.
More fun that way . . . no?
I'm free from 8. That cool?

29/06/2005   20.14
From: Gigi
To: Dawn

That works for me! I'll just work late (as usual) and meet you afterwards.
How's about a Brazilian place in Covent Garden called Guanabara.
We can eat, drink and dance there?
Shall I book?

30/06/2005   08.33
From: Dawn
To: Gigi

Do it! See you there 7.30
Can't wait x

The Date

I have always fantasised about women. And I don't mind admitting it because I know that all of my friends do as well. All women do at some point. They might fantasise about it and not like it afterwards, but we all do it. So why don't we all join hands, say 'There is nothing wrong with thinking about fannies' and allow ourselves to talk about it openly?

It doesn't mean you are bisexual; it just means you let your mind wonder. And if you carry it out once in a while it simply means you're willing to embrace what your desires tell you every now and then. And anyway, girls' bodies are gorgeous, so why the hell not? That's why I met Gigi.

It was a week since I'd spent my evening with Gillian and Gavin. I was still coming down from it. Gillian and I had been texting and emailing loads, continuously expressing how delighted we were at how successful our encounter was.

If I'm honest, my quota of female lusting had been more than exhausted. But Gigi and I had been trying to arrange a night out for two months and there was no way I could cancel. Even though I don't think I would have batted an eyelid if Angelina Jolie had licked my inner thigh.

As arranged we met outside Guanabara in Covent Garden, at 7.30. I knew it was her as she was the only Japanese person in the foyer. She was older than I had expected, which shocked me a little. She'd never actually told me her age, and I had never asked, so I didn't feel deceived, just surprised. My vision had been of a petite girl around my age. But Gigi was around 5 foot 4, sturdy and closer to forty than thirty.

She was wearing a lacy black top which wasn't very successful at hiding the red satin trim of her black lacy bra. On the bottom a short black skirt covered a small amount of her well-built legs, and knee-length black stacks gave her a good few inches more than God did. She looked great. Not what I had been expecting, but I loved her instantly.

In a way her age comforted me. Meeting another 26-year-old female for a date would have felt weird, possibly girly and giggly. But Gigi gave off a vibe that she was experienced and confident with the set up. Which meant that I was too.

She walked in front of me as we made our way to our table. A dude on some bongos was creating a beat that was impossible for us not to dance to as we walked. Her strides were small, more of a shuffle, probably on account of her short legs. As she walked she tapped her hands in the air to the beat of the music. She had rhythm and I liked her little arms.

It was very loud so we had to shout at each other across our table. This would have been fine if they hadn't taken an hour to come with our drinks, so we were dehydrated and strained by the time they arrived. It was a shame, it got the evening off to a slow start.

She warned me that she got drunk quickly and ordered a cocktail. I had a JD/DC – I've never really been a cocktail drinker, I find them way too sugary.

Her voice had a strong New York accent. It was gentle but firm. I could tell she was strong minded but she wasn't intimidating, not to me anyway. But that could have been because we were on a date.

She was a director for a city firm and I'm sure that on a nine to five basis she wasn't the pussycat that she was with me. Put it this way, if I was her PA I wouldn't want to mess up her coffee order.

Despite all this she had a real cuteness about her. Freckly cheeks complemented her dimples when she smiled, and wisps of hair that had shook loose from her pony tail gave a soft outline to her rounded face.

She hadn't lied; when her cocktail came she was clearly under its influence before the liquid had moved less than a centimetre down the glass. 'I'm already drunk' she announced openly as we munched on our shared platter of bits and bobs.

I was nearly at the end of my first drink and not feeling it at all. It was one of those nights where I could drink the bar dry and not get slightly drunk. I shouldn't have gone out really. The mood just wasn't taking me. Luckily Gigi's company was so easy that being sober in a place full of crazy Brazilian party animals wasn't too much of a strain.

'Have you used the website much since you've lived in London?' I asked her, desperate to know if I was the only girl she had met on the Net.

'Yes, I love it. I used it recently actually. To arrange something.' She stopped talking and munched on a fishcake.

'Oh really? To arrange what?'

'I don't know if I should tell you.' She looked apprehensive but I could tell she was bursting to relay all the sordid details.

'How prudish are you?' She asked.

'I pick up birds on the Internet to satisfy my sexual desires. I'm not very prudish at all,' I said and she laughed.

'OK. A few months ago I used it to organise a threesome with a couple!'

She was clearly unsure what my reaction would be. The last thing in the world she thought I was going to come back with was, 'Holy fucking shit, I did exactly the same thing last week!'

We howled with laughter and clinked our glasses. It was quite an uncanny coincidence. And one which smashed the ice and let controversial conversation pour on through.

I'd got through two drinks but still wasn't affected. She, on the other hand, was still on drink one and was quite steadily getting hammered. She had an amazing way of being cute and flirty but bold and outspoken at the same time. Comments like 'The most satisfying moment I have had with a girl was when I finally managed to bed a friend of mine in New York, and was in a position to say "sit on my face!" without it being a fantasy!' Would be followed shortly by some hair twiddling, a sweet giggle and possibly some subtle bottom lip biting.

Gigi wasn't what one would describe as beautiful but she was fabulous without a shadow of a doubt. She spends thousands of pounds on fur coats, handbags and jewellery. Half her wardrobe is Gucci and her straight up attitude to sex makes her impossible not to admire.

It was refreshing to spend time with someone who wasn't ashamed to be experimental and be honest about it. Like me she was adamant that she was not bisexual. Neither of us had any intentions, desires nor interest in having ongoing sexual relationships with women. We both love men, want to be with men and neeeeeeed men.

Although a lot of the evening was spent talking about our girl-on-girl experiences, we also spent a large amount of time reeling off our best and worst male ones. We shared an oral fixation, so were able to compare techniques on how to pleasure a penis for maximum impact. Very educational it was too!

Gigi has a fantasy: to have a threesome with two other girls. This is where I could gloat, as I did that last year with a couple of friends of mine. It was awesome. A totally unexpected, unplanned and mind blowing experience that none of us have any idea how it started. Never to be repeated but never to be forgotten.

She was so jealous and I loved telling her all about it. Made me feel very proud. But I still wasn't horny. Gillian and Gavin had seriously wiped me out the week before, and a midweek visit from The Soldier (see acknowledgments for details) satisfied me even further. I was all sexed out and there was no way I could force it.

All my talk of girl-on-girl-on-girl was clearly turning Gigi on and she started to get very tactile with me. It was coming up to 2.30 a.m. and I was tired, not drunk, and still about as horny as a pretzel. The last thing I wanted to do was offend her but I just wasn't feeling it.

'Shall we have another drink?'

'No, Gigi, I'm done. I think we should go.'

She jumped to her feet. There was no doubt that her intentions were to go home together.

'Look, Gigi, I think you're great and I'd love you to come back with me but I'm just not horny, so nothing sexual is going to happen, OK? Sorry to be so bold but I don't want to give any wrong impressions.'

She looked gutted. Not because of the rejection so much as the way that it made her feel like she was being presumptuous. I was so angry with myself for saying it. It was so rude. I could have at least waited until we got home and said I was too tired. It was arrogant of me to presume that she would want me at that stage. I should have kept my mouth shut. I put my arm around her, gave her a huge cuddle and apologised about a thousand times. She took it really well and I asked her to come back regardless.

Back at my house it was a little awkward. Fine, I'd said that I wasn't randy, but then we didn't know each other all that well, we'd essentially gone out on a date and we were suddenly in my room undressed and ready to go to sleep.

Luckily, Gigi was a lot drunker than I was so I don't think she felt as uneasy. She asked me if it was OK for her to take her bra off, and I told her to get naked and not be so silly. Jesus, just because I didn't want to have sex didn't mean I expected her to sleep in her dancing gear. And besides, I wanted to see her body.

It was cute. She was small and chunky but well proportioned. He boobs were big with very dark nipples and her tummy was potted and round.

She got into bed and was asleep in moments. I watched her for a while. She was pretty and sweet and slept all curled up with her head on her hands. I kissed her cheek gently and went to sleep myself.

Next morning our alarms went off at 7 a.m. Lilu had made her way in between us so the three of us spent a few moments stretching and coming to terms with the early hour.

Gigi got up and we had a lovely cuddle before she left to get a cab. It was all very easy.

I lay back on my bed with Lilu and held her close to me. My favourite thing in the world is cuddling my cat in my bed. And even after all the dates I've been on, I still look forward to that moment the most. After a fun night with someone is over and I can be in my own place, doing things at my own pace and with my own space. Well, sharing it with Lilu obviously.

My date with Gigi proved something to me: I'm not sexually predatory with women like I am with men. All of my female sexual encounters (the couple excluded) have come out of unplanned sexual situations. I go with what happens at the time and in the moment and I can't force it. It doesn't come naturally to me to flirt with women. I think about women a lot but they are just thoughts, nothing beats the touch of a man. And from the experiences I have had, I wouldn't agree with anyone who said that girls know what to do and therefore the sex is better. I can hold my hands up and say proudly that the majority of men know exactly what they're doing and they are bloody brilliant at it.

From now on if I ever get asked if I'm bisexual I will comfortably say, 'No, I'm not bisexual. I'm just sexual.'

LOGGING OFF . . .

Six months after beginning this adventure I now feel like it's come to a natural close. My emotions have been taxed, I've laughed so hard I nearly lost my eyeballs, and sexually . . . well sexually you can probably guess what I feel I've accomplished there.

I think I've pushed my own personal boundaries and therefore feel really calm. I want an exciting life and am aware that what I do with my time determines whether or not I have that. Therefore, just to keep things interesting, I put myself into situations that I know will challenge me. It works – and these last few months have been the ultimate example of that.

Every date was a challenge. I would be an absolute liar if I said I didn't get nervous before each one. However, even if the date was a disaster, I always came away from them feeling stretched – yeah, sorry, bad choice of words, let me rephrase – like I had learned something about myself. My patience was tested, my integrity, braveness and social abilities were all run through the mill and I have to say that I've come out of it feeling very good about who I am. Because I know what I can handle, and with what I'm comfortable and not comfortable. I am relaxed in situations that are mutual, simple as that. It might sound obvious but it isn't really.

When you date so much in such a short period of time, you realise what you put up with when you're only sporadically meeting new people. What I mean is that if Herr Fingers, for example, was the only guy I'd dated in months, I might have been tempted to give it another go, even though I knew that I was never going to be interested. Because I gave myself the choice, I didn't have to settle for something that didn't make me happy, and this has meant relationships with real longevity have developed. And I hope that this gives anyone who feels like they don't have many options the impetus to get out there. With the Internet it's possible for everyone, you just need to embrace it.

In terms of the relationships I've formed, I don't believe it could have gone any better. Plato and I still see each other as often as we can. I still tell him that he is one of my favourite people and I mean it without equivocation. He is the most honest, gentle and genuine person I have ever met. He is selfless and generous and unmistakably sincere and he makes me laugh like I'm being tickled. He continues to tell me hilarious stories of his inabilities to be normal, and I come away with wrinkle marks and bellyache every time I see him. This whole experience was made better by my friendship with him.

Flash and I go out for dinner lots and recently went away to Dubai for a seven star weekend. The guy is so much fun and such easy company. Nothing shocks him; I love that. I told him all about Gillian and Gavin and he was great about it. I thought he might have been offended, but no . . . the randy little bugger had a story that topped it. He is incredibly sexy and we love hanging out; this relationship will continue as it is for as long as it can, and I hope that's a while. And just for the record . . . my Cockdar could not have been any further off the mark . . . seriously . . . so, so far off! Woo ha!

Gillian and I are in constant contact; we send each other texts all the time. She gets all excited when I'm on the telly and I know she is so looking forward to reading the book. Our friendship will carry on, and will hopefully get better and better, but I wouldn't repeat our erotic liaison. It's not that I didn't enjoy it, just that the experience satisfied a part of me. I didn't only meet them for sexual reasons, I met them to test myself, to see how brave I am, and the result of the experiment left me contented. I don't have the desire to be extreme at the moment, those kind of sexual situations will probably be as they were for me before: random and unplanned. I won't say they won't happen again – Jesus, I could never say that – but I don't feel the need to set up opportunities like that for myself. For the time being anyway . . .

Gigi is as fab as I thought she was, we have stayed in touch and I would love us to be close. Yet it will be in a purely platonic capacity. Having said that, my only sexual experiences with girls have come out of spontaneous moments with friends . . . Enough said! I've learnt not to restrict myself by saying never.

The Wolf and I shared a few months of naughty text messages, but we didn't get round to another date. Monsieur Cunni, whom I obviously wanted to see again for a repeat performance, went back to France shortly after, so we only saw each other that once. But hey, I can't deny that I haven't spent many a night going over that one in my head. Every girl's dream, I imagine!

The Big Bumbino emailed me a few epics thanking me for looking after his gash but I only replied once saying that I hoped the stitches held it together OK. I know what babies are like, they become very dependent if you give them too much love . . .

The Little Leprechaun, The Gopher, Herr Fingers and Del Boy all took rejection well when I told them that we wouldn't be going out again, and the BFG was kind enough not to bore me with his stupidly long words anymore, so I respect them all for that.

I never heard from Master Pendant again after our erratic parting at Baker Street, and Tash eventually stopped heavy breathing into my answer phone about a month after the night he took the top layer of skin off my face with his beard.

As for The Gentleman . . . well there are so many things right and so many things wrong about him that I really don't know where I'm at. I can't deny that our time together was amazing – and I think about him a lot – but the distance is something with which I can't compete and so I tend not to put too much effort into what is probably a pointless cause. An instant message conversation when he arrived back in America gutted me. I knew it was impossible but I didn't want to admit it. It's always fun to think one day . . .

Instant Message From: The Gentleman

Did you find your bag?

Instant Message From: Dawn

Yes I did. We didn't really say goodbye. I had a great time. When will I see you again?

Instant Message From: The Gentleman

I won't be coming back to London for quite a while now. So I guess we wont be seeing each other...unless...

Instant Message From: Dawn

We buy webcams?

Instant Message From: The Gentleman

No, stupid. Unless you come here?

Instant Message From: Dawn

I have too much on, I need to be here right now.

Instant Message From: The Gentleman

And there lies the problem. Your life is there and my life is here. That's not going to change ... is it?

Instant Message From: Dawn

No, I am not sure that it is.

Instant Message From: The Gentleman

So that's that then?

Instant Message From: Dawn

I don't think I can answer that right now.

He emailed me straightaway on 7/7 to ask if I was safe, and we have contact at least once a fortnight, but it's tough to know how to be. Usually I would be flirty and sexy but there is something different about me and him. Something serious, which makes building a relationship hard because I think we both know that the closer we get, the harder it will be. I haven't felt like 'that' about anyone in a long time, but despite this I don't have any intentions or desires to give up anything to be with him, and that's how I think it would be. I'm a 26-year-old single girl with no house, no nine to five job, and – apart from Lilu – no commitments or responsibilities. He, on the other hand, is 36, owns a business and properties in New York, Atlanta and in about five other worldwide destinations. So guess who would have to give up their life for the relationship to work? I really can't see any compromise there, and I have no intention of giving anything up for anyone just yet.

I may not be a homeowner but I'm having so much fun and I value my independence more than any plot of land. Well, that is unless my dream of moving to New York for a short while actually happens – then Lord knows how things might develop. Again, I won't say never.

For now I'm still dancing in my singledom. Being able to take opportunities like my rendezvous with the Couple, and shoot off for spontaneous weekends like I did with Plato and Flash is a great feeling – and one which I'm not keen to put an end to in the near future.

So as I push the lid down on my shiny new laptop I will be saying goodbye to Internet dating for the time being. I strongly recommend it to anyone who wants to spread their social wings, but it is a commitment, and a tiring mission. I'm blind-dated out for now and just want to spend time with my friends.

My relationship with Lilu is still my favourite thing, and the right hand side of my bed remains hers for now. Well, apart from the occasional Friday night guest – but that's a story for another time . . .